RETAIL MERCHANDISING MATHEMATICS:
principles and procedures

MARY D. TROXELL

Retail Merchandising Consultant

Prentice-Hall, Inc., *Englewood Cliffs, New Jersey 07632*

Library of Congress Cataloging in Publication Data

Troxell, Mary D.
    Retail merchandising mathematics.

    Includes index.
      1. Business mathematics—Retail trade.
I. Title.
HF5695.5.R45T74   513'.93   79-1105
ISBN   0-13-775205-9

Editorial/production supervision and interior design
by Wendy Terryberry and Sonia Meyer
Cover design by: George Alon Jaediker
Manufacturing buyer: Harry P. Baisley

Printed in the United States of America

10 9 8 7 6 5 4 3 2 1

Prentice-Hall International, Inc., *London*
Prentice-Hall of Australia Pty. Limited, *Sydney*
Prentice-Hall of Canada, Ltd., *Toronto*
Prentice-Hall of India Private Limited, *New Delhi*
Prentice-Hall of Japan, Inc., *Tokyo*
Prentice-Hall of Southeast Asia Pte. Ltd., *Singapore*
Whitehall Books Limited, *Wellington, New Zealand*

CONTENTS

CHAPTER 2

INTRODUCTION TO RETAIL MERCHANDISING   *15*

CHAPTER 3

ELEMENTS OF MERCHANDISING PROFIT   *31*

CHAPTER 4

THE SEASONAL MERCHANDISE PLAN AND OPEN-TO-BUY   *61*

CHAPTER 5

THE PURCHASE ORDER AND TERMS OF SALE   *97*

CHAPTER 6

MERCHANDISE PRICING AND MARKUP   *131*

CHAPTER 7

REPRICING MERCHANDISE: MARKDOWNS, ADDITIONAL MARKUPS AND EMPLOYEE DISCOUNTS   *167*

CHAPTER 10

PERIODIC REPORTS ON THE MERCHANDISING OPERATION *249*

PREFACE

The fundamental language of retail merchandising consists primarily of numbers and related figure facts such as dollars, units, and percentages. A basic knowledge of the mathematical interrelationship of profit factors, as these pertain to the day-to-day operation of a retail organization of any size, is essential to profitable merchandising. Recent studies have revealed that an alarming number of such mid-management merchandising, personnel as assistant buyers, buyers, and even merchandising managers are so lacking in merchandising mathematical competency as to render them incapable of solving all but the simplest of work-related problems. This is a sad commentary on the effectiveness of academic programs of merchandising study or retail store executive training and development programs.

Retail Merchandising Mathematics has been developed primarily to prepare career-oriented students for employment at such entry level merchandising positions in retail organizations as assistant buyer, assistant manager, or merchandising clerical. In addition, this book can serve as a guide in developing retail store junior executive training programs; it can provide, as well, an excellent procedural source of reference for young buyers with limited work experience, managers of chain units, or merchants who operate small independent stores.

The major purposes of this text are to introduce students to retail merchandising principles and terminology; provide them with the basic merchandising equations and other arithmetic calculations frequently used in the merchandising operations; acquaint them with the various principles, practices, and techniques employed by retail merchants in the planning and control of their stock assortments; instruct them in the use and function of typical retail store merchandising forms and reports; and help them develop a degree of competency in applying basic mathematical formulas to the solving of merchandising problems.

The contents of this book are realistic because they are based on the author's considerable personal experience as a buyer and merchandiser in medium- to large-volume retail organizations; her personal experience as a professor and coordinator of retail merchandising programs of study in both two- and four-year colleges; the opinions and advice of the many retail executives with whom the author has maintained close, professional working relationships; the fact that all material has been thoroughly class-tested; and the favorable comments of students, graduates, faculty associates, and reviewers.

Retail Merchandising Mathematics has been developed as a text or *handbook,* with the added advantages of a *workbook.* In each chapter, after a major topic has been introduced and discussed, practice problems that test the students' understanding of that particular topic are presented. At the end of each chapter new terms are listed in a Summary of Key Terms and their definitions are restated. Also at the conclusion of each chapter are objective and short answer Review Questions, followed by Review Problems, each with workspace for the calculation of answers. The pages on which the Review Questions and Problems appear may be removed when completed, handed in for grading purposes, and later replaced in the book for study and reference.

In the first of the ten chapters there is a brief and thorough review of decimals and percentages, with related practice exercises. Accuracy in handling these arithmetic concepts is an absolute essential in arriving at correct merchandising calculations. The second chapter serves as an introduction to the retail merchandising function, exploring various sizes and types of stores and their organization for carrying out the merchandising activity. Responsibilities of personnel in the Merchandising Division and important staff aides to that Division are also discussed here. Succeeding chapters explore fundamental retail merchandising principles and procedures in sequential learning order, starting with the Seasonal Merchandise Plan and concluding with periodic financial and managerial reports on the merchandising operation.

An Instructor's Manual, including solutions to Practice and Review Questions and Problems, a diagnostic test, arithmetic review test, and midterm and final examination complete with answers, is available.

The author wishes to express her appreciation of the help she has received from many people in the preparation of this text-workbook. Thanks go to business and academic associates who generously shared their valuable time, materials, and experience. Special thanks must go to the hundreds of students who field-tested experimental versions of this text and whose enthusiastic response and interest provided the incentive needed to complete it.

CHAPTER 1

REVIEW
OF ARITHMETIC

Mathematics is the science of numbers and measurements in terms of figures. It is a science that must be thoroughly mastered by anyone who wants a career in merchandising. Merchandise planning and evaluation are done almost completely in the language of numbers.

Today, various calculating machines and mechanical devices are used by business organizations to handle mathematical calculations. All those calculators and devices do, however, is the routine counting work. They do not think. Thinking will always remain the responsibility of people.

To be a good merchandiser, you must know the fundamentals of arithmetic. Only when you can handle whole numbers, fractions, decimals, and percentages rapidly, accurately, and confidently will you be able to think and work efficiently in this field. Although you may have already mastered these various types of arithmetic calculations, a quick review of decimals and percentages, which are widely used in merchandising calculations, may help you sharpen your skills and improve your speed.

Here are some tips. For maximum accuracy in arithmetical calculation, write each number clearly and distinctly; do not take the chance of making a mistake by being unable to read your own handwriting or of others being unable to read it. Make sure that you write the numbers of a problem in their proper position: addition, subtraction, and multiplication problems are usually figured vertically, with the numbers lined up on the right-hand side; division problems are usually figured horizontally; decimal points are placed according to specific rules. Simple tips, yes—but even simple mistakes in arithmetic can be very expensive both to you and to your store.

DECIMALS

A *decimal* is a fraction whose denominator is some power of 10 (10, 100, 1,000, etc.) and which is signified by a decimal point placed at the left of the first figure of the number. For example:

$$.1 \quad = \frac{1}{10}$$

$$.01 \quad = \frac{1}{100}$$

$$.001 \quad = \frac{1}{1,000}$$

$$.0001 = \frac{1}{10,000}$$

The decimal point separates a whole number from a part of that whole number expressed as some power of 10. For example, 1.15 equals 1 and 15/100s of 100. In U.S. currency, where pennies represent hundred parts of a dollar (100 pennies equal one dollar), $1.15 means one dollar and 15/100s of a second dollar, or one dollar and fifteen cents.

Adding Decimals

To add decimals, place the numbers to be added in vertical columns, with each decimal point directly below the one in the number above it. It is the decimal points that must be aligned in a straight row, not the right-hand side of the figures, as in addition of whole numbers. Draw a horizontal line beneath the last number in the column. Put the answer beneath this line, with the decimal point of the answer being placed directly below that of the decimal points of the numbers that have been added.

Problem:

2.42	2.420
.4	.400
11.8	11.800
+ 2.587	+ 2.587
17.207	17.207

Notes:

Align figures so that all decimal points are in a straight vertical line. Then add up the figures just as though there were no decimal points. To avoid possible errors because of the placement of the numbers, zeros can be placed after the numbers so that they all align on the right, as per the example at the immediate left.

To prove the accuracy of your calculation, use the same method that is used to prove a calculation in the addition of whole numbers, that is, by adding the figures in the opposite direction.

Subtracting Decimals

To subtract decimals, first write down the larger number. Then put the smaller number (the one to be subtracted) directly under the larger number, lining up the decimal points in a vertical line. Draw a horizontal line under the second number. Calculate as you would in a problem involving whole numbers, and indicate the remainder under the line—putting the decimal point in the remainder directly below those above the line.

Problem:

19.49	19.4900
− 8.6431	− 8.6431
10.8469	10.8469

As in the addition of decimals, zeros can be added to the right of the decimal points to make this calculation more accurate. This has been done in the example immediately to the left. Adding zeros in this way does not change the value of the numbers in any way.

To prove the accuracy of your calculation, use the same method that is used to prove a calculation in the subtraction of whole numbers; that is, by adding the difference figure to the smaller number (the one being subtracted) the answer should be the first or larger number, as in this example:

$$\begin{array}{r} 10.8469 \\ + \ 8.6431 \\ \hline 19.4900 \end{array} \quad \text{or} \quad 19.49$$

PRACTICE PROBLEMS—Adding and Subtracting Decimals

1. Add each of the following (use separate sheet for figuring):

   (a) .25, .75, .374, .625, .03 = _____

   (b) 3.75, 28.2, .087, 14.7891 = _____

   (c) .012, 1.34, 12.989, 141.3, .375 = _____

   (d) .125, .2875, 1.47, 24.9, 9.009 = _____

   (e) 493.6, 2.901, .43, .975, 14.75 = _____

2. Subtract each of the following (use separate sheet for figuring):

   (a) 9.45 from 11.00 = _____

   (b) 247.59 from 9,421.63 = _____

   (c) .1322 from 5.62 = _____

   (d) .093 from .1203 = _____

   (e) 4.697 from 6.2433 = _____

Multiplying Decimals

To multiply decimals, write down the figures just as though you were putting down a multiplication problem in whole numbers. Do not try to align the decimal points. Calculate the problem as though it were a problem in whole numbers. Then, after you have obtained an answer, add together the number of places to the right of the decimal point in the multiplicand (first number) and the number of places to the right of the decimal point in the multiplier (second number). This total is the number of places that the decimal point should be placed to the left in the answer.

Problem:

$$\begin{array}{r} 3.24 \\ \times\ \ .75 \\ \hline 1620 \\ 2268\ \ \\ \hline 2.4300 \end{array}\quad\text{or}\quad 2.43$$

Notes:

The decimal point is two places to the right in the multiplicand, and two places to the right in the multiplier. This means that the decimal point is placed 4 places to the left of the last figure in the answer (product).

To prove the accuracy of your calculation, use the same method that is used to prove a calculation in the multiplication of whole numbers. Since this involves using division, read the section about dividing decimals before trying to prove a multiplication problem in decimals.

$$2.43 \div .75 = .75\overline{)2.43.00}$$

$$\begin{array}{r} 3.24 \\ \underline{225} \\ 180 \\ \underline{150} \\ 300 \\ \underline{300} \end{array}$$

PRACTICE PROBLEMS—Multiplying Decimals

Multiply each of the following sets of figures in the space provided.

1. (a) $3.20   (b) $19.75   (c) $201.90   (d) $285.10   (e) $19.03
        X 4   X 7   X 14   X 12   X .43

2. (a) 24.6   (b) 8.76   (c) 2.041   (d) 6.257   (e) 876
        X .4   X 2.6   X .07   X .11   X .27

3. (a) 24.628   (b) .21364   (c) 2.69   (d) 1.064   (e) 1.0004
        X 97.5   X 9.6   X 12.3   X 78.2   X .205

4. (a) $425.00   (b) $412.92   (c) $39.33   (d) $81.54   (e) $810.14
        X 37   X 16   X 4   X 13   X 7

Dividing Decimals

To divide a decimal by a whole number, proceed as in regular division, being sure to place the decimal point in the answer space directly above the decimal point in the number to be divided, as in this example:

$$12.75 \div 15 = 15\overline{\smash{\big)}\,12.75}$$

$$\begin{array}{r} .85 \\ 15\overline{\smash{\big)}\,12.75} \\ \underline{12.0} \\ 75 \\ \underline{75} \end{array}$$

To divide a decimal by a decimal, proceed as in regular division, with one additional step: move any decimal point in the divisor (the dividing number) to the right of its last number, then move the decimal point in the dividend the same number of places to the right, adding zeros as necessary.

To prove the accuracy of your calculation, use the same method that is used to prove a calculation in the division of whole numbers—that is, multiply the answer by either the divisor or dividend, and you should get the remaining figure.

$$\begin{array}{r} .85 \\ 12.75 \div 1.5 = 1.5_{\curvearrowright}\overline{\smash{\big)}\,12.7_{\curvearrowright}50} \\ \underline{120} \\ 75 \\ \underline{75} \end{array}$$

PRACTICE PROBLEMS—Dividing Decimals

Divide each of the following (use separate sheet for figuring):

(a) $24.72 by 8 = _____

(b) $196.92 by 9 = _____

(c) 25.0047 by 7 = _____

(d) $576 by .006 = _____

(e) $4,215 by .15 = _____

(f) .31552 by 4.64 = _____

(g) 642.812 by 321.406 = _____

(h) $96.48 by .75 = _____

(i) $174.96 by 1.44 = _____

(j) $2,671.38 by .051 = _____

PERCENTAGES

A *percentage* is a part or specified number of parts of 100 when 100 is considered the whole or base figure. Percentage is indicated by a percent sign: %.

Percentages are used frequently in all kinds of business dealings. Discounts, interest, commissions, and taxes are all expressed in percentages. Percentages are particularly useful for making comparisons. In retail merchandising, net sales or net income is frequently used as the base figure, and costs of goods, expense of operations, and amount of profit are expressed as percentages of that base figure. Then relationships between current figures can be checked against past and planned figures to give the merchant a detailed picture of the state of his/her business as compared to last year and/or plan.

Percentages are added, subtracted, multiplied, and divided in exactly the same way that decimals are. Since percentages are parts of 100, the same rules that apply to the placement of the decimal point in calculating decimals apply to the placement of the percentage point in calculating percentages. The only difference is that a percent sign is always used in the answer.

Therefore, instead of discussing addition, subtraction, multiplication, and division, this section will concentrate on the several common calculations involving percentages.

Converting Percentage into a Fraction or Decimal

1. To change a percentage into a fraction, first remove the percent sign, divide the percent number by 100, and then reduce the resulting fraction to its lowest terms. For example:

$$60\% = 60 \div 100$$
$$= \frac{60}{100}$$
$$= \frac{3}{5}$$

2. To change a percentage to a decimal, first remove the percent sign and then move the decimal point *two places to the left,* adding or subtracting zeros as needed. For example:

$$50\% = 50/100s$$
$$= .50$$
$$= .5$$

3. To change a fractional percentage to a decimal, first change the fractional percentage into its equivalent decimal percentage. Then change the decimal percentage to a regular decimal as in the preceding paragraph. For example:

$$3/5\% = .6\%$$
$$= .006$$

Note: "3/5%" is three-fifths of one part of 100. It is only 6/1,000 of the whole.

Converting a Decimal or Fraction into Percentage

1. To change a decimal into a percentage, move the decimal point *two places to the right,* adding zeros as necessary, and add the percent sign. For example:

$$.05 = 05.$$
$$= 5\%$$

2. To change a fraction to a percent, divide the denominator (the figure below the line) of the fraction into its numerator (the figure above the line). The result will be a decimal. Then change the decimal into a percentage by following the instructions above. For example:

$$7/8 = 8\overline{)7.000}$$

$$
\begin{array}{r}
.875 \\
\underline{64} \\
60 \\
\underline{56} \\
40 \\
\underline{40}
\end{array}
$$

$$= .875$$
$$= 87.5\%$$

To Find What Percentage One Number Is of Another

Percentage can be calculated through the use of an algebraic equation. If two of the three figures used in the equation are known, the third can be calculated. For example:

Problem 1:   17 is what percent of 68?

Equation: 17 is to 68 as X is to 100%

Solution:

$$\frac{17}{68} = \frac{X\%}{100\%}$$

$$68X = 17 \times 100\%$$

$$= 1,700\%$$

$$X = \frac{1,700\%}{68}$$

$$= 25\%$$

Problem 2:   400 is 25% of what amount?

Equation: 400 is to X as 25% is to 100%

Solution:

$$\frac{400}{X} = \frac{25\%}{100\%}$$

$$\frac{400}{x} = \frac{1}{4} \qquad \text{(reduced to lowest terms)}$$

$$1X = 4 \times 400 \qquad \text{(cross-multiplying)}$$

$$= 1,600$$

Note: In calculating percentage, the answer may be an even number or carried out from one to any number of places to the right of the decimal point. Often, one number does not divide evenly into another number. In such cases, an arbitrary rule is usually established as to whether the answer is to be carried out to one, two, or more places to the right of the decimal point. In usual retail practice, percentages are carried out to 100ths of a percent. This means that the answer is figured through the third place to the right of the decimal point. If the third number is 5 or over, the second number is increased by one. If the third number is less than 5, the second number remains unchanged. In either case the third number is then dropped.

To Calculate Percentage of Increase or Decrease

To find the percentage of increase or decrease between two amounts, first find the difference between the two amounts. Then divide the difference by the *original* or former amount, known as the *base*.

a. Here is an example of calculating percent of increase:

Problem 1: If sales volume was $125,000 in 1977 and $100,000 in 1976, by what percent did the volume increase between 1976 and 1977?

Equation: $25,000 is to $100,000 as X is to 100%

Solution:

$$\frac{\$25,000}{\$100,000} = \frac{X}{100\%}$$

$$\frac{1}{4} = \frac{X}{100\%} \qquad \text{(reduced to the lowest common denominator)}$$

$$4X = 1 \times 100\% \qquad \text{(cross-multiplying)}$$

$$X = \frac{100\%}{4}$$

$$= 25\%$$

b. Here is an example of calculating percent of decrease:

Problem 2: If operating expenses were $20,000 in 1977 and $25,000 in 1976, what was the percentage of decrease in expenses between 1976 and 1977?

Equation: $5,000 is to $25,000 as X is to 100%

Solution:

$$\frac{\$5,000}{\$25,000} = \frac{X}{100\%}$$

$$\frac{1}{5} = \frac{X}{100\%} \qquad \text{(reduced to the lowest common denominator)}$$

$$5X = 1 \times 100\% \qquad \text{(cross-multiplying)}$$

$$X = \frac{100\%}{5}$$

$$= 20\%$$

PRACTICE PROBLEMS—Percentages

1. Change the following percents to fractions, and reduce to lowest terms. Use separate sheet for figuring.

   (a)   33% = _____ = _____

   (b)   47 1/2% = _____ = _____

   (c)   50% = _____ = _____

   (d)   1/2% = _____ = _____

   (e)   .1% = _____ = _____

2. Change the following percents to decimals:

(a)   14 1/2% = _____

(d)   155% = _____

(b)   100% = _____

(e)   1% = _____

(c)   3% = _____

3. Change the following fractions to percents:

(a) $\frac{2}{7}$ = _____

(d) $\frac{1}{3}$ = _____

(b) $1\frac{2}{5}$ = _____

(e) $\frac{17}{20}$ = _____

(c) $\frac{3}{8}$ = _____

4. Find the following amounts (do your calculations in space provided):

(a)   26% of $1,426.50

_____
(Answer)

(b)   12 1/2% of $840

_____
(Answer)

(c)   200% of $125

_____
(Answer)

(d)   1/2% of $1,000

_____
(Answer)

(e)   5 1/4% of $400

_____
(Answer)

5. Solve the following problems in the spaces provided:

(a) An all-weather coat was reduced from $80 to $60. What was the percentage of reduction?

_____
(Answer)

(b) The volume in the Men's Furnishings Department last year was $50,000. An increase of 10% is planned for this year. What is the projected volume this year?

_____
(Answer)

(c) During August a manufacturer increased his production from 440 coats last year to 550 coats this year. What was the percent of increase?

_____
(Answer)

(d) Last year, 550 dolls were sold in a toy department. This year, doll sales declined by 60%. How many dolls were sold this year?

_____
(Answer)

(e) A vendor received $88.40 for a group of costume earrings. How many pairs of earrings did he sell if the price he received was $5.20 a dozen?

_____
(Answer)

(f)   A buyer purchased 250 sweaters for a special sales event. If 42% of them were cardigans, how many cardigans did she purchase?

_____
(Answer)

(g)   A buyer found that 2% of the toys in his stock were damaged. They were replaced with new merchandise. How many toys are there in stock if 58 were replaced?

_____
(Answer)

(h)   The buyer for the Jewelry Department totaled the department sales for last Saturday and found that Ms. Horn sold $650 worth of merchandise, Ms. Jones had sales of $1,100 and Ms. Rolf had sales of $925. What percentage of the sales was done by each salesperson?

_____
(Horn)

_____
(Jones)

_____
(Rolf)

6.   Solve the following problems (use separate sheet for figuring):

(a)   3% of $1,827 = _____

(b)   15% of $625.80 = _____

(c)   .5% of $716 = _____

(d) 107% of $385 = _____

(e) 1.12% of $575 = _____

(f) 42.5% of $11.98 = _____

(g) $17.28 = 25% of _____

(h) $37.56 = 2.5% of _____

(i) $441 = 22.5% of _____

(j) 84 = 12.5% of _____

(k) 912 = 50% of _____

(l) 6.21 = 92% of _____

(m) $7.13 is_____% of $7.75

(n) $60.40 is _____% of $2,416

(o) $875 is _____% of $3,500

ARITHMETIC REVIEW PROBLEMS

1. A concern has five salespeople, each of whom receives, in addition to a base salary, a commission of 8% on the amount he/she sells in excess of the average sales of the five. For November their sales were:

    (A) $1,850.75
    (B)   1,797.26
    (C)   1,268.30
    (D)   1,582.48
    (E)   1,326.61

    (a) Which salespeople received commissions?

    _____
    (Answer)

    (b) How much did each receive in commissions?

    (A) _____   (D) _____

    (B) _____   (E) _____

    (C) _____

2. Mr. Henry earns $360 a month, which is 20% more than Mr. Brown earns. What is Mr. Brown's salary?

    _____
    (Answer)

3. If $1.65 represented the 10% tax on each ticket to a benefit performance, what was the total cost of each ticket?

    _____
    (Answer)

4. Mr. Phillips earned $600 in April, from which his employer withheld $114 for taxes. His expenses for April were $120 for rent, $120 for food, $88 for clothing and $128 for sundry other expenses. How much did he have left?

    _____
    (Answer)

5. How many feet of wire would be needed to fence a field 215 feet square if the fence is to be six strands of wire high on all sides?

_____
(Answer)

6. A certain building has 108 windows, each window containing 24 panes of glass. What would be the cost of replacing the glass in all windows at 98¢ a pane?

_____
(Answer)

7. If a hosiery buyer had $600 to invest in socks, how many pairs can he buy at 50¢ per pair?

_____
(Answer)

8. In a test an automobile ran 29 miles in 30 minutes. At this rate, how many miles would it run in 7 1/2 hours?

_____
(Answer)

9. In a community having a population of 7,500 people, 150 are over 65 years old. What percent is this of the total population?

_____
(Answer)

10. If an agent's sales commission of 5% on one sale amounted to $185, what was the total amount of that sale?

_____
(Answer)

CHAPTER 2

INTRODUCTION TO RETAIL MERCHANDISING

One of the most common misconceptions about retailing is that the terms "retailing" and "merchandising" are synonymous. They are not. *Retailing* is a nonmanufacturing business engaged in purchasing consumer goods from a wide variety of sources and assembling them in convenient locations for the purpose of profitable resale to ultimate consumers. *Merchandising,* on the other hand, is the primary function of all retail operations because it involves the buying and selling responsibilities of each firm. All other retail functions, such as those having to do with finance, credit, personnel, advertising, store maintenance, and so on, are secondary or supporting functions of the main store's function, which is merchandising.

FUNDAMENTAL CONCEPTS

There is no one universally accepted definition of merchandising. Neither is this particular activity confined to retailing. Producers, too, merchandise their products to customers. Some producers regard the term as being synonymous with marketing. Others consider it the function of product planning and development. Retailers, however, associate the term with the planning and control of their merchandise assortments in order to meet certain predetermined monetary objectives of the firm. While the primary objective may be profit, this can be achieved only if the retailer is consumer-oriented and employs techniques and devices for determining and satisfying the expressed and latent needs and wants of the firm's potential target group or groups of customers.

Merchandising Objectives

From the customers' point of view, adequate stock assortments include what has become known as the five "rights," which include:

1. the *right* merchandise (for specific purposes);

2. at the *right* time (when the goods are needed—neither too early nor too late);

3. in the *right* quantities (in the amounts needed);

4. at the *right* place (conveniently located; where one would expect to find them);

5. at the *right* prices (the prices customers are both willing and able to pay).

Unbalanced inventories and lost sales opportunities result from failure to achieve these five "rights" in any merchandise assortment.

Retail merchandising involves setting up merchandise departments or classifications (see Chapter 8) as planning and control units, each under the supervision and direction of a department buyer or manager. These middle-management executives are responsible for the planning and maintenance of assortments that are successful in meeting customer demand. They are also responsible for providing the firm with a markup that, in addition to covering costs and expenses relating to the department's operation, contributes a designated share to the overhead expenses and profit of the organization as a whole.

Importance of Figure Relationships

Successful merchandising implies the effective coordination of all available merchandising activities. In most retail organizations, coordination is the responsibility of the store's buyers, who, in addition to being chief executives in their respective departments, must also be thoroughly familiar with all aspects of their markets and the products to be found in each.

Since buyers and department managers are responsible for developing sales that result in a reasonable profit, achievement of this goal requires not only a comprehensive knowledge of ethical buying practices and procedures, but also versatility in handling the interrelationships between the factors that influence profit—sales volume, cost of merchandise sold, and operating expenses. These factors and their interrelationships will be discussed in detail in Chapter 3.

Most merchandising facts are expressed in numbers rather than in words and it is important that merchandising students have a thorough technical training in the computation and interpretation of figure facts, particularly as they relate directly to ultimate business profit or loss. Reports are in terms of figures—dollars, units, and/or percentages. Purchases, operating expenses, terms of sale, markup, markdowns, inventory values, sales volume, stock shortages or overages, transportation costs, and soon, are always expressed in terms of numbers. Certain commonly used terms, such as color, classification, vendor, season letter, and so on, are converted to number codes for record purposes. With the rapidly spreading use among retailers of electronic data processing and reporting, numbers have become the shorthand method by which merchandising information is communicated.

The merchandising executive is judged by his/her merchandising accomplishments, as indicated in the departmental monthly operating statement, when these are compared to seasonal plans, all of which are stated in figures. Profitable merchandising is the result of understanding the interrelationship of the mathematical factors affecting the buying and selling of merchandise and the ability of the buyer to successfully manipulate these factors so that a reasonable profit results.

ORGANIZATION FOR MERCHANDISING

Although merchandising is the primary function in a retail operation of any size its ultimate success is dependent on the operational efficiency of other supporting retail functions.

In the Small Store

Maintaining merchandise in the five "rights" relationships is as much the major function of the smallest retail operation (often called a *Mom-and-Pop* store) as it is of the largest store. In the early days of retailing, as well as in the thousands of small stores located around the country today, merchandising is the primary function of the merchant himself/herself. While he/she must direct selling and advertising, keep records of all transactions, and find and often have to personally maintain a suitable space in which to operate, he/she usually assigns these duties to members of the family or a few hired helpers whenever possible. He/she seldom, however, delegates the planning and activities necessary to balance stocks to customer demand in order to achieve profit objectives.

In Medium- to Large-Volume Stores

Through the years, as many stores have grown in physical size as well as in sales volume, it became apparent that it was necessary to hire specialists to handle various store functions, such as bookkeeping, maintenance of the premises, and often sales promotion activities. As stores continued to grow in physical size and sales volume, it became apparent that separate store divisions needed to be set up to handle each of the basic functions. Increasing sales volume, more scattered markets, changing economic conditions, and keener competition have made the job of the buyer (sometimes referred to as department head or department manager) more difficult and complex. Out of this evolved the Merchandising Division with responsibility for both buying and selling. Former nonmerchandising retail activities that once may have been carried on by the merchant became the responsibilities of such nonmerchandising divisions as Control (all financial matters), Sales Promotion (advertising, display, and publicity), Store Operation (including maintenance), and in the case of quite large stores, Personnel.

The number of divisions and buying departments varies with the size and type of retail organizations. Smaller stores often combine divisions in accordance with the particular needs of the business or the availability of personnel with the necessary interests and talents. In large stores, with many merchandising departments, the Merchandising Division is often headed by a General Merchandise Manager, who has a number of subordinate Divisional Merchandise Managers (referred to in the trade as D.M.M.s), each supervising a number of related departments, such as Ladies' Apparel departments, Infants' and Children's departments, Fashion Accessories departments, Home Furnishings departments, and so on (see Exhibit 2-1).

In Chain Store Systems

A *chain* is a series of retail outlets that are centrally owned and merchandised from an office rather than by a parent or main store. Merchandising responsibilities in chains vary somewhat from that previously described as applying in independent stores. The major difference is that the responsibility for buying and that for selling are entirely separate in a chain organization. Buying is done centrally by specialists for the entire chain while responsibility for selling rests solely with the manager of each unit in the chain. Central buyers prepare standardized assortment plans, determine resources, negotiate terms of sale, and prepare a buying "list" or "catalog" from which the store managers and their department managers may select and place orders for specific items and quantities. This applies primarily to nonapparel merchandise, which is usually stored in a central or regional warehouse and requisitioned from there by individual store managers and their department managers.

EXHIBIT 2-1   TYPICAL DIVISIONAL BREAKDOWN IN A DEPARTMENT STORE

I. *Ladies' Apparel Departments*
    Coats including Rainwear
    Women's Dresses (half-sizes, 12½-26½,
      and straight sizes, 36-52)
      Budget
      Moderate
      Better
    Misses' Dresses (even numbered sizes
      4-20)
      Budget
      Moderate
      Better
    Junior Dresses (odd numbered sizes
      3-17)
    Women's Sportswear
    Misses' Sportswear
      Budget
      Moderate
      Better
    Junior Sportswear
    Blouses
    Aprons and Uniforms
    Maternity Wear
    Furs
    Bridals
    Pre-teen Apparel

II. *Children's Apparel Departments*
    Infants' Wear
    Infants' Toys
    Infants' Furniture
    Girls' Ready-to-Wear, sizes 3-6X
    Girls' Ready-to-Wear, sizes 7-14
    Subteen Apparel
    Boys' Apparel, sizes 3-6X
    Girls' Underwear, Hosiery, Accessories
    Children's Shoes

III. *Intimate Apparel Departments*
    Ladies' Daywear (lingerie)
    Ladies' Sleepwear
    Corsets and Bras
    Robes and Leisurewear

IV. *Men's and Boys' Wear Departments*
    Men's Clothing
    Men's Furnishings and Hats
    Men's Toiletries and Cosmetics
    Men's Sportswear
    Boys' Wear
    Men's and Boys' Shoes and Slippe

V. *Accessories Departments*
    Hosiery
    Jewelry: Costume and Fine
    Handbags
    Fashion Accessories
      Neckwear and Scarfs
      Handkerchiefs
      Umbrellas
      Belts
      Gloves
      Sunglasses
    Millinery
      Budget
      Better
    Wigs
    Women's Shoes
    Cosmetics, Toilet Articles,
      Drug Sundries

VI. *Smallwares Departments*
    Notions
    Silverware
    Clocks
    Art Needlework
    Books and Magazines
    Stationery and Greeting Cards
    Cameras and Photo
      Equipment

VII. *Domestic Departments*
    Piece Goods
      Yard Goods
      Patterns
      Sewing Notions

EXHIBIT 2-1   (continued)

VII. *Domestic Departments* (continued)
    Household Textiles
        Table Linen
        Bath Shop
        Sheets, Pillowcases,
           Mattress Pads
        Blankets, Comforters,
           Spreads

VIII. *Home Furnishings Departments*
    Furniture and Bedding
        Upholstered and Non-
           upholstered Furniture
        Mattresses, Springs, Studio
           Beds
    Floor Coverings
        Rugs and Carpets
        Linoleum
    Draperies and Curtains
    Lamps and Mirrors
    China and Glassware
    Major Household Appliances
        Refrigerators and Freezers
        Stoves
        Washing Machines and Dryers

VIII. *Home Furnishings* (continued)
    Housewares (including small
        appliances)
    Gift Shop
    Radios, Phonographs, Stereos,
        Television, Pianos, Records,
        Musical Instruments

IX. *Other Merchandise Departments*
    Toys and Games
    Sporting Goods
    Luggage
    Candy
    Gourmet Foods
    Bakery

X. *Basement:*
    Includes many of the above
        departments, but handles
        lower-priced lines and
        sometimes seconds.

In the case of apparel and most private brand merchandise, however, central buyers do preliminary planning, buying, and reordering for the entire chain based on sales forecasts and stock requirements of each unit. The merchandise purchases are then received, marked, allocated, and shipped to each unit from a central distribution point. This is called *Central Merchandising.* Here again the individual store manager and department manager are responsible for sales. They may, however, make recommendations to the central buyers and distribution center as to type and description of the stock needed to better satisfy local demand.

Since each unit of a chain is considered a separate entity, it is responsible for its own merchandising activities, sales, and profitability. Rarely is merchandise transferred from one unit of the chain to another.

Chains may be national, regional, or local as far as location is concerned. If the chain has stores located throughout the country, such as Sears, Roebuck and Co., The J. C. Penney Co., and Montgomery Ward, it is known as a *national chain.* National chains are usually merchandised by regional offices, rather than by the main headquarters office, both because of the great number of stores involved and the variations in customer demand that exists between various regions of the country, such as Northeast, Northwest, Southwest, Midwest, and so on.

Regional chains usually have fewer stores than do national chains. Since their stores are located in a limited geographical area, such as Joske's of Texas, Maas Bros. of Florida, or Younker Bros. of Iowa, variations in demand between stores is not as great as that experienced by national chains. They also operate out of central offices which are usually conveniently located with respect to most of their unit stores, thereby reducing many of the communication and transportation problems of the national chains.

In the Branch System

A *branch store* is a retail store that is owned and merchandised by a parent or main store. Because most branches of a parent store are apt to be located fairly close to each other as well as to the parent store, and because they are under the direct control of the parent store and its Merchandising Division, merchandise assortments and services in each branch store are usually more closely tailored to local requirements than are the fairly standardized assortments found in units of a chain.

In a typical branch-operating retail organization, buyers housed in the parent store plan initial assortments, stock requirements, buy for the branches as well as for the parent store, and determine what and how much merchandise is to go to each. In each branch unit there is a department manager in charge of one or more departmental areas. For example, in each branch there may be one department manager for all the departments comprising a Merchandising Division as indicated in Exhibit 2-1. A Group Manager supervises a limited number of department managers in a branch store just as a D.M.M. supervises a limited number of department buyers in the parent store. Group Managers, in turn, are responsible to the branch Store Manager. Branch department managers, as a rule, are not permitted to buy merchandise, although they may sometimes take markdowns with the permission of the department buyer in the parent store. However, since they can control merchandise reorders and can request specific merchandise, department managers can adjust, to a degree, the quantities and assortment mix in order to more effectively serve local demand.

In the case of very large volume branches and/or those that may be at a considerable distance from the parent store, merchandising of the branch usually becomes more autonomous. In such cases, buyers in the parent store, Group and branch department managers, and the Store Managers cooperate in drawing up seasonal sales and stock plans for each branch. Separate Open-To-Buy and Operating Statements (see Chapter 10) may also be prepared for each branch in some cases.

Organizational Chart of Merchandising Division

Exhibit 2-2 shows typical lines of authority and responsibility within the Merchandising Division of a medium- to large-volume store. This exhibit indicates the vertical line of authority from the General Merchandise Manager down to departmental sales and stock personnel. Continuous straight lines represent lines of authority; dashed lines represent staff (advisory) responsibility.

Responsibilities of Merchandising Executives

Although the student may have already become familiar with the responsibilities of Merchandising Division personnel, it seems appropriate at this point to briefly review those responsibilities.

The General Merchandise Manager. The General Merchandise Manager (G.M.M.) is head of the Merchandising Division and its chief executive authority. In a four-functional retail organization, this major executive, together with the President and/or General Manager, and the heads of the other functional divisions of the store—Controller, Sales Promotion Director, and Operations Manager—are referred to as "top management" and are responsible for formulating major store policies. The chief responsibility of the General Merchandise Manager is to interpret these policies to the personnel under his/her supervision and see that the policies are implemented throughout the entire Merchandising Division.

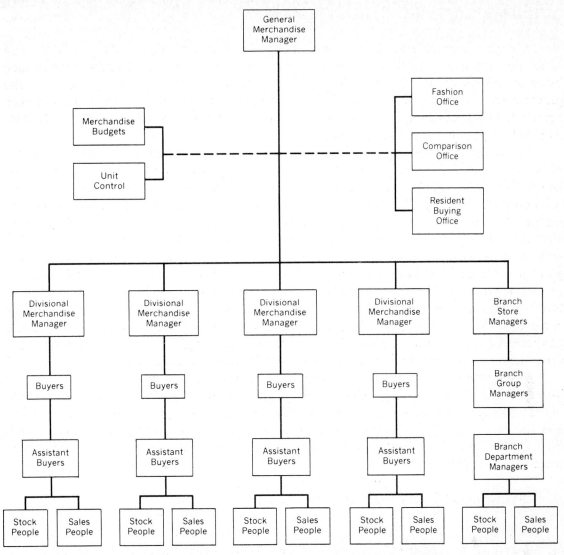

EXHIBIT 2-2 TYPICAL ORGANIZATIONAL PLAN FOR A MERCHANDISING DIVISION

Merchandising policies established by a store's top management team result in formation of the image customers have of that store (See Exhibit 2-3). Image-building policies pertain to the following:

- depth and breadth of assortments;
- price ranges;
- degree of fashion emphasis;
- brand policies;
- quality of merchandise handled;
- selling services;
- customer services;
- markdown policies;
- meeting competitors' prices;
- promotional activities;
- general atmosphere in which the merchandise is presented.

EXHIBIT 2-3   ANALYSIS OF THE STORE'S IMAGE

I. Merchandise Features

1. *Quality*	No standard set or enforced; sub-standard goods may be carried	Attempt, through buyers, at serviceable quality	Much merchandise tested for quality	Store carries best the market affords
2. *Price Ranges*	Low	Medium to low	High to medium	High
3. *Values Provided*	Poor	Fair	Good	Excellent
4. *Variety of Lines Offered*	Very restricted (single lines, such as prescription drugs, slacks, paintings, men's ties)	Related product lines (in apparel for example)	General merchandise lines (both apparel and home furnishings) and possibly foods and auto equipment	Seller of both merchandise and services (insurance, travel, repairs, rentals, etc.)
5. *Continuity in Lines*	Odd lots—no continuity	Some regular assortments but emphasis on specials temporarily available	Regular assortments featured	Open stock; continuity long maintained
6. *Breadth and Depth of Assortments in Each Line*	Narrow with little depth	Best sellers in depth	Broad assortments but little depth	Broad and deep assortments
7. *Degree of Exclusiveness*	Staple and standard goods available elsewhere	Top national brands featured, also available elsewhere	Chief emphasis on private brands	Much exclusive merchandise obtained from confined sources
8. *Taste Level*	No special attention paid to good taste	Popularity the measure of taste	Some goods that appeal to the discriminating customer	A high degree of discrimination and sophistication in goods offered
9. *Timing of Fashions*	Odd lot fashion bargains	Stress on mass accepted fashions	Stress on styles increasing in popularity	Leadership; many newly introduced styles
10. *Relationship with Suppliers*	Convenient depot for goods of which producers have a surplus	Shops for bargains in the market; price appeal emphasized	Seeks cooperative agreements on regular goods with some price specials and special orders.	Close relationships with name producers; feature confined lines and styles

II. Promotion Features

1. *Advertising*	Blatant and hard to believe	Pedestrian; uninteresting	Worth reading	Very informative and always believable

EXHIBIT 2-3 (continued)

2. *Windows*	Cluttered and messy	Gain attention but not interest	Gain attention and interest but may not move customer to enter store	Create attention, interest and desire, evidenced by customer entering the store
3. *Publicity*	Nothing unusual going on	Lots of ballyhoo but little real information	Occasional important events	Some newsworthy event nearly always in progress

III. Service Features

1. *Credit*	Cash only	Charge accounts as an accommodation	Regular, rotated and instalment accounts available	Credit buying opportunity stressed
2. *Delivery*	"Take-with" only	Charge for all deliveries	Charge on small sales under a minimum	Free on all purchases
3. *Adjustments and Returns*	Difficult to obtain	Restrictions enforced	Liberal	"The customer is is always right"
4. *Personal Assistance to Customers*	None—self service	Little—self selection in most lines	Salespeople available of average ability	Experienced salespeople who are professional customer advisors
5. *Efforts at Customer Persuasion*	Little attempt to either assist or persuade—mostly order filling	Goal to help customers buy but not to persuade	Persuasion attempted if believed to be in both the customer's and the store's interest	Hard sell—considerable pressure to make each sale
6. *Attitude toward Individual Customers*	All parts of the crowd to be handled with dispatch	Certain people and groups given the "red carpet" treatment	All treated same but courteously	Attempt to treat every customer as an honored, special guest
7. *Atmosphere of the Store*	Run-down, old, dingy, dirty, stuffy	Functional but ordinary	Fresh, new, clean, modern look, comfortable for shopping	Opulent, rich, elegant
8. *Social Standing*	Where the bargain hunters shop	Where the middle class shops	Where more discriminating customers shop	Where the community leaders and celebrities shop

In some retail organizations the General Merchandise Manager has an assistant whose chief responsibility it is to function as a liaison between G.M.M. and the various D.M.M.s in relation to evaluating merchandise plans and results, as well as sales promotional efforts.

The Divisional Merchandise Manager.   The Divisional Merchandise Manager is the middle-management representative, in that he/she supervises and coordinates a group of departments handling related merchandise and is responsible for the profitable operation of those departments. He/she represents the General Merchandise Manager to the buyers in presenting and interpreting merchandise policies, plans, and procedures. In turn he/she acts as a liaison or channel of communication between the buyers and store management.

The Buyer.   In general, each buyer is responsible for (1) implementing all policies and procedures as dictated by the store's top management; (2) operating a department successfully; (3) attracting customers to the department; and (4) making a satisfactory profit.

Specifically the buyer is responsible for:

- drawing up seasonal merchandise plans;
- buying merchandise;
- pricing and repricing of all merchandise;
- approving orders and reorders;
- maintaining proper vendor relations;
- planning, scheduling, and coordinating departmental advertising and all other promotional plans;
- maintaining merchandise assortments in a desired relationship to sales;
- directing transfers of merchandise between parent and branch stores.

The Assistant Buyer.   The Assistant Buyer assists the departmental buyer in:

- developing, reviewing, and revising seasonal merchandise plans;
- supervising salespeople under supervision of the buyer;
- performing all duties delegated to him/her by the buyer, such as preparing ads, placing reorders, taking stock counts, taking markdowns, transferring merchandise, returning merchandise to vendors, and so on.

In one large New York-based branch-operating store each buyer has three assistants. The third assistant, lowest in rank and known as the Branch Assistant, is in charge of all the department's transactions and communications with its branches. The second assistant, next highest in rank, is known as the New York Assistant and is in charge of the New York store's selling department and its personnel. He/she returns merchandise to vendors, takes markdowns as ordered by the buyer, is responsible for parent store ads, signs, and display, and has other duties assigned by the buyer. The first assistant is the highest in rank and is known as the Buying Assistant because he/she is usually in charge of and buys for at least one classification represented in the department's stock, writes reorders, frequently looks at producers' lines, substitutes for the buyer on some occasions, and evaluates unit control sales and stock reports.

The Merchandise Clerical.   In very large stores that have a centralized unit control operation, the buyer of each large volume department usually is assigned a Merchandise Control Clerk, who keeps duplicate records in the buyer's office of certain stock and sales information for the day-to-day ready reference of the buyer. This is a staff rather than a line position, but one to which merchandise trainees are frequently assigned as a way of becoming quickly familiar with the operation of a merchandise department. It is an excellent early learning rung on the merchandising career ladder. The Merchandise Clerical is responsible for maintaining dollar and unit records of and issuing periodic reports to the buyer on all merchandise transactions as these take place in both the parent and branch stores. Such records and reports include:

- merchandise on order by vendor, classification, style number, and price;
- merchandise received from vendors by classification, style number and price;
- daily unit sales by classification, price line, vendor, style number, cost, or any other breakdown the buyer may need in order to maintain inventory at planned levels;
- daily customer returns broken down as for sales (above);
- all price changes;
- transfers of stock;
- sales and stock reports as requested.

Interdependence of Store Divisions

Although merchandising is the primary function of any retail operation, the Merchandising Division is heavily dependent on the other functional divisions of the store for realization of its objectives. Perhaps this is why the buyer is sometimes referred to as "the hub of the retail wheel."

For example, while the department buyer determines what items will be advertised, the size of each ad, the media to be used, and when the ad will run, the *Sales Promotion Division* is responsible for the copy, the artwork, the layout of each ad, and the subsequent follow through in terms of necessary displays, signs, publicity, and so on, to facilitate the success of the promotional effort as a whole.

The *Control Division* is responsible for control of the buying and selling activities of the Merchandising Division within predetermined budgetary limits and the current financial condition of the store. The Controller (division head) must make sure the store has the financial resources to satisfy the merchandising objectives of each department so that it may proceed with making buying commitments (see Chapters 4 and 5). Sometimes this involves borrowing from banks or investors. The Control Division is also responsible for control of funds received from credit, cash, or C.O.D. sales through its Accounts Receivable Department. It is also responsible for paying employees for the services they have rendered (Payroll), and vendors for merchandise, supplies, and services provided (Accounts Payable). In addition, the Control Division is responsible for keeping both physical and book inventory records (see Chapters 8 and 9).

The *Operations Division* is responsible for maintaining the store premises (called "the plant") in the manner and with the atmosphere that is satisfactory to the store's target group/groups of customers. It can enhance the store's image and greatly facilitate the sale of merchandise by supplying:

- well-trained and efficient sales and service personnel;
- desirable customer services, such as Adjustments, Personal Shopping, Delivery, Credit, and Mail and Telephone Ordering services, etc.;
- efficient Receiving and Marking departments;
- an effective Protection department;
- efficient Alteration workrooms.

STAFF AIDES TO THE MERCHANDISING DIVISION

The Merchandising Division of most stores has a number of staff services available to aid it in the planning of stocks, in their actual purchase, and in promoting their sale once the goods reach the store.

The Resident Buying Office

Perhaps the most important aide to the Merchandising Division is its Resident Buying Office, located in a major market area. The primary function of a Resident Buying Office, which is solely a service organization, is to provide all types of merchandise assistance to member stores, each of which pays a fee for services rendered.

Some of the more important services offered their client stores by resident buying offices are:

- providing market specialists who help client store buyers find the merchandise for which they are looking when the latter are in the market, and keeping buyers alerted to market developments and trends when they are in their home store through bulletins, telephone calls, and so on;
- conducting clinics for client store buyers at the start of each new market season;
- offering Central Merchandising services in some instances;
- arranging for group purchases so that all store participants may share in the advantages of a large-volume purchase;
- placing orders for buyers upon their requests;
- following up on orders buyers have placed to ensure prompt delivery;
- offering sales promotional assistance upon request;
- figure exchange among client stores as planning and evaluation guides.

The Unit Control Office

Unit control systems, as discussed in Chapter 8, refer to procedures for recording the number of units of merchandise bought, sold, in stock, and on order during any given period. These records and the periodic reports drawn from them may be processed manually or, more recently, through electronic data-processing systems and procedures. The latter, although more expensive to buy and operate, are preferred because they enable merchandising executives to have practically on-the-spot information about consumer preferences, trends, and stock positions in relation to sales. In fact, with a computer terminal in a buyer's office, instantaneous information on sales, stock on hand and on order, and rate of sale of a style, classification, or price line may be obtained on the terminal screen by the turn of a knob or switch as on a television set.

Unit control systems may be centrally operated for the store as a whole, which is usually the case with large stores that employ automated systems. Small stores tend to operate under a decentralized system in which case each merchandise department keeps its own records on a manual basis.

The Fashion Office

A Fashion Office may consist of a single individual or a whole department, depending on the sales volume of the store and the number of its branches. The job of the Fashion Office (usually headed by a woman whose title is Fashion Coordinator or Fashion Director) is to collect and assess information on fashion trends from all available sources both within and outside the store, and to make such information available to the store's merchandising, advertising, and display executives. The Fashion Office is also responsible for informal modeling of store stock throughout the store, for putting on fashion shows both inside and outside the store, for assisting with special promotions within the store, and serves the store as its chief source of publicity.

The Comparison Office

The Comparison Office acts as the eyes and ears of a store's Merchandising Division, keeping track of and reporting on competitors' stock and ads in comparison with merchandise offered by the home store. This type of service is a valuable aide to the Merchandising Division, since comparisons are based on the shopper's viewpoint as a customer rather than on that of a merchandising professional.

The Testing Bureau

Only the largest department and specialty stores and national chains can afford to maintain a special Testing Laboratory where prospective purchases and/or in-stock merchandise is examined in terms of its performance in use. Since the cost of the necessary equipment and staff makes the maintenance of such a project too expensive except for the largest retail organizations, such as The J. C. Penney Co. and R. H. Macy Co., smaller retail firms use commercial testing laboratories as the need arises.

The Research Office

A Research Office is found mainly in large, branch-operating retail firms and chain operations, and its head usually reports directly to the President or Chief Executive Officer (C.E.O.) of the store. Although best known for checking out potential locations for new stores, the Research Office can also be useful in any area of the store's operation. As a staff aide to the Merchandising Division, for example, this office may analyze customer traffic patterns to improve departmental layout, or analyze the operating results of certain departments in an effort to improve their profit.

SUMMARY OF KEY TERMS

Branch Store. A retail store that is owned and merchandised by a parent or main store.

Central Merchandising. Central buyers do preliminary planning, as well as buying and reordering for subscribing stores on the basis of actual sales and stock reports made periodically to central merchandising headquarters.

Chain Store. A series of retail outlets that are centrally owned and merchandised from an office rather than by a parent or main store.

Mom-and-Pop Store. Small retail operation usually run by the proprietor with few or no hired assistants.

National Chain. A chain operating many unit stores throughout the country.

Regional Chain. A chain operating fewer unit retail stores in a limited geographical area.

Resident Buying Office. A service organization, located in a major market area, that provides all types of merchandising assistance to its member stores.

Retail Merchandising. The planning and control of merchandise assortments in order to meet predetermined objectives of the firm.

Retailing. Nonmanufacturing business engaged in the selection and purchase of consumer goods from a wide variety of sources which are assembled in convenient locations for the purpose of profitable resale to ultimate consumers.

Unit Control. Procedures for recording the numbers of units of merchandise bought, sold, in stock, and on order during any given period.

REVIEW QUESTIONS-Introduction to Retail Merchandising

1. From a customer's point of view, what is considered an adequate assortment of merchandise?

2. Why is it important that merchandising students be trained in the computation and interpretation of figure facts?

3. What is meant by the term "Mom-and-Pop" store? Give several examples of this type of store in your locality.

4. Describe the process called "central merchandising."

5. Name and briefly describe what is involved in five merchandising policies that have a direct effect on a store's image.

6. Name and briefly describe five areas of a buyer's responsibility.

7. Indicate the rungs in the merchandising career ladder from bottom to top.

8. Explain why a buyer is sometimes called "the hub of the retail wheel."

9. Name and briefly describe the work of at least three staff aides to the Merchandising Division.

CHAPTER 3

ELEMENTS OF MERCHANDISING PROFIT

Business profit may be defined as the excess of dollar income over dollar expenditures, and, as such, is the key to economic growth and development in any free-enterprise system. In its broadest sense, profit is the reward to be gained for risking investment of capital in a business undertaking.

If retail merchants are to maintain their competitive position in today's highly competitive economy, they must be profit minded. Growth and expansion require huge amounts of capital because of steadily rising costs of goods, labor, equipment, and land or rent. Consistently good operating profits can provide some of this needed capital, but rarely all of it. Outside investment capital and bank loans are usually required if the firm is to effectively grow and prosper. Potential investors or lenders, therefore, must be assured that because of a firm's consistently good profit record, forward-looking management, and growth potential, they can expect a satisfactory return on their investments, as well as ultimate repayment of their loans in full. The inability of many of this country's oldest and best-known retail firms to finance their further growth and expansion has caused a number of them in recent years to seek mergers with other, better-capitalized firms or to sell out to conglomerates or retail syndicates.

PROFIT AS A RETAIL MERCHANDISING OBJECTIVE

A retail organization is in the business of buying goods for profitable resale to ultimate consumers. In most cases a retail firm's sole source of income is that which is generated by the activities of its Merchandising Division, in the form of sales volume. In order to achieve merchandising profit, therefore, the income received from net sales must exceed the total cost of the merchandise sold during a given period, in addition to the operating expenses incurred during the same period.

Buyers are directly responsible for the selection of specific lines of merchandise so tailored to the needs, wants, taste level, and pocketbooks of the store's present and potential customers that maximum sales will result. Merchandise managers are responsible for supervising the activities of a designated group of buyers and their selling departments. Buyers, merchandise managers, department managers, and store managers are evaluated annually on the basis of the sales volume they achieve and perhaps even more important on the amount of profit each selling department contributes to the profit of the store as a whole. In retailing vernacular, net operating profit or loss is referred to as the "bottom line" and, as such, is considered a primary yardstick in measuring the degree of retail merchandising success.

Federal and some state income tax regulations require that every business firm prepare an annual Profit and Loss Statement (abbreviated P and L), which is an itemized summary of its total income, expenditures, and resulting profit or loss for a fiscal period. Exhibit 3-1 is typical of a Profit and Loss Statement in general use by retailers. Some firms prepare their Profit and Loss statements at more frequent intervals, such as quarterly or semi-annually.

In addition to preparing periodic Profit and Loss statements, the Accounting Department of most retail organizations prepares and issues for each of the firm's selling departments, a detailed monthly report on income from sales, inventory on hand and on order, operating expenses incurred, and resulting profit or loss from operations. These reports are known as Operating Statements and are illustrated, as well as discussed in greater detail, in Chapter 10.

Departmental buyers, merchandise managers, department managers, and store managers carefully study the reports on actual merchandising results attained for the following reasons:

- to compare actual result figures with previously budgeted figures;
- to help identify specific strengths and weaknesses in their own operations, in comparison with the results achieved by similar operations in other stores;
- as viable indications of the direction in which their own operations are currently taking;
- for indications of any changes that should be made in management or store policies if a more profitable operation is to result.

This chapter is devoted to a study of the basic factors directly affecting merchandising profit, the component parts of each, and the significant relationships that exist among these factors.

BASIC PROFIT FACTORS AND THEIR COMPONENTS

Profit, you will recall, refers to the excess of dollar income over dollar expenditures. Should expenditures exceed income, the difference is referred to as a loss.

The factors directly affecting merchandising profit are:

- *operating income:* dollar income derived from customer purchases; usually referred to, in retailing, as net sales or sales volume
- *cost of merchandise sold:* the actual cost of all merchandise that was sold during a given period of time
- *operating expenses:* expenses incurred in maintaining the place(s) of business from which the goods are sold

EXHIBIT 3-1 PROFIT AND LOSS STATEMENT
February 1-July 31, 1979

			$	%
Gross Sales		$110,000		
Less Returns and Allowances		10,000		
NET SALES			$100,000	100.0
Inventory @ Cost, Feb. 1		$ 20,000		
Gross Purchases @ Billed Cost	$73,000			
Less Returns to Vendors	4,000			
Net Purchases @ Billed Cost		69,000		
Transportation Costs		1,000		
Total Cost of Goods Handled		$ 90,000		
Inventory @ Cost, July 31		25,000		
Gross Cost of Goods Sold		$ 65,000		65.0
Cash Discounts Earned	.	3,000		3.0
Net Cost of Goods Sold		$ 62,000		62.0
Net Workroom Costs		1,000		1.0
TOTAL COST OF GOODS SOLD			63,000	63.0
GROSS MARGIN			$ 37,000	37.0
Direct Operating Expenses				
Advertising	$ 3,200			
Buyer & Ass't Salaries	4,300			
Buyer's Travel	500			
Selling Salaries	9,100			
Delivery	400			
Miscellaneous	2,900			
Total Direct Expenses		$ 20,400		
Indirect Operating Expenses				
Administration	$ 2,500			
Utilities	500			
Maintenance	2,200			
Occupancy	3,200			
Miscellaneous	1,700			
Total Indirect Expenses		10,100		
TOTAL OPERATING EXPENSES			30,500	30.5
NET OPERATING PROFIT			$ 6,500	6.5

For a better understanding of how each of these three basic factors affects profit, it is necessary to break each down into its component parts and learn about the effect of each component on the final bottom line, or profit, figure.

Operating Income

As previously stated, sales made to customers are a retailer's major, if not only, source of income. Major components of operating income are: gross sales, customer returns, and customer allowances. Operating income or net sales are derived from consideration of these three components.

Gross Sales. The term gross sales refers to the dollar value of all sales made during a given period of time.

Formula:

Gross sales = Total of all sales made to customers
during a specified period of time.

Problem:

Last Saturday a Handbag Department had sales of 30 bags at $14 each, 25 at $25 each, and 6 at $35 each. What were that department's gross sales for the day?

Solution:

$$
\begin{array}{ll}
\text{30 pieces at \$14 =} & \$\ \ 420 \\
\text{25 pieces at \$25 =} & +\ \ \ 625 \\
\text{6 pieces at \$35 =} & +\ \ \ \underline{210} \\
\text{Gross sales =} & \$1,255
\end{array}
$$

Customer Returns.   When customers return merchandise for either cash or charge refund, a deduction from sales must be made since each return of merchandise represents a cancellation of a sale previously recorded, and an identical increase in stock on hand.

Formula:

Customer returns = Total value of merchandise returned by
customers for cash refund or charge
credit during a specified period of time.

Problem:

Last week a store's Coat Department accepted as returns from customers one $150 coat, one $100 coat, and two $80 coats. What was the total dollar amount of customer returns for the week?

Solution:

$$
\begin{array}{ll}
\text{1 coat at \$150 returned} & \$150 \\
\text{1 coat at \$100 returned} & +\ 100 \\
\text{2 coats at \$80 returned} & +\ \underline{160} \\
\text{Total customer returns} & \$410 \\
\text{for the week}
\end{array}
$$

Allowances to Customers.   In the course of business it sometimes becomes necessary to grant a customer some type of partial rebate on a purchase in order to get her/him to keep that merchandise. As in the case of returns of merchandise by customers, such customer allowances decrease previously recorded sales by an identical amount. Stock on hand, however, in this case, is not increased, since customers retain the merchandise rather than returning it to the store.

In actual practice, the dollar amount of all allowances given customers during any period is combined with the dollar amount of merchandise returned by customers during that period. The combined figure then appears as a single offset to gross sales on the Profit and Loss Statement.

Formula:

Customer allowances = Total amount of individual partial
refunds or credits given customers
on purchases previously made

Problem:

Last week, in addition to returns of merchandise by customers, as noted in the preceding problem, a total of $65 in allowances was granted to other customers. What was the total dollar amount of last week's customer returns and allowances?

Solution:

Customer returns last week	$410
Customer allowances last week	+ 65
Total customer returns and allowances for the week	$475

Retail merchants are vitally concerned with customer returns and allowances since these represent reductions in sales income previously reported and anticipated. For this reason most retailers indicate customer returns and allowances on their income statements, both in dollars and as a percentage of gross sales.

Formula:

$$\text{Customer returns and allowances } \% = \frac{\text{\$ Customer returns and allowances}}{\text{\$ Gross sales}}$$

Problem:

If the Coat Department referred to above had gross sales for the week amounting to $5,000, and customer returns and allowances for that week amounted to $475, what was the percentage of these returns and allowances?

Solution:

$$\text{Percent of customer returns and allowances} = \frac{\$475}{\$5,000}$$
$$= 9.5\%$$

Net Sales. *Net sales* is the term for the dollar difference between gross sales and total customer returns and allowances. In calculating Operating Profit (or Loss), net sales is synonymous with operating income.

Formula:

Net sales = Gross sales − customer returns and allowances

Problem:

From the figures indicated in the preceding problem, find net sales for the week.

Solution:

$$\text{Net sales} = \$5,000 - \$475$$
$$= \$4,525$$

PRACTICE PROBLEMS—Sales

1. If gross sales in the Teen Department were $135,552 and customer returns and allowances $2,713.44, what was the percentage of customer returns and allowances?

           _____
           (Answer)

2. Net sales in the Men's Furnishings Department totaled $46,780. If customer returns and allowances amounted to $2,340 for the same period, what were the gross sales?

           _____
           (Answer)

3. Gross sales for July in the Sportswear Department amounted to $87,650. Customer returns and allowances for the month amounted to 10%.

    (a) What was the dollar amount of returns and allowances?   (a) _____
                                                                   (Answer)

    (b) What were the net sales?   (b) _____
                                                                     (Answer)

4. If gross sales of the Bon Ton Department Store amounted to $3,000,000 last year, and customer returns and allowances totaled $111,360:

(a) What were the net sales?

(a) _____
    (Answer)

(b) What was the percentage of customer returns and allowances?

(b) _____
    (Answer)

5. If net sales of the Housewares Department were $32,400 and customer returns and allowances were calculated to be 10%, what were the department's gross sales?

_____
(Answer)

Cost of Merchandise Sold

The second basic profit factor is *cost of merchandise sold*. It is a derived figure, representing the aggregate (total) costs of all the merchandise that was sold during a given period of time. In calculating cost of merchandise sold, the following figures must be taken into account: (1) cost of net purchases; (2) dollar value of the beginning and ending inventories; and (3) any other merchandise costs that might apply.

Cost of Net Purchases. The actual cost of merchandise purchases is affected by the following factors:

a. *Billed Cost of Purchases.* The term *billed cost* refers to the price a vendor charges for each item of merchandise shipped to the store, as indicated on the vendor's invoice (or bill) for that merchandise. On income statements "Billed Cost of Purchases" refers to the aggregate costs of all merchandise received from vendors during the period, as indicated by vendors' invoices for those purchases.

As a general rule, the billed cost figure retailers use in calculaing cost of merchandise sold represents the net cost of that merchandise, or the gross cost of purchases minus the aggregate cost of all merchandise that the store might have returned to vendors during the period.

b. *Inbound Transaction Costs.* Unless otherwise stated on the purchase order, it is a usual trade practice for retailers to pay part or all of the transportation charges incurred in getting merchandise from the vendor's shipping point to the store. Transportation costs increase the cost of merchandise. Inbound transportation charges, plus the billed cost of merchandise, is referred to as *delivered cost of merchandise.*

Freight or other transportation costs should not be confused with delivery expense. The former refers to getting merchandise from vendors to the store (see Chapter 9). The latter refers to the delivery of merchandise to customers who have made purchases in the store and is therefore an operating expense (see p. 43).

c. *Cash Discounts on Purchases.* Discounts may be granted a store by a vendor if the store pays the vendor's invoice within a specified time period (see Chapter 5). These discounts are offered in terms of a percentage off the billed cost of merchandise only. Cash discounts may or may not be taken advantage of by a retail store, depending on that store's cash flow position.

Cash discounts, if actually taken by a store, serve to reduce the cost of purchases by an identical amount. If offered but not taken, cash discounts have no effect on cost of purchases.

For example, if a vendor offers a 3% cash discount on an invoice for $500, and the store pays that invoice within the specified discount period, a savings of $15 in the billed cost of the merchandise results.

d. *Workroom and/or Alteration Costs.* For discussion of this factor see p. 40.

Formula:

Net cost of purchases = Billed cost − returns to vendors
+ inbound transportation costs
− cash discounts earned

Problem:

For May the bookkeeper for a Children's shop reported the following figures: billed cost of gross purchases, $8,000; returns to vendors, $250; freight costs, $160; cash discounts earned, $210. What was the net cost of purchases for the month?

Solution:

Net cost of purchases = Billed cost of total purchases − total
returns to vendors + inbound transportation costs − cash discounts earned

= $8,000 − $250 + $160 − $210

= $7,700

Net Cost of Merchandise Sold. The cost of merchandise sold cannot be determined solely on the basis of net cost of purchases. Additional factors, such as the cost value of the beginning and ending inventories for the period must also be considered, as well as any other pertinent related costs of the merchandise.

Every retail operation at the beginning of a new fiscal time period has an inventory of goods on hand. This is referred to in the trade as the *beginning,* or *opening, inventory.* Likewise, at the end of each fiscal period there is an inventory left on hand. This is generally referred to in the trade as the *ending* or *closing inventory.* The net cost of merchandise sold during any given period is determined by adding together the cost values of the beginning inventory, the net purchases and net transfers in, and inbound transportation charged, and subtracting from that total figure (called *cost of merchandise handled*) the cost of the ending inventory and any cash discounts earned on purchasers.

Formula:

Net cost of merchandise sold = Cost of beginning inventory
+ cost of net purchases
+ cost of net transfers in
+ inbound transportation
− cost of ending inventory
− cash discounts earned

Problem:

The cost value of a small dress shop's March 1 inventory was $5,000. The billed cost of net purchases during March amounted to $7,500, and transportation charges amounted to $150. The cost of the March 31 inventory was $6,000, and cash discounts earned on purchases amounted to $600. What was the net cost of merchandise sold in March?

Solution:

March 1 inventory at cost	$ 5,000
Net March purchases at cost	+ 7,500
Transportation charges	+ 150
Total cost of merchandise handled in March	$12,650
March 31 inventory at cost	− 6,000
Gross cost of merchandise sold in March	$ 6,650
Cash discounts earned	− 600
Net cost of merchandise sold in March	$ 6,050

Other Merchandise Costs. Sometimes, because of accepted practices or the nature of certain types of merchandise, additional merchandise costs may be necessarily incurred in order to put the merchandise in first-class, salable condition. Retailers refer to such costs as *workroom and alteration costs*—costs absorbed by a selling department and not directly passed on to customers. Such costs are not to be confused with alterations requested by and paid for by customers. Examples of costs necessary to put merchandise in more salable condition are: polishing or assembling furniture, resewing ripped seams or belt loops, replacing broken zippers, or pressing badly wrinkled merchandise in ready-to-wear departments. Nor are workroom and alteration costs a profit-affecting factor in every selling department. Whether it is or not depends primarily on the nature of the merchandise handled. For example, a Stationery Department would probably never have such costs because of the nature of the merchandise handled. However, in Men's Clothing departments, workroom and alteration costs are a significant profit factor, since it has become a traditional practice for such departments to offer customers free trouser and sometimes sleeve length alterations. On the other hand, rarely are such free alterations offered by women's ready-to-wear departments.

Since workroom and alteration costs are not significant profit factors in all selling departments, it has become an accepted practice to treat this figure, where applicable, as an addition to net cost of merchandise sold (gross cost minus cash discounts earned), thereby arriving at a total cost of merchandise sold figure.

Formula:

Total cost of merchandise sold = Cost of beginning inventory
+ billed cost of net purchases
+ cost of net transfers in
− cost of ending inventory
− cash discounts earned
+ workroom and alteration costs

Problem:

A Better Sportswear Department, for a six-month period, showed the following figures: beginning inventory, $12,000; billed cost of net purchases, $80,000; transportation charges, $2,000; cash discounts earned on purchases, $6,000; ending inventory at cost, $11,000; workroom costs, $500. What was the total cost of merchandise sold?

Solution:

Beginning inventory at cost	$12,000
Billed cost of net purchases	+ 80,000
Transportation charges	+ 2,000
Total cost of merchandise handled	$94,000
Ending inventory at cost	− 11,000
Gross cost of merchandise sold	$83,000
Cash discounts on purchases	− 6,000
Net cost of merchandise sold	$77,000
Workroom charges	+ 500
Total cost of merchandise sold	$77,500

PRACTICE PROBLEMS—Cost of Merchandise Sold

1. A Luggage buyer purchased 12 tote bags from the Reliable Luggage Co. at $90 a dozen. Freight charges amounted to $3.70, and the cash discount offered was 2%. Find the net cost of the purchase if the invoice was paid in time to take the cash discount.

_____
(Answer)

2. A Sportswear buyer received an invoice for the following merchandise from the B&C Manufacturing Co.:

> 18 pairs of slacks costing $10.75 each
> 12 skirts costing $12.75 each
> 18 blouses costing $11.75 each

Shipping costs amounted to 8% of billed cost.

(a) What was the total billed cost of this purchase?

(a) _____
(Answer)

(b) What were the shipping costs in dollars?

(b) _____
(Answer)

(c) What was the delivered cost of this merchandise?

(c) _____
(Answer)

3. A Lingerie Department had a July 1 inventory of $6,330 at cost. The billed cost of merchandise received during July amounted to $2,000, merchandise returned to vendors amounted to $86, and shipping costs were $100. What was the cost of merchandise handled in July?

_____
(Answer)

4. A Cosmetics buyer received the following merchandise and covering invoice from the Whitehall Manufacturing Company:

> 9 dozen eye liners at $24 dozen cost
> 18 mascara sets at $36 dozen cost
> 12 jars eye cream at $27 dozen cost

Shipping costs amounted to $6. Cash discount allowed by the vendor was 3%.

(a) What was the billed cost of this shipment?

(a) _____
(Answer)

(b) What was the delivered cost?

(b) _____
(Answer)

(c) What was the net cost of this purchase if the invoice was paid in time to earn the cash discount?

(c) _____
(Answer)

5. The Housewares Department in Gable's Department Store showed the following figures for a six-month period: beginning inventory at cost, $46,000; billed cost of net purchases, $114,000; inbound freight costs, $6,000; cash discounts earned on purchases, $9,200; ending inventory at cost, $56,000. What was the net cost of the merchandise sold during the period?

_____

(Answer)

Operating Expenses

The third basic profit factor is *operating expenses,* which may be defined as expenses incurred by retailers in maintaining a place or places of business, paying employee salaries, and providing customer services. Operating expenses are charged entirely or prorated to each of a store's selling departments and therefore represent an important profit factor.

There are two major categories of retail store operating expenses:

Direct or *controllable operating expenses* are those directly related to the operation of a specific department and would cease if that department ceased to exist. Examples of direct or controllable expenses include salaries of departmental selling, nonselling, and executive personnel; selling supplies; advertising; delivery to customers; buyer's market trips; and space rental.

Indirect or *fixed operating expenses* are those that are storewide in nature and would continue to exist even if the selling departments ceased to exist. Examples of indirect or fixed operating expenses include: store maintenance, insurance, depreciation, salaries of senior executives, and utilities.

Direct or controllable expenses are easily identified and charged directly by the store's Accounting Department to the selling departments that incur them. Indirect or fixed expenses, being storewide in nature, are charged to each selling department on a prorated basis as determined by top management—usually as a specified percentage of net departmental sales.

Formula:

Operating expenses = Direct expenses + indirect expenses

Problem:

In April the Gift Department had net sales of $6,000. Direct expenses were as follows: selling salaries, $600; buyer's salary, $340; advertising, $300; supplies, $20. Indirect expenses were 10% of net sales.
(a) Find the indirect expenses.
(b) Find the total operating expenses of the department.

Solution:

(a) $6,000
    × .10
  $600.00   indirect expenses

(b) $ 600
  + 340
  + 300
  + 20
  $1,260 direct expenses

 $ 600
+ 1,260
$1,860 total operating expenses

Effect on Profit

The three basic factors just examined—operating income, cost of merchandise sold, and operating expenses—are called *profit factors*, because each has a direct bearing on the extent of profit realized from a merchandising operation.

Determining Profit or Loss. Figure facts representing each of these three factors—net sales, cost of merchandise sold, and operating expenses—are used in determining a fourth or result figure which retailers refer to as *net operating profit (or loss)*—the *"bottom line."*

Formula:

$$\text{Net operating profit (or loss)} = \text{Net sales} - \text{cost of merchandise sold} - \text{operating expenses}$$

Problem:

Find the net operating profit of a Notions Department with net sales, $10,000; total cost of merchandise sold, $5,500; and operating expenses, $3,500.

Solution:

$$\text{Net operating profit} = \$10,000 - \$5,500 - \$3,500$$
$$= \$1,000$$

Operating profit varies up or down as one or more of the basic profit factors vary.

	A	B	C
Net sales	$10,000	$9,000	$10,000
Total cost of merchandise sold	− 5,500	− 5,500	− 5,000
Operating expenses	− 3,500	− 3,500	− 3,000
Operating profit	$ 1,000	$ -0-	$ 2,000

How to Increase Profits. Retailing is a very volatile business. Current conditions frequently vary from those anticipated when operating plans were originally formulated. The successful retailer is constantly aware of the interrelationship between the three factors—net sales (operating income), total cost of merchandise sold, and operating expenses—and operating profit. In this connection he/she quickly makes any adjustments necessary to assure maximum profits.

While there are no hard and fast rules for a retailer to follow in order to merchandise at a profit, the following can be considered guidelines for achieving improved profits:

- *increase net sales* with only a proportionate increase in the cost of merchandise sold, and little or no increase in operating expenses;
- *decrease cost of merchandise sold* without decreasing sales (see Pricing Merchandise, Chapter 6, and Terms of Sale, Chapter 5);
- *decrease direct operating expenses* without endangering quality of service to customers.

PROFIT AND LOSS STATEMENTS

Keeping continuous, detailed records of the three basic profit factors—income from sales, all costs of merchandise acquired for resale purposes, and operating expenses—is the responsibility of a retailer's Accounting Department. In departmentized stores, separate records are kept for each selling department. In nondepartmentized stores, these records are kept for the store as a whole.

As previously indicated, income and expenditure figures for each department are summarized in periodic reports known as Profit and Loss statements. It is not the author's intention to delve into the underlying bookkeeping procedures, but simply to point out to students how the data those statements contain are used by merchandising executives to improve the profitability of their operations.

Final Periodic Profit and Loss Statement

The basic purpose of a periodic Profit and Loss Statement is to indicate whether a specific department or store has operated at a profit or loss during a specific period of time, and the extent of that profit or loss. The format of this type of report is structured around the details of what we have just been studying—net sales, total cost of merchandise sold, and operating expenses, resulting in operating profit or loss.

Retailers introduce into the P&L statement an additional figure called *gross margin,* a figure that represents the difference between net sales and total cost of merchandise sold. Gross margin (sometimes referred to as *gross margin of profit*) indicates the amount remaining out of income, after paying all costs of merchandise sold, that is available to cover operating expenses and provide a reasonable profit. If operating expenses are less than gross margin, the difference is called *net operating profit.* If expenses exceed gross margin, the difference is called *net operating loss.*

Formula:

$$\$ \text{ Gross margin} = \$ \text{ net sales} - \$ \text{ total cost of merchandise sold}$$

Problem:

Net sales in the China and Glassware Department last year amounted to $400,000. Total cost of merchandise sold was $225,000. What was the gross margin?

Solution:

$$\$ \text{ Gross margin} = \$400{,}000 - \$225{,}000$$
$$= \$175{,}000$$

Gross margin percentage is calculated by dividing dollar gross margin by net sales for the same period.

Skeleton Profit and Loss Statement

A quick and extremely useful method for reviewing, at frequent intervals, where a specific department or store stands with regard to profit from operations utilizes only summary figures for the five basic components of the final, more detailed Proft and Loss Statement. Details of the various transactions relating to each component are eliminated in what is referred to as a "Skeleton Statement."

Skeleton Statement figures are obtainable from the perpetual book inventory records kept by a store's Accounting Department (see Chapter 9) or from other periodic reports issued by that department. Skeleton P&L statements are expressed in dollars and/or as percentages of net sales, the latter being explained later in this chapter.

Example:

		Figure
Net sales	$35,000	1
Cost of merchandise sold	− 18,000	2
Gross margin	= $17,000	3
Operating expenses	− 13,500	4
Net operating profit	= $ 3,500	5

From the Skeleton Statement above it can be seen that among its five components:

- figures 1 minus 2 equal 3;
- figures 3 minus 4 equal 5;
- given any two of the first three or last three figures, the third can always be determined.

Components of Profit or Loss as Percentages of Sales

Dollar departmental or storewide profit and loss figure facts (either in skeleton or final detailed form) are useful for many purposes. However, dollar figures do not provide the information necessary for comparing and evaluating the profitability of one department's operation with that of another, nor of one store with another. To make such comparisons more realistic, most retail stores convert major dollar profit and loss figure facts into percentages of net sales and then use both dollars and percentages in evaluating each merchandising operation.

In converting the dollar value of each of the various profit elements into a percentage, *net sales are always considered to be the base figure representing 100%* (see p. 6).

Formulas for Determining Percentages:

$$\text{Cost of merchandise sold } \% = \frac{\$ \text{ Cost of merchandise sold}}{\$ \text{ Net sales}}$$

$$\text{Gross margin } \% = \frac{\$ \text{ Gross margin}}{\$ \text{ Net sales}}$$

$$\text{Operating expense } \% = \frac{\$ \text{ Total operating expenses}}{\$ \text{ Net sales}}$$

Problem 1:

Prepare a Skeleton P&L Statement in both dollars and percentages from the following figures: net sales, $20,000; total cost of merchandise sold, $10,000; gross margin, $10,000; operating expenses, $8,000; and net operating profit, $2,000.

Solution:

		Computation	%
Net sales	$20,000	Whole amount	100.0
Total cost merchandise sold	− 10,000	$\dfrac{\$10,000}{\$20,000}$	− 50.0
Gross margin	= $10,000	$\dfrac{\$10,000}{\$20,000}$	50.0
Operating expenses	− 8,000	$\dfrac{\$\ 8,000}{\$20,000}$	− 40.0
Net operating profit	= $ 2,000	$\dfrac{\$\ 2,000}{\$20,000}$	10.0

It should be noted that in calculating Skeleton P&L percentages, as well as dollars, that the first figure minus the second always equals the third, and that this third figure minus the fourth always equals the fifth or final one. Given both the dollars and percentages of net operating profit (figure 5) and gross margin (figure 3), the dollar and percentage values of net sales (figure 1), total cost of merchandise sold (figure 2), and operating expenses (figure 4) can all be determined.

Problem 2:

An operating profit of $2,000 was reported for a Gift Department. This represented 10% of net sales. Gross margin for the same period amounted to $10,000 or 50% of net sales. Find both dollars and percentages of (a) net sales, (b) total cost of merchandise sold, and (c) operating expenses for this department.

Solution:

(a)

10% = $2,000

1% = $\dfrac{\$2,000}{10}$

= $200

100% = $200 × 100

= $20,000

		$	%	
Net sales		$20,000	100.0	(a)
Total cost of merchandise sold		− 10,000	− 50.0	(b)
Gross margin	=	$10,000	50.0	
Operating expenses		− 8,000	− 40.0	(c)
Operating profit	=	$ 2,000	10.0	

(c)

(b)

Total cost merchandise
sold in dollars

= Net sales − gross margin
= $20,000 − $10,000
= $10,000

Total cost merchandise
sold as percent

= Net sales % − gross margin %
= 100% − 50%
= 50%

(c)

$$\text{\$ Operating expenses} = \text{\$ Gross margin} - \text{\$ operating profit}$$
$$= \$10{,}000 - \$2{,}000$$
$$= \$8{,}000$$

$$\text{Operating expenses \%} = \text{Gross margin \%} - \text{operating expenses \%}$$
$$= 50\% - 10\%$$
$$= 40\%$$

As a basis for comparison, percentage figures present a clearer operating profit picture than do dollars alone, as indicated below.

Problem 3:

In April the Costume Jewelry Department in Store A had net sales of $8,800; total cost of merchandise sold was $4,600; and operating expenses amounted to $3,600. For the same month the Costume Jewelry Department in Store B had net sales of $9,200; total cost of merchandise sold was $5,000; and operating expenses were $3,900. Which store had the most profitable operation? Defend your answer.

Solution:

	Store A		Store B	
	$	*%*	*$*	*%*
Net sales	$8,800	100.0	$9,200	100.0
Total cost of merchandise sold	− 4,600	− 52.3	− 5,000	− 54.3
Gross margin	$4,200	47.7	$4,200	45.7
Operating expenses	− 3,600	− 40.9	− 3,900	− 42.4
Net operating profit	$ 600	6.8	$ 300	3.3

Store A had the most profitable Jewelry operation. Operating profit was $300, or 3.5% better than Store B, despite the fact that Store A's dollar sales for the month were lower than Store B's by $400. Store A spent 52.3 cents of every dollar of income from sales on cost of merchandise sold, while Store B spent 54.3 cents. Store A spent 40.0 cents of every dollar of sales income for operating expenses, while Store B spent 42.4 cents.

PRACTICE-PROBLEMS—Operating Expenses and Profit or Loss ($ and %); Skeleton Profit and Loss Statement ($ and %)

1. The Record Department in the Bauer & White Department Store had net sales of $50,000 for the 6-month period ending July 31, and a net loss of 2%. Gross margin was 40%. What were the department's operating expenses in:

(a) dollars?

    (a) _____
           (Answer)

(b) percentage?

    (b) _____
           (Answer)

2. If net sales of a department were $30,000, total cost of merchandise sold $19,000, and operating expenses $9,000, what was the:

(a) dollar profit or loss?

    (a) _____
           (Answer)

(b) profit or loss percentage?

    (b) _____
           (Answer)

3. Gross sales in the Toy Department last month were $65,000. Customer returns were 3.7%. What were the net sales for the month?

_____
(Answer)

4. Determine the operating expense percentage from the following figures:

Gross sales	$188,000
Customer returns	12,000
Advertising	5,520
Selling salaries	41,520
Buying salaries	17,060
Miscellaneous expenses	10,000

_____
(Answer)

5. Find the total cost of merchandise handled during June from the following figures:

June 1 inventory	$8,330
Billed cost of purchases	4,000
Transportation costs	300
Merchandise returned to vendors	500

_____
(Answer)

6. Find the net cost of merchandise sold in June from the following figures:

June 1 inventory	$8,330
Billed cost of June purchases	4,000
Transportation charges	300
Merchandise returned to vendors	500
June 30 inventory	7,800
Cash discounts earned	114

_____
(Answer)

SUMMARY OF KEY TERMS

Beginning (Opening) Inventory. The dollar value of the aggregate (total) stock on hand at the start of each new accounting period.

Billed Cost. The price a vendor charges for merchandise as indicated on the vendor's invoice (bill) for that merchandise.

Bottom Line. A trade colloquialism for net operating profit or loss.

Business Profit. The excess of dollar income over dollar expenditures.

Cost of Merchandise Handled. The trade term for the sum of (1) the cost value of the beginning inventory, (2) the cost value of net purchases, (3) total transportation costs, and (4) net transfers in during a specified period.

Cost of Merchandise Sold. The aggregate or total cost of all merchandise sold during a specified period.

Customer Allowances. Price allowances or rebates granted customers in order to get them to keep merchandise previously purchased which they would otherwise have returned for full credit.

Customer Returns. Merchandise previously purchased by customers that is subsequently returned for full credit.

Delivered Cost of Merchandise. The billed cost of merchandise, plus inbound transportation costs paid by the store.

Direct or Controllable Operating Expenses. Expenses that are directly related to the operation of a specific department and would cease if that department ceased to exist.

Ending (Closing) Inventory. The dollar value of the aggregate (total) stock on hand at the close of the last business day in each accounting period.

Gross Margin. The difference between net sales and total cost of merchandise sold.

Gross Margin Percentage. Dollar gross margin for a period divided by dollar net sales for the same period.

Gross Sales. The dollar value of all sales made during a specified period of time.

Indirect or Fixed Operating Expenses. Expenses that are storewide in nature and would continue to exist if any of the store's selling departments ceased to exist.

Inventory. The trade term for stock on hand, generally expressed in terms of total value, either at cost or retail.

Net Operating Profit (or Loss). The difference between gross margin and total operating expenses. Often referred to as the bottom line.

Net Sales. The dollar difference between gross sales and customer returns and allowances. Sometimes referred to as operating income.

Operating Expenses. Those incurred in maintaining a place or places of business, paying salaries, and providing services.

Profit and Loss Statement. Itemized summary of firm's total income, expenditures, and resulting profit or loss for a fiscal period.

Profit Factors. Those having a direct bearing on the extent of profit realized from a merchandising operation.

Retail. The price at which merchandise is offered for sale to customers.

Vendor. A supplier of merchandise to retailers. A general term for manufacturers, wholesalers, jobbers, producers.

Workroom and Alteration Costs. Costs that are necessarily incurred in putting merchandise in salable condition and which are absorbed by a selling department instead of being passed on directly to customers.

REVIEW QUESTIONS—Elements of Merchandising Profit

1. The factors directly affecting merchandising profit are:

    (1)

    (2)

    (3)

2. In retailing vernacular, net operating profit or loss is referred to as the _____

    _____.

3. The actual cost of merchandise purchases is affected by what four factors?

    (1)

    (2)

    (3)

    (4)

4. How is the total cost of merchandise sold calculated?

5. Explain the difference between direct and indirect operating expenses and give at least two examples of each.

6. Differentiate between total cost of merchandise handled and total cost of merchandise sold.

7. Discuss the means by which a merchant may increase his/her profit percentage.

8. The trade term for stock on hand is _____.

9. The price a vendor charges for merchandise, as indicated on the invoice for that merchandise, is referred to as _____ _____.

10. Customer allowances is just another term for customer returns. True _____ False _____

REVIEW PROBLEMS—Elements of Merchandising Profit

(Correct each percentage to the second place past the decimal point.)

1. In August the Boys' Department showed the following figures:

Net sales	$28,000
Cost of merchandise sold	18,000
Net operating profit	1,000

(a) What was the dollar gross margin?

_____
(Answer)

(b) What was the gross margin percentage?

_____
(Answer)

(c) What was the dollar amount of operating expenses?

_____
(Answer)

(d) What was the operating expense percentage?

_____
(Answer)

2. Net sales in the Lamp Department for the six-month spring season were $150,000. Net cost of merchandise sold was $92,000 and operating expenses were $49,000.

(a) What was the dollar net operating profit for the period?   (a) _____
                                                                      (Answer)

(b) What was the operating profit percentage?   (b) _____
                                                      (Answer)

3. For a six-month period the Junior Sportswear Department had billed costs of merchandise received amounting to $95,000, shipping costs of $2,500, workroom costs of $500, and earned cash discounts of $7,600. What was the total cost of the goods received during this period?

_____
(Answer)

4. If a Fur Department's gross sales for August were $95,000 and customer returns were $4,900, what was the percentage of customer returns?

_____
(Answer)

5. The owner of a children's shop purchased from a vendor:

$$16 \text{ dresses at } \$33.00 \text{ a dozen}$$
$$6 \text{ dresses at } \$31.50 \text{ a dozen}$$
$$57 \text{ dresses at } \$40.00 \text{ a dozen}$$

Transportation costs came to 25% of the billed cost of the merchandise.

(a) What was the billed cost of this purchase?

(a) _____
   (Answer)

(b) What was the total cost of this purchase?

(b) _____
   (Answer)

6. If a boutique showed the following figures for its first year of operation:

Operating expenses	$25,500
Net sales	75,000
Net cost of merchandise sold	45,000

(a) What was its gross margin in dollars?

(a) _____
   (Answer)

(b) What was its percentage of gross margin?

(b) _____
   (Answer)

(c)   What was its net operating profit or loss in dollars?   (c) _____
                                                                              (Answer)

(d)   What was its net operating profit or loss in percentage?   (d) _____
                                                                              (Answer)

7.   If gross margin in the Drapery Department was $105,000, operating expenses $96,000, and net operating profit 4% of net sales, what were the net sales?

_____
(Answer)

8.   With net sales of $25,000, a Coat Department showed a net loss of $1,000. Its gross margin was 40%.

(a)   What was the dollar amount of its operating expenses?   (a) _____
                                                                              (Answer)

(b)   What was its operating expense percentage?   (b) _____
                                                                              (Answer)

9. From the figures given in problem 8, suggest three possible revisions in policy or procedure by which the buyer might attempt to convert this loss into a profit. Justify each suggestion.

(1)

(2)

(3)

10. A Menswear Department with sales for the year of $585,000 showed the following figures:

Billed cost of net purchases	$315,000
Shipping costs	1,800
Cash discounts earned	1,890
Workroom costs	5,500
Opening inventory @ cost	21,500
Closing inventory @ cost	22,000

(a) What was the total cost of the merchandise sold?

(a) _____
(Answer)

(b) What was the gross margin percentage?

(b) _____
(Answer)

CHAPTER 4

THE SEASONAL MERCHANDISE PLAN AND OPEN-TO-BUY

As has been pointed out, the major factors directly affecting merchandising profit are (1) operating income, (2) total cost of merchandise sold, and (3) operating expenses. Achievement of a reasonable profit from merchandising operations is a primary retail goal. If the profit as well as other objectives are to be realized, retail stock assortments must be carefully planned and controlled. The seasonal merchandise plan is the retailer's prime planning tool.

A seasonal *merchandise plan* is a projection of the sales that can be reasonably anticipated during a specified future period of time and the stock estimated to be necessary to achieve those sales.

A merchandise plan is similar in purpose to that of a personal budget. In merchandise budgeting, estimated expenditures for the purchase of stock and payment of necessary operating expenses during a specified period are balanced against estimated income from sales made to customers during that period. In a personal budget, proposed expenditures during a given period of time are balanced against anticipated personal income during the same period. In either case the purpose of budgeting is the same: to anticipate and set limits on expenditures to keep them in line with anticipated income.

For example, in setting up your own personal budget as a student, you first list your anticipated income during the next academic period. This should include income from all sources: allowances, loans, scholarships, part-time employment, and so on. Next, you estimate and list all anticipated expenditures for the same period: tuition, cost of textbooks and other required course materials, transportation, laundry, clothing and other personal needs, recreation, medical and dental expenses, and insurance. If the total of anticipated expenditures exceeds anticipated income, reductions will have to be made in one or more of the itemized expenditures to bring the total in line with income. The best budget, of course, is one in which total anticipated income so exceeds total essential expenditures that a margin of safety, or savings, exists. In merchandise budgeting, this differential is called *operating profit*, as discussed in the preceding chapter. In personal budgeting it is usually referred to as *savings* or *discretionary income*.

The major goals of merchandise planning are:

(1) to have at all times an inventory that is neither too large nor too small for anticipated customer demand;

(2) to schedule the delivery of purchases to the store so that the merchandise is available neither too early nor too late for customer demand;

(3) to keep purchases in line with the store's ability to pay for them;

(4) to have funds available for the purchase of new goods when they may be needed.

THE SEASONAL MERCHANDISE PLAN

It is important to note that since most retail stores today use the Retail Method of Valuation Inventory (see Chapter 8), unless otherwise specified, all figures used hereafter as examples or in problems represent the retail value of merchandise—*not* the cost value.

Seasonal merchandise plans have two main purposes: (1) they serve as guides for individuals responsible for achieving desired sales and profit results; and (2) they provide store management with a yardstick against which actual merchandising results can be measured and evaluated.

Planning Procedures

Most merchandise plans are prepared for six-month periods with further breakdowns into monthly or weekly subdivisions. Most stores operate on the basis of a fiscal (rather than a calendar) year that begins February 1 of one year and ends January 31 of the following year. The first period, designated as the Spring season, extends from February 1 through July 31. The second period, designated as the Fall season, extends from August 1 through the following January 31. With the Spring season starting February 1 instead of January 1, the month of January can be used to clear stocks of winter and Christmas stock remainders to make room for new Spring-oriented goods. And with the Fall season starting August 1 instead of July 1, July can be given over to clearing out summer stock to make room for Fall merchandise. This timing is of particular importance in fashion departments because producers start shipping Spring merchandise in February and Fall merchandise in August.

Format Used. While there is no standard format used for drawing up seasonal merchandise plans, Form 4-1 can be considered typical of those in general use by medium-volume stores. Planning forms used in small stores may be less formal and detailed, while those used by very large-volume stores may be more detailed. Regardless of the amount of detail involved, virtually all merchandise plans call for three entries relating to each of the basic elements being planned:

- last year's actual performance figure (labeled "L.Y.")
- planned figures for this year (labeled "plan"); and
- this year's actual results (labeled "T.Y.").

Many stores allow space for additional entries, such as revisions in the originally planned figures, should they become necessary, and percent of increase or decrease in planned sales this year as compared to the same period last year.

Responsibility for Planning. In departmentized stores, where each department is considered a separate accounting unit, seasonal merchandising plans are developed for each department. In nondepartmentized stores, seasonal merchandising plans are developed for the store as a whole.

SIX MONTH MERCHANDISING PLAN

Dept. Name _____ Dept. No. _____

		PLAN (This Year)	ACTUAL (Last Year)
	Initial markup (%)		
	Gross margin (%)		
	Cash discount (% cost purch.)		
	Season stock turnover (rate)		
	Shortage reserve (%)		
	Advertising expense (%)		
	Selling salaries (%)		

SPRING 197–		FEB.	MAR.	APR.	MAY	JUNE	JULY	SEASON TOTAL
FALL 197–		AUG.	SEP.	OCT.	NOV.	DEC.	JAN.	
SALES	Last Year							
	Plan							
	Percent of Increase							
	Revised							
	Actual							
RETAIL STOCK (BOM)	Last Year							*
	Plan							*
	Revised							*
	Actual							*
MARKDOWNS	Last Year							
	Plan (dollars)							
	Plan (percent)							
	Revised							
	Actual							
RETAIL PURCHASES	Last Year							
	Plan							
	Revised							
	Actual							

Comments

*Represents stock end of period.

Merchandise Manager _____   Buyer _____

Controller _____

FORM 4-1

The store's accountant or Accounting office provides last year's and this year's actual figures for each basic element of the plan, as well as last year's and this year's planned figures for the supplementary elements of the plan (see Form 4-2). Buyers or department managers, working in conjunction with their merchandise managers, are usually responsible for developing planned figures for each of the basic elements. It is generally considered advisable to involve buyers and department managers in the preparation of their own departmental plans, for two reasons:

1. They have specialized knowledge of existing conditions and trends in their respective markets, of customer demand cycles, and of the varied details comprising direct operating expenses of the department.

2. Since they are held responsible for achieving the goal figures set forth in their respective plans, they are likely to be more motivated in achieving those goals if they originally participate in establishing them.

Finally, the plans go to top management for review, revision if necessary, and final approval.

In stores having a number of large-volume branches located at a distance from the parent store, separate departmental merchandise plans are usually drawn up for each branch. In stores with only a few small-volume branches located near the parent store, usually a single departmental plan is drawn up, combining all branch operations with the parent department.

Dept. Name __Misses' Dresses__ Dept. No. __42__

SIX MONTH MERCHANDISING PLAN		PLAN (This Year)	ACTUAL (Last Year)
	Initial markup (%)	48.5	47.5
	Gross margin (%)	42.3	41.8
	Cash discount (% cost purch.)	8.0	7.8
	Season stock turnover (rate)	2.8	2.6
	Shortage reserve (%)	1.5	1.8
	Advertising expense (%)	2.8	3.0
	Selling salaries (%)	8.0	8.5

SPRING 197—		FEB.	MAR.	APR.	MAY	JUNE	JULY	SEASON TOTAL
~~FALL 197—~~		~~AUG.~~	~~SEP.~~	~~OCT.~~	~~NOV.~~	~~DEC.~~	~~JAN.~~	
SALES	Last Year	12,100	14,200	17,300	15,500	14,100	10,800	84,000
	Plan							
	Percent of Increase							6.0%
	Revised							
	Actual							
RETAIL STOCK (BOM)	Last Year	34,500	35,500	39,000	35,000	34,000	29,000	21,000*
	Plan							*
	Revised							*
	Actual							*
MARKDOWNS	Last Year	2,000	2,500	2,800	2,200	2,200	2,100	13,800
	Plan (dollars)							
	Plan (percent)							14.0%
	Revised							
	Actual							
RETAIL PURCHASES	Last Year	15,100	20,200	16,100	16,700	11,300	4,900	84,300
	Plan							
	Revised							
	Actual							

Comments

*Represents stock end of period.

Merchandise Manager _____ Buyer _____

Controller _____

FORM 4-2

Mary D. Troxell, *Fashion Merchandising*, 2nd ed. (New York: Gregg Division, McGraw-Hill, 1976), p. 220.

Basic Elements of the Plan

Although seasonal merchandising plans vary somewhat from store to store with respect to format, scope, and detail, the two essential elements appearing on all of them are sales and stock. Because most plans also provide for the monthly or weekly planning of markdowns and purchases, sales, stock on hand, markdowns, and purchases are referred to as the *basic elements* of any merchandising plan. All other merchandising goal figures that a store may choose to include as objectives in seasonal planning are referred to as *supplemental elements* and are discussed later in this chapter.

Planning Sales. Sales planning represents the most critical merchandising decision a retail merchant must make because as the major, if not the only, source of retail income, sales hold the key to potential profit. Sales are usually planned in dollars of retail value, since sales are made at retail prices. Sales may also be planned in units of merchandise by classification, price line, or both, as discussed in Chapter 8.

Estimating sales that can be reasonably anticipated in a future period involves careful evaluation of factors that may affect the sales volume of a department or a store during that period. Major factors to be considered are:

1. *External factors:* those outside the store and its control, such as:
   - international, national, and local economic conditions;
   - changes relating to the demographies of the population within the store's trading area, such as income level, age mix, and life-style;
   - the competitive situation;
   - price trends and market conditions;
   - change in dates of holidays, such as Easter;
   - difference in number of selling days in the period this year as compared to last year.
2. *Internal factors:* those within the store and its control, such as:
   - last year's sales for the corresponding period;
   - general trend in the home store's total sales;
   - changes in store policies;
   - changes in department's location and/or space;
   - opening of new branches and/or closing of existing ones;
   - number and extent of promotions being planned for the upcoming period.
3. *Fashion trends:* guidelines indicating the direction in which fashion demand is moving, such as:
   - are current fashions moving toward or away from widespread fashion acceptance?
   - effect of changing life-styles on the type of merchandise handled in the department;
   - impact of technological advances on merchandise handled;
   - effect of fashion trends and styling of other types of merchandise on each department's sales potential in the upcoming period.

A review of sales figures for the corresponding period last year is a useful guide in forecasting sales for an upcoming period. These figures should, however, be considered *merely as a guide* because of the tremendous effect on a department's or a store's sales potential of changing economic conditions, product styling, consumer life-styles, and other socioeconomic factors. This is particularly true for departments or stores that primarily handle fashion or seasonal merchandise, since the very nature of that type of merchandise implies constant and often rapid change in styling and customer acceptance from one year to the next.

Seasonal sales goals are usually subdivided into monthly goals. Estimating the sales potential of each month of an upcoming season involves careful consideration of such influential factors as:

- the previous year's sales for the same months;
- the percentage that each month in the past has normally contributed to the total season's sales;
- average industry performance figures as these are available from such sources as the Federal Reserve System, the store's resident buying office, trade associations, and trade periodicals;
- the shifting dates of certain key holidays, such as Easter;
- special promotional events being planned to take place during the period under consideration;
- special circumstances that may have occurred last year but which may be ignored in this year's planning: for example, bad weather, delivery problems, or newspaper strikes, etc.

Form 4-3 is an example of how the six-month Merchandising Plan would look after total season and monthly net sales had been planned.

Planning Stocks. Once sales have been estimated for each month or week of the period, the next step is to estimate the stock needed at the beginning of each month (abbreviated B.O.M.) or the end of each month (abbreviated E.O.M.) if those monthly planned

Dept. Name __Misses' Dresses__ Dept. No. __42__

SIX MONTH MERCHANDISING PLAN		PLAN (This Year)	ACTUAL (Last Year)
	Initial markup (%)	48.5	47.5
	Gross margin (%)	42.3	41.8
	Cash discount (% cost purch.)	8.0	7.8
	Season stock turnover (rate)	2.8	2.6
	Shortage reserve (%)	1.5	1.8
	Advertising expense (%)	2.8	3.0
	Selling salaries (%)	8.0	8.5

SPRING 197–		FEB.	MAR.	APR.	MAY	JUNE	JULY	SEASON TOTAL
FALL 197–		AUG.	SEP.	OCT.	NOV.	DEC.	JAN.	
SALES	Last Year	12,100	14,200	17,300	15,500	14,100	10,800	84,000
	Plan	12,500	17,500	16,000	16,500	15,000	11,500	89,000
	Percent of Increase	3.3	23.2	−7.5	6.5	6.4	6.5	6.0%
	Revised							
	Actual							
	Last Year	34,500	35,500	39,000	35,000	34,000	29,000	21,000*

FORM 4-3

Mary D. Troxell, *Fashion Merchandising,* 2nd ed. (New York: Gregg Division, McGraw-Hill, 1976), p. 224.

sales figures are to be achieved. Actually, the E.O.M. stock for one month is identical with the B.O.M. stock for the following month unless some rare or catastrophic event should take place between the close of business on the last day of one month and the store opening on the first day of the following month. For purposes of discussion in this text, B.O.M. stocks are used, rather than E.O.M. stocks, unless otherwise specified.

Like sales, stocks may be planned in terms of dollars or units of merchandise by classification, price line, or both.

Considerations in stock planning. Major factors to be considered when planning B.O.M. stock levels are:

- the same external, internal, and fashion factors as those considered in sales planning;
- planning B.O.M. stock levels so that the *average* stock on hand throughout the period will result in a desired stock turnover rate;
- to have a B.O.M. stock on hand adequate to meet customer demand until stock replacements for goods sold can be secured;
- planning for stocks to be peaked *just prior* to anticipated peaks in consumer demand for the merchandise involved;
- planning reduced stocks as each selling season approaches its close and consumer demand decreases.

Stock-sales relationships. Retail merchants are guided in stock planning by two important stock-sales relationships: (1) monthly stock-sales ratios; and (2) a desired rate of seasonal stock turnover.

1. *Stock-sales ratio* is the trade term for the figure relationship that exists between the stock at the beginning of a month or other period and sales planned for the same period. A stock-sales ratio is sometimes referred to as the number of months that would be required to dispose of a given B.O.M. stock at the rate at which sales have been either planned or made for the month in question.

Stock-sales ratios vary widely from one month to the next, from department to department, from store to store, and from one type of merchandise to another. They depend primarily on the cycle of demand for various types of merchandise and the merchandising policies of each store, particularly those policies that have to do with the depth and breadth of assortments carried. Table 4-1 indicates the diverse nature of typical monthly stock-sales ratios for three different types of merchandise. The reason that the Men's Furnishings Department has consistently higher stock-sales ratios (that is, higher B.O.M. stocks in relation to sales planned for the month) than do the other two departments is because of the much wider range (different types) of merchandise carried in that department, as well as the number of sizes that must be carried in each type. For example, most Men's Furnishings departments carry the following types of merchandise, each in a wide range of sizes, styles, fabrics, and colors:

- dress shirts, sport shirts, formal shirts;
- ties;
- hosiery;
- undershorts and undershirts;
- sleepwear and robes;
- jewelry;

Table 4-1. Typical Monthly Stock-Sales Ratios

Month	Women's Dressy Coats	Lingerie	Men's Furnishings
January	2.1	4.7	6.3
February	2.6	4.6	6.7
March	2.3	5.5	5.7
April	2.4	5.2	6.3
May	3.8	3.8	6.2
June	4.7	4.3	3.8
July	3.9	4.3	6.0
August	4.5	3.9	5.6
September	5.0	5.0	5.1
October	3.3	4.7	5.6
November	2.7	4.0	3.6
December	1.9	1.8	1.5

Mary D. Troxell, *Fashion Merchandising,* 2nd ed. (New York: Gregg Division, McGraw-Hill, 1976) p. 227.

and in recent years cosmetics and fragrances. In contrast, the Women's Coat Department carries extremely limited types of merchandise—untrimmed and fur-trimmed dressy, casual, and tailored coats—in a narrow range of sizes, fabrics, and colors.

The stock-sales ratio is an important concept or tool in stock planning because it, more than any other figure, directly relates stock requirements to planned sales.

Formula (for calculating B.O.M. stock when planned sales and stock sales ratio are known):

B.O.M. stock = Planned sales × stock-sales ratio

Problem:

A Men's Furnishings Department planned sales for February at $3,300. If the February stock-sales ratio for this department was 6.7, what should be the dollar value of its February B.O.M. stock?

Solution:

$ B.O.M. stock = $ Planned sales × stock-sales ratio
= $3,300 × 6.7
= $22,110

Formula (for calculating stock-sales ratio when planned sales and B.O.M. stock are known):

$$\text{Stock-sales ratio} = \frac{\$ \text{ B.O.M. stock}}{\$ \text{ Net sales}}$$

Problem:

The Spring merchandise plan for The Card and Gift Gallery indicated planned stock for March of $10,000 and a March 1 inventory of $40,000. What was the stock-sales ratio for March?

Solution:

$$\text{Stock-sales ratio} = \frac{\$ \text{ B.O.M. stock}}{\$ \text{ Net sales}}$$

$$= \frac{\$40,000}{\$10,000}$$

$$= 4$$

Conversely, the amount of B.O.M. stock that is needed can be determined if planned sales and desired stock-sales ratio are known.

2. *Stock turnover* is defined as the ratio between net sales during a given period and the average stock for the same period. Stock turnover rates differ from stock-sales ratio in the following respects:

- The period covered in calculating stock-sales ratio is a single month, whereas stockturn is usually calculated for a much longer period, such as an entire season or year.
- The stock figure used in determining stock-sales ratio represents stock at a specific time, such as the beginning of a month. In calculating stock turnover, however, the stock figure used represents the *average* that is maintained over an extended period of time.
- In calculating stock-sales ratio the inventory figure is divided by net sales, whereas in calculating stock turnover net sales are divided by average stock.

It should be carefully noted that to achieve a desired stock turnover figure for any given period, monthly stocks must be kept in line with budgeted stock-sales ratios.

The more rapidly its stock is sold, the more profitably a retail store operates since stock turnover indicates the rate at which money invested in inventory is turned into income as sales are made from that stock. A good rate of stock turnover is desired and the result of careful planning and good management. Most buyers are evaluated on the rate of stock turnover they have been able to achieve during each fiscal season or year.

The rate of stock turnover varies widely from store to store and from department to department in any given store, depending on:

- the type of merchandise handled (seasonally oriented goods "turn" more rapidly than do nonseasonally oriented goods);
- the price range of the merchandise handled (lower-priced goods "turn" more rapidly than do higher-priced goods);
- the depth and breadth of assortments carried (shallower, narrower stocks "turn" more rapidly than do deeper, broader stocks).

Data that are useful in planning stock turnover goals are available from a variety of sources. Performance records can be compared to "average" and "goal" figures for similar departments in similar volume stores, as indicated in the *Merchandising and Operating Reports* issued annually by the National Retail Merchants Association. Also, a store's resident buying office often makes such figures available to its client stores. Form 4-4 is an example of how a Six-Month Merchandising Plan might look after seasonal and monthly net sales and B.O.M. stock had been planned.

SIX MONTH MERCHANDISING PLAN

	PLAN (This Year)	ACTUAL (Last Year)
Initial markup (%)	48.5	47.5
Gross margin (%)	42.3	41.8
Cash discount (% cost purch.)	8.0	7.8
Season stock turnover (rate)	2.8	2.6
Shortage reserve (%)	1.5	1.8
Advertising expense (%)	2.8	3.0
Selling salaries (%)	8.0	8.5

SPRING 197—		FEB.	MAR.	APR.	MAY	JUNE	JULY	SEASON TOTAL
~~FALL 197—~~		~~AUG.~~	~~SEP.~~	~~OCT.~~	~~NOV.~~	~~DEC.~~	~~JAN.~~	
SALES	Last Year	12,100	14,200	17,300	15,500	14,100	10,800	84,000
	Plan	12,500	17,500	16,000	16,500	15,000	11,500	89,000
	Percent of Increase	3.3	23.2	−7.5	6.5	6.4	6.5	6.0%
	Revised							
	Actual							
RETAIL STOCK (BOM)	Last Year	34,500	35,500	39,000	35,000	34,000	29,000	21,000*
	Plan	32,000	39,000	36,000	35,000	33,000	26,000	21,000*
	Revised							*
	Actual							*
	Last Year	2,000	2,500	2,800	2,200	2,200	2,100	13,800

FORM 4-4

Mary D. Troxell, *Fashion Merchandising*, 2nd ed. (New York: Gregg Division, McGraw-Hall, 1976), p. 225.

The average annual rate of stock turnover of various types of goods varies widely from one type of store to another, one department to another, and from one type of goods to another. The following chart indicates the variation in the average rate of stock turnover between certain merchandise departments according to the National Retail Merchants Association.

Type of Merchandise	Average Rate of Annual Stockturns
Adult female apparel	4.6
All dresses	4.5
Small electrical appliances	3.7
Men's furnishings	3.3
Adult male apparel	2.8
Toys	2.7
Books	2.6
Bridals and formals	2.6
Men's footwear	2.1
Women's footwear	2.0
Children's footwear	1.6
Floor coverings	1.5

The following chart indicates the approximate annual rate of stock turnover in different types of retail establishments:

Type of Store	Average Rate of Annual Stockturns
Gasoline service station	21
Supermarkets	17
Paint and wallpaper stores	5
Drug stores	4
Ready-to-wear stores	4
Furniture stores	3
Shoe stores	2

Stock turnover can be improved by:

- keeping stocks in line with budgetary restrictions;
- examining all items making up an assortment and identifying both the slow- and fast-moving items in the assortment;
- prompt reordering of fast-moving stock;
- disposing of slower-moving stock through better display and/or selling techniques and taking markdowns, if necessary to clear;
- continually clearing out, through markdowns, odds and end of merchandise not being reordered.

The sales dollars released through disposing of slow-sellers should be used to build up the stock of fast-selling items.

Formula (for calculating turnover when average stock[1] and sales for the period are known):

$$\text{Stock turnover rate} = \frac{\$ \text{ Net sales}}{\$ \text{ Average stock}}$$

Problem:

For the year a Boys' Department had net sales of $200,000. The average stock for this period was $50,000. What was the rate of stock turnover?

Solution:

$$\text{Stock turnover} = \frac{\$ \text{ Net sales}}{\$ \text{ Average stock}}$$
$$= \frac{\$200,000}{\$50,000}$$
$$= 4$$

[1] Average stock is obtained by adding together the beginning inventory, the closing inventory, and all available intermediate inventory figures, and dividing that total by the number of figures used. For example, to find the average stock for a six-month period in which all first-of-the-month inventory figures are available, as well as the inventory that remains on hand at the close of the period (the ending inventory), all these figures should be added together and divided by 7—the number of figures used—to obtain the average inventory value for the six-month period.

Formula (for calculating average stock when inventories are known):

$$\text{Average stock} = \frac{\text{Sum of beginning and ending plus all intervening stock figures}}{\text{Number of figures used}}$$

Problem:

If a Misses' Dress Department had the following inventories, what was the department's average inventory for that three-month period?

May 1	$35,000
June 1	33,000
July 1	26,000
Aug. 1	21,000

Solution:

$$\text{Average stock} = \frac{\$35,000 + \$33,000 + \$26,000 + \$21,000}{4}$$

$$= \frac{\$115,000}{4}$$

$$= \$28,750$$

Conversely, the dollar value of average stock that should be carried can be determined if planned sales for the period are divided by the desired rate of stock turnover.

Formula (for calculating average stock when planned sales and turnover rate are known):

$$\text{Average stock} = \frac{\text{Planned sales for period}}{\text{Turnover rate}}$$

Problem:

A Hosiery Department planned sales of $200,000 for a six-month period and wanted to achieve a stock turn of 4. What should be the average stock carried in the period under consideration?

Solution:

$$\text{Average stock} = \frac{\$200,000}{4}$$

$$= \$50,000$$

PRACTICE PROBLEMS—Stock Sales Ratio; Stock Turnover

1. What is the planned stock-sales ratio of the Fashion Accessories Department when the October 1 stock is planned at $19,000 and October sales are planned at $9,000?

(Answer)

2. If planned sales for April in the Costume Jewelry department are $130,000 and the planned stock-sales ratio for the month is 2.4, what should be the dollar value of the stock on April 1?

           _____
           (Answer)

3. The planned sales in the Lingerie Department for the six-month period February through July was $142,000. If a stock turnover rate of 4 was planned for this period, what should be the dollar value of the average stock carried during the period?

           _____
           (Answer)

4. From the following figures, calculate:

(a)   the average stock for the year

    (a) _____
        (Answer)

(b)   the annual rate of stock turnover

    (b) _____
        (Answer)

Gross sales	$497,500
Customer returns	47,500
Inventory 8/1/77	85,200
Inventory 10/1/77	105,000
Inventory 12/1/77	250,000
Inventory 2/1/78	53,000
Inventory 4/1/78	90,000
Inventory 6/1/78	80,000
Inventory 8/1/78	76,000

5. Sales for the six-month period in a Handbag Department were $250,500. The monthly inventories at retail for this period were:

February 1	$90,000
March 1	87,500
April 1	92,000
May 1	90,000
June 1	84,000
July 1	79,000
July 31	62,000

(a) What was the average stock for the period?

(a) _____
     (Answer)

(b) What was the stock turnover rate for the period?

(b) _____
     (Answer)

(c) If April sales amounted to $23,000, what was the stock-sales ratio for April?

(c) _____
     (Answer)

6. The Cosmetics Department's stock was planned for January 1 at $22,500. Sales for the month were planned at $5,900. Determine the stock-sales ratio for January.

_____
(Answer)

7. Planned sales in the Lingerie Department for November are $260,000 and the planned stock-sales ratio is 3.1. What should be the dollar value of the stock on November 1?

_____
(Answer)

8. Planned sales in the China Department for June are $225,000 and the planned stock-sales ratio is 1.8. What should be the dollar value of the June 1 stock?

_____
(Answer)

Planning Markdowns. The third basic element of a seasonal merchandise plan, with which most planners are concerned, is markdowns. The term *markdown* refers to the dollar difference between the current retail price at which items of merchandise are marked and the lower retail price to which they are being marked.

Markdown policies. A certain percentage of any retail stock will always have to be marked down before it can be sold. But markdowns reduce the retail value of the stock on hand, thereby reducing the dollar income to be derived from sales of items whose retail price has been reduced from that at which it was originally marked when first brought into stock. For this reason, most retail merchants attempt to control markdowns by stiplulating in their seasonal merchandise plans the maximum that can be taken either monthly or for the season as a whole. Markdowns are planned at retail dollar value or as a percentage of net sales or both.

Some retailers, however, prefer not to plan markdowns when drawing up seasonal plans. These retailers prefer to regard markdowns as a "hedge" against being overstocked in case actual sales are less than those that were planned. Furthermore, they reason that markdowns, like markup and stockturn, should be treated as an *average,* supplemental figure for the season as a whole, instead of a monthly figure, which at best can be only an estimate arbitrarily allocated to each of the months involved. And some retailers are of the opinion that if markdowns are planned either as a seasonal percentage of net sales and/or in dollars that buyers or department managers will take them regardless of whether they are justified or not.

Because of rapidly changing consumer demand with regard to highly seasonal or fashion-influenced goods, markdowns are generally larger in departments or stores handling these types of merchandise than in those handling merchandise of a more staple nature, such as housewares or floor coverings.

As percentage of sales. Markdowns as a percentage of planned sales usually will vary widely from month to month any season, due to the cyclical nature of consumer demand for various types of merchandise and each individual store's merchandising policies relating to the taking of markdowns. They will also vary widely on a yearly basis from one type of merchandise to another. For example, markdowns as a percentage of net sales are usually higher for fashion goods than they are for staple goods. They are usually higher in departments handling moderately high to high unit price merchandise than in those handling moderately low to low unit price merchandise. Here are some typical figures, as compiled from *Merchandise and Operating Results,* published by the National Retail Merchants Association.

	Markdown %
All Dresses (misses', juniors, and women's sizes)	18.2
Women's Footwear	18.0
Adult Female Apparel	15.5
Bridals and Formals	14.9
Children's Footwear	12.7
Adult Male Apparel	9.5
Toys	9.5
Floor Coverings	8.6
Female Sleepwear and Robes	8.1
Men's Footwear	7.8
Men's Furnishings	5.6
Small Electric Appliances	4.6
Books	3.0
Cosmetics	1.9

Formulas (for determining markdown percentage):

(a) Dollar markdowns = $ Net sales $\times$ markdown %

(b) Markdown % $= \dfrac{\$ \text{ Markdowns}}{\$ \text{ Net sales}}$

Problems:

In preparing his Fall season merchandise budget, a Stationery buyer reviewed departmental markdown figures for the corresponding season last year in which net sales totaled $75,000 and markdowns during the period totaled $3,450. After study of markdown percentage figures for similar departments in similar stores, however, the buyer decided his previous year's markdowns had been too high.

(a) What was last year's markdown percentage? (b) If he plans sales this Fall season at $75,000 (the same as last year's actual sales) and markdowns at 4.0%, what would be the dollar amount of this year's planned markdowns?

Solutions:

(a) Last year's markdown % $= \dfrac{\$3,450}{\$75,000}$

$= 4.6\%$

(b) This year's planned $ markdowns $= \$75,000 \times 4.0\%$

$= \$3,000$

Having determined the total dollar markdowns for the entire six-month period, the buyer would then apportion the $3,000 among the individual months, bearing in mind that $450 fewer markdowns should be taken in the upcoming period on the same sales base of $75,000.

Form 4-5 is an example of how the six-month merchandising plan might look after sales, beginning-of-the-month stocks, and markdowns had been planned.

Planning Purchases. Having determined planned sales, stocks, and markdowns for an upcoming period, the planner is now able to plan the fourth and last basic element of a merchandise budget: stock purchases. The reason for planning purchases is to maintain a desired balance between stock and sales throughout a given period.

Dept. Name __Misses' Dresses__   Dept. No. __42__

		PLAN (This Year)	ACTUAL (Last Year)
SIX MONTH MERCHANDISING PLAN	Initial markup (%)	48.5	47.5
	Gross margin (%)	42.3	41.8
	Cash discount (% cost purch.)	8.0	7.8
	Season stock turnover (rate)	2.8	2.6
	Shortage reserve (%)	1.5	1.8
	Advertising expense (%)	2.8	3.0
	Selling salaries (%)	8.0	8.5

SPRING 197–		FEB.	MAR.	APR.	MAY	JUNE	JULY	SEASON TOTAL
FALL 197–		AUG.	SEP.	OCT.	NOV.	DEC.	JAN.	
SALES	Last Year	12,100	14,200	17,300	15,500	14,100	10,800	84,000
	Plan	12,500	17,500	16,000	16,500	15,000	11,500	89,000
	Percent of Increase	3.3	23.2	−7.5	6.5	6.4	6.5	6.0%
	Revised							
	Actual							
RETAIL STOCK (BOM)	Last Year	34,500	35,500	39,000	35,000	34,000	29,000	21,000*
	Plan	32,000	39,000	36,000	35,000	33,000	26,000	21,000*
	Revised							*
	Actual							*
MARKDOWNS	Last Year	2,000	2,500	2,800	2,200	2,200	2,100	13,800
	Plan (dollars)	1,800	2,000	2,600	2,000	2,000	2,100	12,500
	Plan (percent)	14.4	11.4	16.3	12.1	13.3	18.3	14.0%
	Revised							
	Actual							
	Last Year	15,100	20,200	16,100	16,700	11,300	4,900	84,300

FORM 4-5

Mary D. Troxell, *Fashion Merchandising,* 2nd ed. (New York: Gregg Division, McGraw Hill, 1976), p. 228.

The trade term *planned purchases* indicates the amount of merchandise that is planned for *delivery* to the department or store during any given period without exceeding the planned closing stock for that period. And, like sales and stock, purchases may be planned either in dollars or units of merchandise. In this text, however, we will be referring to purchases planned in dollars and on a monthly rather than a seasonal basis.

Medium- and large-volume stores usually plan their purchases on a monthly basis. Chains frequently plan their purchases on a weekly basis. Small stores often plan theirs for periods longer than a single month, perhaps for an entire selling season or for the period between market trips. In any case, all planned purchases are derived in exactly the same way: by simple arithmetic computation.

Purchases should never be based on guesswork or planned independently of sales and stock plans. Instead they are arithmetically derived from planned sales, stock, and markdown figures, representing a "need minus have" situation—stock the department or store will "need" to acquire, minus stock it "has" or already owns at the beginning of each period. Planned purchases should not be confused or equated with open-to-buy, which is discussed later in the chapter.

Methods of calculating. The calculation of planned purchases begins with planned sales for a given month. To that figure is added planned markdowns for the same month. The sum of these two figures represents the amount by which the value of the B.O.M. stock is expected to be decreased throughout the month and will "need" to be replaced. To these two figures—sales and markdowns—is added the value of the planned stock for the end-of-the-month (E.O.M.) which, you will recall, is identical with the B.O.M. stock for the following month. The sum of these three figures—planned sales, markdowns, and E.O.M. stock—then represents total stock needs for the month being planned, as calculated on the basis of already budgeted figures. But since a store or department will always

Dept. Name __Misses' Dresses__   Dept. No. __42__

SIX MONTH MERCHANDISING PLAN		PLAN (This Year)	ACTUAL (Last Year)
Initial markup (%)		48.5	47.5
Gross margin (%)		42.3	41.8
Cash discount (% cost purch.)		8.0	7.8
Season stock turnover (rate)		2.8	2.6
Shortage reserve (%)		1.5	1.8
Advertising expense (%)		2.8	3.0
Selling salaries (%)		8.0	8.5

SPRING 197—		FEB.	MAR.	APR.	MAY	JUNE	JULY	SEASON TOTAL
~~FALL 197—~~		~~AUG.~~	~~SEP.~~	~~OCT.~~	~~NOV.~~	~~DEC.~~	~~JAN.~~	
SALES	Last Year	12,100	14,200	17,300	15,500	14,100	10,800	84,000
	Plan	12,500	17,500	16,000	16,500	15,000	11,500	89,000
	Percent of Increase	3.3	23.2	−7.5	6.5	6.4	6.5	6.0%
	Revised							
	Actual							
RETAIL STOCK (BOM)	Last Year	34,500	35,500	39,000	35,000	34,000	29,000	21,000*
	Plan	32,000	39,000	36,000	35,000	33,000	26,000	21,000*
	Revised							*
	Actual							*
MARKDOWNS	Last Year	2,000	2,500	2,800	2,200	2,200	2,100	13,800
	Plan (dollars)	1,800	2,000	2,600	2,000	2,000	2,100	12,500
	Plan (percent)	14.4	11.4	16.3	12.1	13.3	18.3	14.0%
	Revised							
	Actual							
RETAIL PURCHASES	Last Year	15,100	20,200	16,100	16,700	11,300	4,900	84,300
	Plan	21,300	16,500	17,600	16,500	10,000	8,600	90,500
	Revised							
	Actual							

Comments

*Represents stock end of period.

Merchandise Manager __T. J. Evans__   Buyer __Jane Dean__

Controller ____

FORM 4-6

Mary D. Troxell, *Fashion Merchandising*, 2nd ed. (New York: Gregg Division, McGraw Hill, 1976), p. 231.

have stock on hand at the beginning of each month, the value of that stock must be subtracted from the total stock "needs" for the month. The difference between the value of the total stock that will be needed during any given month and the value of the stock that is anticipated as being on hand at the beginning of that particular month represents planned purchases, or the amount of merchandise that can be brought into stock during the month, according to *planned* figures.

Form 4-6 is an example of how a six-month merchandising plan would appear after sales, beginning-of-the month stocks, markdowns, and retail purchases had been planned.

Formula (for calculating monthly planned purchases in retail dollars):

Planned purchases = Planned sales for month + planned markdowns for month + planned E.O.M. stock − planned B.O.M. stock

Problem:

If a Junior Dress Department had the following budgeted figures:

Planned sales for May	$16,500
Planned markdowns for May	2,000
Planned stock May 31	33,000
Planned stock May 1	35,000

what would be the planned purchases for the month?

Solution:

Planned purchases for May = Planned sales + planned markdowns
+ planned E.O.M. stock
− planned B.O.M. stock

= $16,500 + $2,000 + $33,000
− $35,000

= $51,500 − $35,000

= $16,500

Converting retail value to cost value. Some retailers plan purchases at cost as well as at retail. The cost value of a retail figure is easily obtained by simply multiplying the retail figure by the cost complement of the planned initial markup percentage—shown here as a supplemental element of the seasonal merchandising plan.

Formula (for converting retail planned purchases to cost):

Planned purchases at cost = Planned purchases at retail
× (100% − initial markup %)

Problem:

If a department's planned purchases at retail were $10,000 for July and initial markup was planned at 49.0%, what would be the cost value of planned purchases for July?

Solution:

Planned purchases at cost = Planned purchases at retail
× (100% − initial markup %)

= $10,000 × (100.0% − 49.0%)

= $10,000 × 51.0%

= $5,100

PRACTICE PROBLEMS—Planned Markdowns; Planned Purchases

1. A buyer took the following markdowns during August:

   40 sportshirts from $18 to $12.99
   60 sportshirts fom $15 to $9.99
   80 T-shirts from $10 to $6.99

   (a) Sales volume for the month was $24,000. What was
   the August markdown percentage?

   (a) _____
   (Answer)

   (b) If markdowns had been planned at 3.5% for August,
   how does the actual markdown compare to plan?

   (b) _____
   (Answer)

2. If February markdowns in a Notions Department amounted to $2,755 and net sales
   were $47,500, what was the markdown percentage for the month?

   _____
   (Answer)

3. A Toy Department buyer planned the following budget for November:

Planned stock November 1	$ 80,000
Planned sales, November	120,000
Planned markdowns, November	6,000
Planned stock December 1	100,000

What were the planned purchases at retail for the month?

_____
(Answer)

4. The Fall merchandise plan for a Junior Sportswear Department indicated the following figures for October:

Planned sales	$75,000
Planned markdowns	6,500
Planned stock September 30	68,000
Planned stock October 31	54,000
Planned markup	49.0%

(a) Find the planned purchases at retail for October.

(a) _____
(Answer)

(b) Find the planned purchases at cost for October.

(b) _____
(Answer)

5. Initial markup in a Budget Lingerie Department is planned at 48.5%. July sales are planned at $12,000 and August sales at $15,000. The stock-sales ratio is planned at 1.5 for July and 2.0 for August. Markdowns are planned at $900 for July.

(a) What are the planned purchases for July at retail?

(a) _____
(Answer)

(b) What are the planned purchases for July at cost?

(b) _____
(Answer)

6. A Housewares Department had the following planned and actual figures:

Planned stock November 1	$115,000
Planned stock December 1	145,000
Planned markdowns November	3,500
Planned sales November	46,000
Actual stock November 1	110,000
Actual sales November	45,000
Actual stock December 1	145,000
Actual markdowns November	3,000

(a) Determine the original planned purchases for November.

(a) _____
(Answer)

(b) Determine the revised planned purchases for November.

(b) _____
(Answer)

SUPPLEMENTAL ELEMENTS
OF THE SEASONAL PLAN

While the basic elements of a Seasonal Merchandise Plan—sales, stocks, markdowns, and purchases—are usually planned on a monthly or weekly basis, certain other merchandising goals are usually established on a seasonal basis and actual performance figures are regularly checked against those goals.

Usually considered most important of seasonal goals is Initial Markup percentage. *Initial Markup* refers to the difference between the delivered cost of an item and the retail price placed on it when it is first brought in to stock. Initial markup can be expressed both in dollars and as a percentage of net sales.

The procedure for arriving at initial markup percentage as a seasonal goal is discussed in Chapter 6. While some stores may establish monthly markup goals, the majority find a single seasonal goal figure satisfactory for the following reasons:

1. buyers mark their purchases into existing department price lines (see Chapter 6);
2. the planned markup should always be considered an *average* figure to be maintained throughout a season by balancing lower-than-goal markup on some purchases with higher-than-goal markup on others;
3. achieved markup percentages vary little from month to month during any one season unless the department runs a number of special sales at low markups.

Instead of establishing a seasonal percentage goal figure for initial markup, or sometimes in addition to it, many stores plan gross margin percentage (of net sales) when developing their seasonal budgets. Gross margin, as was indicated in Chapter 3, is the retail trade term for the dollar difference between net sales for a given period and the total cost of merchandise sold during that period. *Gross margin percentage,* also discussed in Chapter 3, is calculated by dividing dollar gross margin for the period by dollar net sales for the same period.

Gross margin is a very important figure in merchandise planning as well as in computing operating profit or loss. This is because it represents the dollars left over from sales income, after deducting cost of sales, with which to pay all operating expenses and achieve a reasonable operating profit (see Chapter 3).

Other seasonal profit-related goals that retailers may find it advantageous to establish for some of their departments are:

*   shortage reserve as a percentage of net sales (see Chapter 9);
*   cash discount earned as a percentage of the cost of purchases (see Chapter 5);
*   net alteration and workroom costs as a percentage of net sales;
*   customer returns as a percentage of gross sales;
*   transportation costs as a percentage of the cost of purchases (see Chapters 5 and 10);
*   stock turnover rate;
*   certain operating expenses that have a close relationship with planned sales, such as selling salaries and advertising;
*   markdowns if they are *not* considered a basic element of the seasonal plan and distributed on a monthly or weekly basis.

OPEN-TO-BUY

While the seasonal merchandise plan is the retailer's prime planning tool, open-to-buy is the retailer's prime control tool. The term *Open-to-Buy* (abbreviated O.T.B.) refers to the value of purchases that can still be made for delivery during any given month or other specified time period without exceeding the value of the inventory planned for the end of that period. O.T.B. reports are usually prepared weekly, biweekly, or monthly by a store's Accounting Department for each of its selling departments, and issued to the departmental buyer or manager for the purpose of controlling purchases so that planned closing stock levels for each accounting period can be met. Form 4-7 is an example of a dollar Open-to-Buy report for the month of May at the end of the second week of that month.

Calculating O.T.B.

O.T.B. is discussed in the same chapter with the seasonal merchandise plan for the following reasons: (1) O.T.B. is the equivalent of planned purchases less orders already placed for delivery during the period, and (2) the two basic figures used in calculating O.T.B. are obtained from that plan: planned monthly sales and planned B.O.M. and E.O.M. stock levels. Other figures involved in the calculation are those resuiting from current operations: actual stock on hand and merchandise on order (Form 4-8).

Following is the formula for calculating O.T.B. at the beginning of a month or other specified period:

Formula:

> O.T.B. = Planned sales + planned markdowns + planned
> E.O.M. stock − B.O.M. stock − merchandise
> on order for delivery during the current period

Problem:

What is the March O.T.B. for a department with the following figures as of March 1?

Planned sales March	= $15,000
Planned markdowns March	= $ 1,000
Planned March 31 stock	= $32,000
March 1 stock	= $30,000
Merchandise on order for March delivery	= $ 5,000

Solution:

Planned sales March	= $15,000
+ Planned markdowns March	= 1,000
+ Planned March 31 stock	= 32,000
= Total stock needed in March	= $48,000
− March 1 stock	= 30,000
= Planned purchases, March	= $18,000
− On-order for March delivery	= 5,000
= O.T.B. as of March 1	= $13,000

Smith & Welsh

DEPARTMENTAL OPEN — TO — BUY REPORT (All Dollar Figures Are Shown To Nearest Hundred)

FIGURES THROUGH 5/14 2nd WEEEK OF PERIOD IV   19 79

Item	Dept Line	T.Y.	L.Y.	T.Y.	L.Y.	T.Y.	L.Y.	T.Y.	L.Y.	T.Y.	L.Y.	T.Y.	L.Y.	T.Y.	L.Y.	T.Y.	L.Y.
Purchases Period/Date	1	755.9	534.2	72.3	63.9	360	63.6	85.6	42.9	1520	80.3	-5.1	5.3	1224	133.3	109.5	37.7
Purchase M.U. % Per/Date	2	53.2	53.1	50.2	49.8	52.4	50.4	506	49.5	50.9	54.4	-	50.4	52.3	537	57.1	53.9
NET SALES Period Date	3	498.8	508.0	64.0	86.9	51.4	39.7	61.2	43.7	71.2	86.5	14.2	14.1	52.0	58.2	77.1	78.8
NET SALES Planned Per/Date	4	503.3	x	77.0	x	52.0	x	46.0	x	90.0	x	11.0	x	60.0	x	79.0	x
Mark-Up Cancellations Memo																	
MARK $ Period to Date	5	60.3	22.4	-	-	16.5	5.4	-	-	16.9	17.0	-	-	8.0	-	9.9	-
DOWNS % Year to Date	6	12.7	10.4	12.6	6.6	20.4	20.5	11.4	14.8	12.9	9.4	16.3	10.3	8.3	8.5	10.3	8.7
Inv. As Of Report Date	7	2259.6	2575.4	282.4	335.0	239.2	293.5	257.5	277.2	308.0	369.3	140.8	157.6	263.2	338.4	329.0	384.2
Planned Stock End/Per.	8	1930.0	1671.0	250.0	190.0	280.0	250.0	210.0	180.0	260.0	365.0	50.0	56.0	230.0	140.0	350.0	310.0
Orders To End/Period	9	814.5	1004.5	99.7	148.0	171.0	144.9	57.1	83.8	172.1	333.0	-	5.3	44.8	133.0	95.4	153.3
Open To Buy At Report Date	10	-664.4	-1375.4	-54.1	-314.8	-76.2	-142.4	-55.6	-105.0	-150.1	-347.3	-86.8	-103.4	-28.0	-171.4	-103.4	-264.4
ORDERS Succeeding Per.	11	404.2	167.1	166.1	47.1	53.1	3.0	47.7	35.0	7.3	14.4	1.8	-	-	-	79.0	9.4
ORDERS Planned "	12	654.0	x	100.0	x	40.0	x	60.0	x	110.0	x	-	x	85.0	x	120.0	x
ORDERS 2nd Succeed. Per.	13	391.0	83.1	86.0	31.1	75.0	36.1	50.0	-	100.0	-	95.0	-	70.0	-	100.0	-
ORDERS Future	14	497.8	793.8	4.8	49.7	309.4	110.2	-	4.5	6.9	19.1	9.4	29.2	-	-	12.4	-

Item	Dept Line	T.Y.	L.Y.	T.Y.	L.Y.	T.Y.	L.Y.	T.Y.	L.Y.	T.Y.	L.Y.	T.Y.	L.Y.	T.Y.	L.Y.	T.Y.	L.Y.
Purchases Period/Date	1	18.8	-.4	23.1	8.9	141.3	109.7										
Purchase M.U. % Per/Date	2	50.9	-	49.0	79.8	517	54.2										
NET SALES Period Date	3	.8	3	11.5	11.3	95.4	88.6										
NET SALES Planned Per/Date	4	-	x	11.3	x	77.0	x		x						x		
Mark-Up Cancellations Memo																	
MARK $ Period to Date	5	5.1	-	-	-	3.9	-										
DOWNS % Year to Date	6	67.0	30.2	-	-	8.1	10.3										
Inv. As Of Report Date	7	24.2	6.4	87.0	90.5	328.3	443.3										
Planned Stock End/Per.	8	40.0	30.0	110.0	110.0	250.0	340.0										
Orders To End/Period	9	.4	3.4	24.6	49.7	149.4	53.2										
Open To Buy At Report Date	10	15.4	37.2	19.1	4.6	-144.7	-161.5										
ORDERS Succeeding Per.	11	2.8	-	3.3	-	43.1	58.2										
ORDERS Planned "	12	7.0	x	12.0	x	120.0	x		x						x		
ORDERS 2nd Succeed. Per.	13	130.0	-	17.0	-	1050	54.0										
ORDERS Future	14	121.0	462.2	-	-	33.9	118.9										

FORM 4-7 OPEN-TO-BUY REPORT

WEEKLY REPORT OF OUTSTANDING ORDERS (All Figures Shown in Hundreds of Dollars)

AS OF END OF 4th WEEK IN PERIOD VII 19 77

DIV. CODE	DEPT. NO.	DELIVERY DUE BY END THIS PERIOD				DELIVERY DUE SUCCEEDING PERIOD				DELY DUE 2ND SUCCEEDING PERIOD				FUTURE DELIVERY				TOTAL COST	COST % RECIP.	DEPT. NO.
		COST FOR.	DOM.	TOTAL	RETAIL TOTAL	COST FOR.	DOM.	TOTAL	RETAIL TOTAL	COST FOR.	DOM.	TOTAL	RETAIL TOTAL	COST FOR.	DOM.	TOTAL	RETAIL TOTAL			
21	141	18.4	37.9	56.3	112.1	.9	11.1	12.0	23.9	.9	12.2	13.1	26.1		11.7	11.7	23.3	93.1	199.04	141
21	171	23.4	48.7	72.1	131.3		1.8	1.8	3.3		1.4	1.4	2.5					75.3	182.12	171
21	172	14.8	8.7	23.5	45.1	.6		.6	1.2									24.1	192.01	172
21	189		78.1	78.1	140.0		111.6	111.6	200.0		106.0	106.0	190.0		29.0	29.0	52.0	324.7	179.24	189
21	233	.2	44.7	44.9	81.4		11.9	11.9	21.6		6.4	6.4	11.6					63.2	181.32	233
21	234		16.7	16.7	29.0		4.4	4.4	7.6									21.1	173.37	234
21	235		21.1	21.1	42.0		3.0	3.0	6.0									24.1	199.20	235
21	240		3.8	3.8	6.7		1.9	1.9	3.3		6.5	6.5	11.4					12.2	176.15	240
21	251		73.5	73.5	121.9		21.7	21.7	36.0									95.2	165.81	251
21	261	48.0	33.9	81.9	161.4	33.1	13.8	46.9	86.7	5.2	13.3	18.5	34.2					147.3	184.81	261
21	412	5.9	11.4	17.3	36.6													17.3	211.82	412
21	413		8.3	8.3	17.2													8.3	206.78	413
21	414	.9	4.6	5.5	13.7													5.5	249.81	414
21	415		2.9	2.9	5.6													2.9	192.72	415
21	997	111.6	394.3	505.9	934.0	34.6	181.2	215.8	389.6	6.1	145.8	151.9	275.8	-	40.7	40.7	75.3	914.3	SUB-TOTAL ACCESSORIES	

An abbreviated formula might be stated as follows:

O.T.B. = Planned purchases for a specified period – all
orders placed for delivery before the end of
the current period but not yet received

O.T.B. may also be calculated for the balance of a month at any point during that month. The procedure is the same as for the entire month except that actual result figures are used instead of planned figures with one major exception—planned E.O.M. stock—which remains the same as in the seasonal plan. Planned sales become those for the balance of the month. Planned markdowns also become those for the balance of the month. B.O.M. stock becomes stock currently on hand.

For example, assume the buyer for the department above wants to know what his O.T.B. is as of March 15. He has the following figures to work with in his calculations:

Actual sales March 1-15	$ 8,000
Actual markdowns March 1-15	$ 500
Planned stock on March 31	$32,000
Stock on order for March delivery	$ 6,000
Stock on hand March 1	$30,000

Solutions:

Planned sales March 16-31	$ 7,000	($15,000 plan – $8,000 actual)
Planned markdowns March 16-31	$ 500	($1,000 plan – $500 actual)
Planned stock March 31	$32,000	(from seasonal plan)
March 1 stock	$30,000	(actual)
Stock received March 1-15	$ 9,000	(net purchases)
On order March delivery	$ 6,000	

Stock on hand March 15 = B.O.M. stock + stock received March 1-15
– actual sales March 1-15–actual
markdowns March 1-15
= $30,000 + $9,000 – $8,000 – $500
= $39,000 – $8,500
= $30,500

O.T.B. balance March = $7,000 + $500 + $32,000 – $30,500 – $6,000
= $39,500 – $36,500
= $3,000

Problem:

From the following figures calculate a Wig shop's open-to-buy, as of February 14, for the balance of the month.

Planned sales balance of month	$1,000
Planned markdowns balance of month	100
Planned stock February 28	2,500
Stock on hand February 14	2,000
Merchandise on order for February delivery	1,000

Solution:

Planned sales balance of month	$1,000
Planned markdowns balance of month +	100
Planned stock February 28 +	2,500
Total stock requirements balance of February =	$3,600
Stock on hand February 14 −	2,000
Purchases allowed for balance of month =	$1,600
Stock O.O. for February delivery −	1,000
O.T.B. for February as of February 14 =	$ 600

If the O.O. figure exceeds the planned purchase figure for the balance of the month, that condition is termed *overbought*. To differentiate between an O.T.B. condition and an overbought condition, the latter amount is enclosed in parentheses. For example, if a department's planned purchases for the balance of May amounted to $1,000 and orders already placed for May delivery totaled $1,500, then the department is overbought for May by $500, or:

$$\text{May O.T.B.} = \text{Planned purchases for May} - \text{merchandise on order for May delivery}$$
$$= \$1,000 - \$1,500$$
$$= (\$500)$$

Calculating O.T.B. can be compared to reconciling one's checkbook balance with the monthly statement most banks provide their checking account customers. Checks issued are comparable to purchase orders for stock that have been placed by the buyer or department manager of a store. Checks that have "cleared the bank" (paid out by the bank) are comparable to those purchase orders that have been filled by the vendors to whom they were issued, the merchandise received, and placed in stock. Occasionally, however, some checks that have been issued have not cleared the bank as of the date the bank's statement was prepared. These are termed "outstanding checks" and are comparable to outstanding purchase orders a buyer has already placed for delivery within a given month but which have not as yet been filled by the vendors to whom they were issued. However, since outstanding checks are the legal obligation of the person issuing the checks, and the outstanding purchase orders the legal obligation of the store which the buyer or department manager represents, they are commitments that must be taken into account in order to arrive, in the first instance, at the balance one actually has in his/her checking account, or, in the second instance, the remaining O.T.B. for that specific month.

Most stores require their buyers to indicate on each purchase order the month in which the merchandise involved is scheduled for delivery. Only in this way can orders be charged against the proper month's O.T.B. In cases where delivery is scheduled for more than one month, buyers are usually required to break down the total retail value of the order into separate monthly O.T.B. commitments. This feature of O.T.B., as a prime inventory control device, forces buyers, through carefully scheduling delivery dates, to time the delivery of their purchases to coincide more closely with peaks in customer demand for the merchandise involved.

For example, assume that in June a Sportwear buyer decides to place an order with a vendor for 30 pieces each of two skirts in the vendor's Fall line. Both skirt styles cost $25.00 each, so the buyer decided to retail each style at the same price of $50.00 each. However, she wanted only one style delivered in August and the other in September. So, in writing up the order, which included both styles, she indicated that the total cost and total retail of the order—$1,500 and $3,000, respectively—be split between the two months with $750 at cost and $1,500 at retail being charged against August O.T.B. and the same amount against September O.T.B.

Converting O.T.B. at Retail to Cost

Thus far we have been discussing O.T.B. at retail value. In some stores, however, O.T.B. is calculated at both cost and retail. Converting retail O.T.B. to its cost equivalent can be done in one of two ways.

1. Planned purchases at retail are first converted to cost, as previously explained, by multiplying the retail figure by the complement of the initial markup percentage indicated as a seasonal goal figure on the merchandise plan. Then the cost of all commitments (O.O.) for the period are totaled and subtracted from planned purchases at cost to give an O.T.B. at cost. Expressed as a formula:

$$\begin{array}{l} \text{Planned purchases at retail} \times (100\% - \text{initial markup \%}) \\ \underline{- \text{ Cost value of all O.O. for the period}} \\ = \text{Cost value of O.T.B. for the period} \end{array}$$

2. If both planned purchases and O.O. for the period are stated at retail value, O.T.B. at cost can be determined by multiplying O.T.B. at retail by the complement of the initial markup percentage as follows:

O.T.B. at cost = Retail O.T.B. × (100% − initial markup %)

Problem:

If an Infants' Department had the following figures for May:

Planned stock at retail May 1	$20,000
Planned sales at retail May	4,000
Planned markdowns at retail May	800
Planned stock at retail June 1	22,000
May on order at cost as of May 1	1,500
Planned initial markup percentage	50%

(a) What were May planned purchases at retail?
(b) What were May planned purchases at cost?
(c) What was the May O.T.B. at cost on May 1?

Solutions:

(a)
Planned sales May	$ 4,000
Planned markdowns May	+ 800
Planned May 31 stock	+ 22,000
Total stock needs May	$26,800
Planned stock May 1	− 20,000
Planned May purchases at retail	$ 6,800

(b) Planned purchases at cost = Planned purchases at retail × (100% − retail markup %)
= $6,800 × (100% − 50%)
= $6,800 × 50%
= $3,400

(c) O.T.B. at cost = Planned purchases at cost − O.O. at cost
= $3,400 − $1,500
= $1,900

89

1. On November 15 a Housewares Department had stock on hand amounting to $52,000 and merchandise on order for November delivery of $8,000. Planned sales for the balance of the month were $16,000 and the closing inventory was planned at $64,000. What was the O.T.B. for the balance of November?

_____
(Answer)

2. From the following figures:

Planned markup %	42%
Planned sales July	$175,000
Planned markdowns July	20,000
Planned stock July 1	250,000
Planned stock July 31	125,000
July on order	60,000

(a) Calculate July planned purchases at cost.

(a) _____
(Answer)

(b) Calculate July O.T.B. at cost.

(b) _____
(Answer)

3. Find the balance of December O.T.B. when stock on hand December 10 amounted to $265,000, planned sales for the balance of the month $171,000, planned markdowns for the balance of the month $11,000, planned December closing stock $150,000, and merchandise on order for December delivery totaled $71,500.

_____
(Answer)

4. Find the balance of the O.T.B. for May when stock on hand May 15 is $16,300, planned sales for the balance of the month $9,000, May on—order $3,000, and the planned stock for June 1 $10,000.

_____
(Answer)

5. If a Fashion Accessories Department had the following figures for September:

Planned sales	$ 9,000
Planned markdowns	400
Planned E.O.M. stock	25,200
Planned B.O.M. stock	24,600
Planned markup	51.5%

(a) Determine planned purchases at retail.

(a) _____
(Answer)

(b) Determine planned purchases at cost.

(b) _____
(Answer)

6. Find the balance of the O.T.B. for February when stock on hand February 7 is $8,150 and planned sales for the balance of the month are $4,500. Merchandise on order for February delivery amounts to $1,500 and the planned ending inventory is $5,000.

_____
(Answer)

SUMMARY OF KEY TERMS

Basic Elements of a Merchandise Plan. Net sales, stock, markdowns, and purchases.

Discretionary Income. Income available after providing for such essentials as food, shelter, clothing, basic transportation, and taxes.

External Factors. Those outside the store and its control.

Fashion Trends. Various indications of the direction in which fashion demand is moving.

Initial Markup. The difference between the delivered cost of merchandise and the retail price placed on it when it is first brought in to stock.

Internal Factors. Those within the store and its control.

Markdown. The dollar difference between the current retail price of merchandise and the lower retail price to which it is to be marked.

Merchandise Plan. A projection of sales that can be reasonably anticipated during a specified future period of time and the stock estimated as necessary in order in achieve those sales.

Open-to-Buy. Purchases that can still be made for delivery during any given month or other specified period after deducting from planned purchases for the period orders already placed for delivery during the same month or period.

Overbought. The condition that exists when merchandise on order for a period exceeds the planned purchases for that period.

Planned Purchases. The amount of merchandise planned for delivery during an given period, without exceeding the planned closing stock for that period.

Stock-Sales Ratio. The figure relationship that exists between the stock at the beginning of a month or other period and net sales for that month or other period.

Stock Turnover. The ratio of net sales during a given period to the average stock for the same period.

Supplemental Elements of a Merchandise Plan. Seasonal goal figures other than sales, stock, markdowns, and purchases that are planned by top management of the firm.

Name _____ Date _____

REVIEW QUESTIONS—The Seasonal Merchandising Plan; Open-To-Buy

1. What are the four major goals of merchandise planning?

   (1)

   (2)

   (3)

   (4)

2. Most stores operate on a fiscal basis of two planning seasons a year, with the first

   beginning _____ and the second _____ of each year.

3. What are the three types of figure entries usually considered in all seasonal merchandise planning?

   (1)
   (2)
   (3)

4. What are the four basic elements included in most seasonal merchandise plans?

   (1)
   (2)
   (3)
   (4)

5. What are the three basic factors that must be taken into consideration when formulating seasonal sales and stock plans for most selling departments?

   (1)
   (2)
   (3)

6. Briefly describe the difference between stock-sales ratio and stock turnover.

7. How can the buyer for a selling department in a medium volume retail store go about increasing his/her rate of stock turnover?

8. How are planned purchases calculated?

9. Name three supplemental goal figures often included in seasonal merchandise planning and briefly explain the importance of each.

10. What is the meaning of the term "open-to-buy"? How is it determined?

REVIEW PROBLEM—Planning Seasonal Sales, Stock, Markdowns, Purchases; Stock-Sales Ratio; Stock Turnover

Development of a Merchandise Budget (A Case Study)

The largest department store in the midwestern city of Wagner was Adams & Baker, with an annual sales volume in 1977 of approximately $5,000,000.

Ralph England was the store's Men's Furnishings buyer. As guidelines in developing a merchandising plan for the 1978 Spring season, he was given the following figures:

Planned sales for the entire fiscal year	$265,000
Planned sales for the 1978 Spring season (as percentage of annual sales)	44%
Increase in planned sales for the 1978 Spring season over 1977 Spring season	10%

Monthly Sales Percentage Goals

February	14.0%	May	17.5%
March	16.0%	June	16.5%
April	20.0%	July	16.0%

B.O.M. Stock-Sales Ratios

February	3.8	May	3.6
March	4.2	June	3.7
April	3.5	July	3.9

Estimated Beginning and Ending Inventory Values for the Six-Month Season

February	$61,940
August 1	$72,300

Markdowns estimated for the Spring season at 5.5% to be allocated monthly as follows:

February	6.6%	May	4.9%
March	4.9%	June	5.2%
April	4.3%	July	7.5%

On the basis of this information, calculate and place your answers to each of the following problems in the appropriate spaces on the six-month merchandise planning form provided.

1. Monthly planned sales figures, rounded off to the nearest hundred dollars.
2. Percentage of increase or decrease in planned sales for each month.
3. B.O.M. stocks, rounded off to nearest ten dollars.
4. Monthly and total season planned dollar markdowns.
5. Monthly and total season planned purchases at retail value, rounded off to the nearest ten dollars.
6. Planned average stock for the season.
7. Planned rate of stock turnover for the season.

Dept. Name _____ Dept. No. _____

SIX MONTH MERCHANDISING PLAN

	PLAN (This Year)	ACTUAL (Last Year)
Initial markup (%)	48.5	47.5
Gross margin (%)	42.3	41.8
Cash discount (% cost purch.)	2.9	2.5
Season stock turnover (rate)		1.41
Shortage reserve (%)	.8	1.1
Advertising expense (%)	1.8	2.0
Selling salaries (%)	6.0	6.8

SPRING 197—		FEB.	MAR.	APR.	MAY	JUNE	JULY	SEASON TOTAL
~~FALL 197—~~		~~AUG.~~	~~SEP.~~	~~OCT.~~	~~NOV.~~	~~DEC.~~	~~JAN.~~	
SALES	Last Year	14,826	16,974	21,105	18,075	18,121	16,879	106,000
	Plan							
	Percent of Increase							
	Revised							
	Actual							
RETAIL STOCK (BOM)	Last Year	63,923	80,520	83,536	75,320	72,926	74,910	75,095*
	Plan							*
	Revised							*
	Actual							*
MARKDOWNS	Last Year	1,200	960	890	985	1,050	1,275	6,360
	Plan (dollars)							
	Plan (percent)							
	Revised							
	Actual							
RETAIL PURCHASES	Last Year	32,597	20,976	13,774	16,691	21,034	18,460	123,532
	Plan							
	Revised							
	Actual							

Comments

*Represents stock end of period.

Merchandise Manager _____   Buyer _____

Controller _____

96

CHAPTER 5

THE PURCHASE ORDER
AND TERMS OF SALE

The whole cycle of merchandise processing starts with the writing of a Purchase Order, which is the first subject covered in this chapter. The paperwork involved in completing the cycle, from the time the merchandise arrives at the store until it is purchased by customers, is discussed in detail in Chapter 9.

THE PURCHASE ORDER

Most stores require that for every order placed with a *vendor* (also known as a "resource"), a written Purchase Order (abbreviated P.O.) be made out. On occasion it may be necessary for a buyer to place a verbal order for merchandise. In such cases, however, practically all stores require that the verbal order be "confirmed" promptly with a duly authorized written P.O.

Importance of the Written Order

The *Purchase Order* is, in effect, a legal contract between a store and a vendor to buy certain specified merchandise under certain specified conditions. Therefore, it must be completely, legibly, and accurately made out. Many stores require that their buyers use only the store's P.O. form and never a vendor's order form when placing orders. The reason for this requirement is that on the back of the vendor's copy of practically all store P.O. forms are listed 16 general contractual terms, provisions, and conditions (Form 5-1). These relate to the billing, packing, and shipping of the merchandise specified on the front of the P.O., and were originally drawn up as basic trade agreements by the National Retail Dry Goods Association (predecessor of the National Retail Merchants Association) to protect the interests of the Association's member stores.

INSTRUCTIONS TO VENDOR

BILLING

1. All 10 Day Datings begin at date of receipt of goods by us.
2. Provide separate invoices for each department.
3. Include packing slip and or duplicate copy of the invoice with each shipment and mark the label of the carton containing them "PACKING SLIP ENCLOSED".
4. In the case of slow freight shipments and billings from remote central offices, mail original invoice to:

   Smith & Welsh

   Packing slip must accompany the merchandise if the invoice is mailed.
5. Invoices for all shipments made on or after the 25th of the month will be dated the first of the following month.

PACKING AND LABELING

1. Sort and pack by style, color and size where applicable and list in detail on the packing slip and/or invoice the number of pieces included of each item.
2. Label each carton, showing the name of the vendor, our address, our department number and our order number or order numbers, if a carton contains merchandise for more than one order.
3. In the case of multiple carton shipments, show the number of cartons included on the label of each carton, i.e., "on 2" for two cartons, "on 3" for three cartons, etc.
4. Do not pack merchandise for more than one department in the same carton.

SHIPPING AND ROUTING

1. Follow permanent instructions of our traffic department unless otherwise directed on this order. If no instructions have been given, consult the buyer or our traffic department.
2. Complete shipment is required unless other arrangements are specified on the order.
3. All orders shipped on a given day must be given to the carrier on one bill of lading with the number of cartons belonging to each department and to each order listed in the body of the bill of lading.
4. Valuation of Parcel Post shipments:
   a. For values up to $25 apply minimum.
   b. For values $25 to $50 apply actual value.
   c. For values over $50 apply $50 value.
5. Valuation of other shipments:
   a. FOB Point of origin.
      Use released value except on clothing.
      Value clothing shipments in full but not in excess of $1,000.
   b. FOB *Chicago, Ill.*
      Valuation at the discretion of vendor.
6. Excess transportation costs will be charged back.
7. This order is subject to the conditions and special instructions on the back.

FORM 5-1 INSTRUCTIONS TO VENDORS

The P.O. becomes the basis for the retailer to determine:

- if the merchandise received is as ordered;
- if the merchandise was shipped as directed and before the cancellation date specified on the order;
- if the vendor's billing is correct;
- the retail price at which the merchandise is to be marked and added to the Book Inventory (see Chapter 9);
- when payment of the vendor's invoice is due.

Although the contractual conditions to be found on the back of the vendor's copy of most store P.O.s may be standardized, information required on the face sheet of the order is not. While the face sheet may differ from one store to another in size, format, and amount of detail, each requires that essentially the same basic information be provided. Multibranch retail firms often use two types of P.O. forms. The "short" form is used for merchandise being ordered for delivery to a single destination and/or for special orders. Form 5-2 is an example of the "short" form in general use today. The "long" form is used to detail merchandise being ordered for each or most of its several branches. It is identical to the short form except that it is elongated horizontally to accommodate details of merchandise ordered for individual branch stores.

Components of the Purchase Order

The face of most P.O.s provides designated spaces in which the following information is to be written:

1. *Department number.*
2. Complete *name and address of vendor* from which merchandise is being purchased.
3. *Vendor's Duns number* is an identification number assigned to a business by a leading credit investigating firm which is universally accepted by the business community as identification for all trading purposes.
4. *Date* order is placed.
5. *F.O.B. point* (see the discussion of shipping terms later in this chapter).
6. *Ship via* (information on routing instructions and carriers to be used obtained from the store's traffic department, and never left to the discretion of the vendor).
7. *Ship to* (address or addresses to which merchandise is to be delivered).
8. *Shipping dates:* (1) specific date before which merchandise is not to be shipped or it will be refused; and (2) specific date by which ordered merchandise must be shipped complete or it will be refused or order canceled. (If these specific dates are not indicated on the P.O., the store is obligated to take the merchandise whenever the vendor ships it.)
9. *Terms and dating* (refer to the percent of cash discount allowed and the period in which this discount is available).
10. *Merchandise ordered* (should be listed separately as follows):
    - vendor's style number;
    - store's classification code;

020822

ORDER NUMBER | REVISED ORDER NUMBER | DEPT. NO | CODE

THIS INFORMATION MUST APPEAR ON ALL PACKAGES AND INVOICES

VENDOR TO BE PAID

VENDOR'S DUNS NUMBER

NAME

STREET

CITY   STATE   ZIP

SHIPPING MFR.
IF OTHER
THAN ABOVE:

DATE OF ORDER | PAGE | PAGES OF

SHIPPING DATE *
MUST BE RECEIVED
COMPLETE BY

DO NOT SHIP
BEFORE

* AUTOMATIC CANCELLATION POLICY

THIS ORDER IS CONSIDERED
CANCELLED AND WILL BE
RETURNED AT THE VENDOR'S
EXPENSE IF NOT RECEIVED
COMPLETE WITHIN SPECIFIED
DATES SHOWN ABOVE

MFR NO

**TRANSFER
TO:**

FOR INTERNAL USE ONLY

NOTE: IF MORE THAN ONE SHEET IS
USED FOR ANY ORDER, ENTER GRAND
TOTALS ONLY ON FIRST PAGE

Smith & Welsh

8th & Market Sts.
Chicago, Ill.

ALL MERCHANDISE ON THIS ORDER IS FOR ONE STORE
ONLY. MARK AND SHIP TO
AT ADDRESS INDICATED BY CHECKED BOX.

☐ F O B STORE
☐ F O B OUR CONSOLIDATOR
☐ F O B POINT OF ORIGIN

F.O.B.

TERMS
AND
DATING

SHIP
VIA:

UNLESS OTHERWISE STIPULATED ABOVE, FOLLOW OUR
PERMANENT ROUTING INSTRUCTIONS

OR MARK FOR →   STORE   BUT SHIP TO

CHARGE PERIOD | TOTAL COST | MARK-UP

APRON NUMBER
APRON DATE
CHKD. BY
DATE CHKD.

DEPT. MGR.   DIV. MDSE. MGR.

CLASSI-FICATION	STYLE NUMBER	TOTAL QUANTITY	UNIT COST	TOTAL COST	UNIT RETAIL	TOTAL RETAIL

DESCRIPTION

1
2
3
4
5
6
7
8
9
10
11
12
13
14
15
16
17
18
19

FORM 5-2 "SHORT" PURCHASE ORDER

- brief description of each style;
- breakdown by size and color, if applicable;
- total units ordered in each style;
- unit cost of each style ordered;
- total cost of each style ordered;
- total cost of the order.

11. *Buyer's signature.*
12. *Divisional Merchandise Manager's signature.*
13. On the Order Checking Department's and buyer's copies—but *not on the vendor's copy*—the following should be indicated:
    - *unit retail* of each style (indicating the retail price to be placed on each style ordered at the time the P.O. is written, known as *preretailing*);
    - *total retail of each style* (unit retail times number of units);
    - *total retail of the order;*
    - *purchase markup* percentage;
    - *delivery breakdown by classification* (If order includes more than one classification, indicate total cost and total retail for each classification. For example, an order involving three classifications for a total of $750 might read: Class 1, $200; Class 6, $400; Class 7, $150.);
    - *delivery schedule by accounting period(s)* to be charged (If an order is written for delivery in more than a single month, the value of merchandise scheduled for delivery in each of the periods should be indicated for use in preparation of the O.O. and O.T.B. report. For example, an order totaling $1,000 might read: January, $600; February, $400.).

Processing the Order

Most store P.O.s consist of multiple copies for distribution to a number of destinations for future action and/or reference. A four-copy P.O., for example, might be distributed as follows:

- original to the vendor;
- one copy to the store's Receiving Department;
- one copy to the store's Order Checking Department;
- one copy retained for the buyer's file of merchandise on order.

The Order Checking Department receives a copy of all store P.O.s and Order Cancellations (see Form 5-3) and files same by departmental number. An Order Check Department clerk is assigned responsibility for the P.O. files of one or more departments. Usually orders placed for delivery in the current month are kept in a "Current On-Order" file, while those scheduled for delivery in future months are grouped together in a "Future On-Order" file.

All Receiving Aprons (see Chapter 9) for incoming merchandise are forwarded to the Order Checking Department to be matched up with a covering P.O. on file there. Once a P.O. can be matched with a Receiving Apron, the Order Check clerk writes on the Apron the following information as obtained from the P.O.:

- unit and total retail figures;
- the amount of the transportation costs and who is responsible for paying them;
- terms of sale and invoice due date.

```
                    Smith & Welsh

                      8th & Market Sts.              DATE
                       Chicago, Ill.
                                                            19

                  CANCELLATION OF ORDER

     ┌                                                  ┐
        TO

     └                                                  ┘


  ───────────────────────────────────────────────────────
                      PLEASE CANCEL
  ┌────┬────┬────────┬──────────┬──────────┬──────┬─────────┬──────────┐
  │    │    │        │ APPROXIMATE│ ORDER NO.│ DEPT.│CLASS No.│DELIVERY DATE│
  │    │    │        │   AMOUNT  │          │      │         │SPECIFIED ON│
  │    │    │        │ CANCELLED │          │      │         │  ORDER   │
  │ALL │PART│BALANCE │           │          │      │         │          │
  └────┴────┴────────┴──────────┴──────────┴──────┴─────────┴──────────┘
                REASONS FOR CANCELLATION
      IF CANCELLING PART OF ORDER SPECIFY WHAT PART




  ┌────────────────────────┬─────────┬────────────────────┐
  │ SIGNED BY              │         │ CHECKED TO ORDER    │
  │                        │  DATE   │    BY               │
  │        DEPARTMENT MANAGER│        │         ORDER CHECKER│
  └────────────────────────┴─────────┴────────────────────┘
```

FORM 5-3 CANCELLATION OF ORDER

If an Order clerk receives an Apron for which no P.O. is on file, it is designated as a "problem," the buyer is notified, and further processing of that merchandise is held up until the Order clerk receives a duly authorized P.O. for the merchandise.

If unit retail prices have not been indicated on a P.O. for which an Apron has been received, it also is designated as a "problem" and further processing of the merchandise is held up until the buyer supplies the Order clerk with the necessary retail price information.

The Order clerk is responsible for checking off, on the appropriate P.O., the items of merchandise that have been received according to information recorded on the Receiving Apron. If the entire order is received as ordered, the P.O. is removed from the current month's On-Order file and placed in the department's "Completed" file. If only part of the order is received, the Order clerk crosses out on the P.O. those items of merchandise that have been received, according to the Receiving Apron, and returns the P.O. to the current month's On-Order file. The balance still due on that particular order is considered an outstanding order, thereby reducing the department's O.T.B. by a like amount as explained in Chapter 4.

Many stores, particularly the larger ones, provide spaces either on the back or on the face of the Order Checking Department's and the buyer's copy of each P.O. for recording the following information with regard to all shipments made against that specific P.O. (see Form 5-4):

Form

020822 ORDER NUMBER | REVISED ORDER NUMBER | DEPT. NO | CODE

DATE OF ORDER | PAGE

THIS INFORMATION MUST APPEAR ON ALL PACKAGES AND INVOICES

SHIPPING DATE

VENDOR'S DUNS NUMBER

VENDOR TO BE PAID

DO NOT SHIP BEFORE | MUST BE COM...

CENTRAL ORDER CHECK COPY

NAME

STREET

CITY | STATE | ZIP

• AUTOMATIC CANCEL POLICY

THIS ORDER IS CO CANCELLED AND W RETURNED AT THE EXPENSE IF NOT COMPLETE WITHIN DATES SHOWN ABOVE

SHIPPING MFR. IF OTHER THAN ABOVE:

MFR. NO.

DEPT. MGR. | DIV. MDSE. MGR.

DATE PASSED	APRON NUMBERS	APRON DATE	TOTAL COST		DATE PASSED
			AMT. THIS APRON		
ORDER CLK.			NEW BALANCE		ORDER CLK.
			AMT. THIS APRON		
ORDER CLK.			NEW BALANCE		ORDER CLK.
			AMT. THIS APRON		
ORDER CLK.			NEW BALANCE		ORDER CLK.
			AMT. THIS APRON		
ORDER CLK.			NEW BALANCE		ORDER CLK.
			AMT. THIS APRON		
ORDER CLK.			NEW BALANCE		ORDER CLK.

FORM 5-4 RECORD OF SHIPMENTS AGAINST A SPECIFIC ORDER

- apron number;
- apron date;
- apron amount;
- identifying number of the Order clerk that processed each shipment;
- dollar amount of balance remaining "open" on that P.O.

Buyers find this procedure especially helpful in checking departmental On-Order and Open-To-Buy reports.

TERMS OF SALE: DISCOUNT AND DATING

When buyers buy merchandise, they not only agree with the vendor on the cost price of each item but they also negotiate other factors that have an important bearing on the actual cost of the goods, which, in turn, affects gross margin and net operating profit.

Major factors to be negotiated are:

- discounts allowed;
- dating for payment of invoices;
- shipping arrangements;
- transportation costs.

A *discount* that is granted by a vendor to a purchaser is defined as a percentage reduction in the quoted or billed cost[1] of merchandise if certain terms are met by the retailer. Discounts granted serve to reduce the amount a store actually pays for the merchandise it purchases for resale purposes. The longer the period of time allowed a store for payment (without penalty) of a vendor's invoice, the more favorable it is to that store's cash flow pattern, and the more likely it will be that the store will be able to pay the invoice out of revenue from sales of those particular goods. Transportation costs that are part or wholly paid for by the store increases the actual cost of the goods. Those that are paid for by a vendor help keep the actual cost of the goods to a minimum.

Buyers are held responsible for obtaining the most favorable terms possible from vendors, to minimize the cost of their merchandise purchases and, in turn, to maximize the important gross margin figure.

Types of Discounts

Discounts vary greatly from one industry to another, from vendor to vendor, and among various classifications within the same merchandising area. For example, the discounts on merchandise purchases for a retail store's Infants' and Children's Department vary tremendusly according to the types of merchandise handled, such as furniture, toys, apparel, and accessories. However, within each segment of any one industry, the discount percent granted is a fairly constant figure. The reason for this is that governmental regulations require each vendor to extend identical benefits to all customers, and failure to do so can involve suits by aggrieved store customers, and possible court-imposed fines. However, in some cases it is common practice for vendors not to extend discounts. In such cases terms are referred to as being "net."

The types of discounts allowed the purchaser by the vendor are many and varied. Major types of discounts are:

- quantity discount;
- trade discount;
- cash discount;
- anticipation;
- cash discount loading.

Quantity Discount. A *quantity discount* is a stated percentage allowed by the vendor off the billed cost of merchandise when a stipulated quantity is purchased. A quantity discount percentage is deductible regardless of when the invoice is paid and is usually granted

---

[1] Wholesale price of goods as it appears on a vendor's invoice. Not to be confused with the "delivered cost" of goods, which includes transportation charges.

on large purchases or purchases accumulated over a specified period of time. Quantity discount is usually based on a sliding scale: the larger the quantity purchased, the greater the discount percentage. Quantity discounts are intended as incentives to induce buyers to make commitments for larger amounts of goods than they might do normally, and are legal under specific provisions of the Robinson-Patman Act. In taking quantity discounts, the buyer must judge the merit of savings in cost price involved as compared to the risk of tying up more than the normal planned purchase allowance or open-to-buy. Although quantity discounts are not customarily offered in some industries, notably Apparel and Accessories, they are common in Home Furnishings and various hard-goods lines.

Formulas (for calculating quantity discount):

1. $ Quantity discount = $ Billed cost × quantity discount %
2. Actual $ cost of merchandise = Billed cost − $ quantity discount

Problem:

An Infants' and Children's Department buyer decided to purchase some cribs from a vendor who quoted a quantity discount of 1.5% on all orders exceeding $1,800 at cost price. If the buyer placed an order for cribs amounting to $2,000, what would be the actual cost of the cribs?

Solution:

1. $ Quantity discount = $ Billed cost × quantity discount %
   = $2,000 × 1.5%
   = $2,000 × 0.015
   = $30

2. Actual $ cost = $2,000 − $30
   = $1,970

Trade Discount. A percentage, or series of percentages, which reduce the list price of merchandise (the theoretical retail price suggested by the vendor) to cost price is known as *trade discount.* This type of discount is used for determining cost on the basis of the list or suggested retail price of the goods in question. It is used primarily by vendors of cosmetics, toys, photo equipment, and various types of premarked (vendor-marked) merchandise. Trade discount is rarely, if ever, used by vendors of apparel. It may also be used for such staple accessories as premarked hosiery and basic underwear when selling to the vending machine trade.

Trade discounts are deducted regardless of when the covering invoice is paid. In some industries this type of discount is quoted as a single percentage, for example $100, less 45%. In others, it is quoted as a series of discounts, for example $100, less 30%-10%-5%. When there is a series of discounts, each is treated as a percentage of the previous balance—not of the original amount.

Fair trade laws enacted by state legislatures in recent years forbid vendors from "fixing" the retail price of goods they sell to retailers. For this reason, retailers no longer have to set the retail price of items at the list prices quoted by vendors. Today it is common practice for buyers to use the billed cost of goods and a desired markup percent in calculating the retail prices they assign to their purchases.

Any one of the following three arithmetic methods for calculating trade discounts in a series may be used. These are known as the:

1. direct method;
2. complement method;
3. "on percentage" method.

Procedures involved in calculating cost by each of these three methods are shown below.

Formula:

$$\text{Billed cost} = \text{List price} - \text{trade discount}$$

Problem:

The trade discounts on a power lawn mower that "lists" at $100 are 25%-10%-5%. Find the billed cost of this item.

Solutions:

$$\text{Billed cost} = \$100 - (25\% + 10\% + 5\%)$$

1. *Direct Method:* the longest method; using maximum arithmetic procedures.

List price	= $100
Less 25% discount	= $100 × .25
	= $100 − $25
List less 25%	= $75
Less 10% discount	= $75 × .10
	= $75 − $7.50
List less 25% + 10%	= $67.50
Less 5% discount	= $67.50 × .05
	= $67.50 − $3.38
List less 25% + 10% + 5%	= $64.12

2. *Complement Method:* a shortcut method, using the complement of each discount percentage.

List price	= $100
Complement of 25% discount	= 75%
Less 25%	= $100 × .75
List less 25%	= $75
Complement of 10% discount	= 90%
Less 10%	= $75 × .90
List less 25% + 10%	= $67.50
Complement of 5% discount	= 95%
Less 5%	= $67.50 × .95
List less 25% + 10% + 5%	= $64.125 or $64.13

3. *"On Percentage" Method:* shortest of three methods, using the percentage product figure, arrived at by multiplying together the complements of each discount percentage.

List price	= $100
Complements of discount percentages	= 75% × 90% × 95%
	= .75 × .90 × .95
	= .64125
List less 25% + 10% + 5%	= $100 × .64125
	= $64.125 or $64.13

Cash Discount. The term *cash discount* refers to the stated percentage off the billed cost of goods that is allowed by some vendors if payment of an invoice is made within a stipulated number of days following the date of the invoice.

A vendor's objective in offering cash discount is to extend to retailers an incentive for paying invoices earlier than the time usually allowed for payment without penalty. The objective of the retailer who takes advantage of such cash discounts is to reduce the actual cost of the merchandise involved. A decrease in the cost of merchandise sold, without a decrease in net sales, results in higher gross margin and, in turn, potentially greater net operating profit.

In most cases merchandise subject to quantity and/or trade discounts is usually subject as well to any cash discounts that may be offered by vendors. Eligibility for taking cash discount is contingent primarily on making payments of invoices no later than the last day of the discount period.

It is important for students to be aware of the fact that although buyers are responsible for negotiating the best possible terms of sale, the decision as to whether or not to take advantage of cash discount by paying invoices within a specified period of time is not theirs to make. Rather, that is a type of major policy decision that can only be made by the firm's top management or at least by its Controller, who is responsible for Accounts Payable and who is in a position to be aware of the firm's current cash flow position as well as any other influential economic conditions.

Not all industries offer cash discounts to the retailer. Also, the percentage of cash discounts allowed on purchases varies widely from one industry to another. Some of the industries that have traditionally offered cash discounts, and the percentage allowed by each, are:

Gloves	6%
Handbags	3%
Millinery	7%
Apparel (ladies')	8%
Home Furnishings	2%

Cash discounts, when offered, are deductible from the net billed cost of each invoice— that is, *after* any quantity and/or trade discounts have been calculated.

Net billed cost is the term used to indicate the net cost of merchandise after quantity, trade, and cash discounts have been taken.

Formula:

$$\text{Net billed cost} = \text{Gross billed cost} - \text{trade or quantity discounts} - \text{cash discount}$$

Problem:

A Domestics buyer bought $2,000 worth of blankets for the store's annual White Sale. The vendor offered a 1.5% quantity discount on all orders over $1,500, in addition to cash discount terms of 2/30 N60. If the vendor's invoice for this purchase was dated June 5, how much should the store remit to the vendor if the invoice was paid on July 2?

Solution:

Gross billed cost	= $2,000
Quantity discount	= 1.5%
Quantity discounted bill	= $2,000 × 1.5% = $30
	= $2,000 − $30
	= $1,970
Date of invoice	= June 5
Date invoice was paid	= July 2
Cash discount allowed	= 2/30 N60

$$\text{Last day for cash discount} = (\text{June } 30 - 5) + (\text{July } 1\text{-}5)$$
$$= 25 + 5 = 30 \text{ days}$$
$$= \text{July } 5$$
$$\text{Cash discount earned} = \$1{,}970 \times 2\%$$
$$= \$1{,}970 \times .02$$
$$= \$39.40$$
$$\text{Amount to remit to vendor} = \$1{,}970 - \$39.40$$
$$= \$1{,}930.60$$

The solution to this problem could also be obtained by multiplying the quantity discounted cost of the merchandise ($1,970) by the complement of the cash discount percentage (98%), as follows:

$$\text{Quantity discounted bill} = \$1{,}970$$
$$\text{Complement of cash discount} = 100\% - 2\%$$
$$= 98\%$$
$$\text{Net billed cost if paid July } 2 = \$1{,}970 \times 98\%$$
$$= \$1{,}970 \times .98$$
$$= \$1{,}930.60$$

Net Terms. A condition of sale in which cash discount is neither offered nor permitted is known as *net terms.* Under these terms payment in full is due within a specified number of days following the date of the invoice. We refer to such a transaction as being a "Net" (abbreviated N) arrangement. It is to be remembered, however, that sometimes quantity and/or trade discounts on purchases may be allowed but no cash discount is offered. In such cases, if the invoice is to be paid without incurring a late payment penalty, the retailer remits to the vendor the billed cost of purchases, less any quantity and/or trade discounts, before the end of the "net" period, as specified on the invoice.

Unless otherwise stated, invoices incur a late payment penalty if not paid within the specified "net" period.

PRACTICE PROBLEMS—Quantity, Trade, and Cash Discounts

1. An order for 5,000 units of an item costing $1.00 each may entitle a buyer to a 10% discount on the purchase. What would be the billed cost if the buyer purchased 5,500 of this item?

(Answer)

2. A vendor offers perfume at a list price of $30, which carries a trade discount of 40%. What would be the billed cost for 12 bottles of this perfume?

(Answer)

3. The trade discount on a sterling silver item is quoted at $48 list, less 25%-10%-5%. What is the billed cost of the item?

_____
(Answer)

4. What is the net cost on an order amounting to $850 if cash discount earned is 4%?

_____
(Answer)

5. Calculate the net cost on the following order for merchandise:

   60 dozen blouses at $60 a dozen; cash discount earned is 3%.

_____
(Answer)

6. An invoice dated August 1 carries terms of 6/10 N30. The billed cost is $1,275.

   (a) When must the bill be paid in order to deduct the discount?   (a) _____
   (Answer)

   (b) What amount must be paid at that time?   (b) _____
   (Answer)

7. If a buyer purchases 120 coats at $52 each and earns an 8% discount, what amount must he pay to the manufacturer?

_____
(Answer)

8. Determine the amount to be paid the vendor on an invoice dated April 1 for an item listed at $230 less 10%-5%-2%, 4/10 N30.

_____
(Answer)

Anticipation. *Anticipation* represents an *additional* cash discount when an invoice is paid prior to the end of the regular cash discount period. Anticipation discount is another term of sale which should be negotiated between the retailer and vendor at the time of purchase; the covering P.O. should specify "Anticipation Allowed." While some vendors do not permit an anticipation discount, some retailers deduct it unless a notation on the vendor's invoice expressly forbids it.

The number of days of anticipation is based on the number of days remaining between the date on which an invoice is actually paid and the last day of the regular cash discount period. The rate of anticipation discount is subject to change, based on prevailing interest rates because, in effect, the vendor has the use of the retailer's money ahead of the date arranged by the terms of sale, and the retailer is charging the vendor "interest" for its use. In mid-1978 the anticipation rate ran from 12% to 20%. Anticipation discount is taken *in addition to any other discounts* that might apply to an invoice. Although anticipation should technically be calculated on the net cost of an invoice (after the cash discount has been deducted), it is common practice to combine the cash and the anticipation discount percentages in order to determine the dollar amount that should be remitted to the vendor. For example:

Formulas:

1. Remit to vendor when anticipation
   is calculated separately
   $$= \text{Billed cost} - (\text{billed cost} \times \text{C.D. \%})$$
   $$= \text{Billed cost} - \$ \text{ cash discount}$$
   $$= \text{Net cost} - (\text{net cost} \times \text{A.D. \%})$$
   $$= \text{Net cost} - \$ \text{ anticipation}$$

110

2. Remit to vendor when anticipation
   % is added to cash discount %   = Billed cost − (billed cost ×
                                      [C.D. % + A.D. %])
                                   = Billed cost − combined discounts

Problem:

The ABC Shade Co. received an invoice in the amount of $1,000 from one of its vendors. This invoice was dated June 10 and carried terms of 5/30 N60, anticipation permitted. If the invoice was paid on June 20, and the prevailing anticipation rate was 12%, how much should be remitted to the vendor if: 1. anticipation is calculated on the *net* amount of the invoice? 2. the cash discount and anticipation rates are combined?

Solutions:

Step 1:   Last day of a 30-day cash discount period would be July 10 (20 days remaining in June + 10 days in July).

Step 2:   If the invoice was paid on June 20, it was anticipated by 20 days (10 days in June + 10 days in July), or 2/3 of a 30-day month. If the anticipation rate was 12% a year or 1% a month, the rate for 20 days, or 2/3 of a month, would be .0067 (2/3 of 1% or .01).

Solution 1:

Net invoice amount = Billed cost − cash discount %
                   = $1,000 − ($1,000 × .05)
                   = $1,000 − $50
                   = $950

To be remitted   = $950 − ($950 × .0067)
                   = $950 − $6.37
                   = $943.63

Solution 2:

To be remitted   = Billed cost − (billed cost × [cash discount % + anticipation %])
                   = $1,000 − ($1,000 × .0567)
                   = $1,000 − $56.70
                   = $943.30

Cash Discount Loading.   *Loading* refers to the practice of intentionally increasing the cost price of purchases in order to attain a cash discount percentage rate in excess of the rate regularly offered by a vendor.

A store's objective in requiring cash discount loading is to obtain a cash discount percentage rate arbitrarily set by store management that is higher than the cash discount regularly allowed by the vendor. The retailer may request the vendor to bill at the loaded cost or the store's Accounts Payable Department will make the necessary adjustment when the invoice is processed.

Cash discount loading tends to either (1) reduce purchase and cumulative markup where the retail price has already been established on the basis of a lower cash discount percentage, or (2) increase the retail price calculated on the basis of an arbitrarily determined, higher cash discount percentage.

Following is an example of cash discount loading:

Formula:

$$\text{Loaded cost} = \frac{\text{Net cost}}{100\% - \text{loaded discount }\%}$$

Problem:

A vendor quotes merchandise at $1,000 cost, with terms of 5/10 N 30. The buyer insists on terms of 8/10 N30, which is the *standard* discount rate for his store. To what amount should the cost price of these goods be revised in order to permit the higher cash discount rate but the same return to the vendor?

Solution:

Under the original terms of 5/10 N30 the vendor would obtain:

$$\text{Actual net cost} = \$1,000 - (\$1,000 \times .05)$$
$$= \$1,000 - \$50$$
$$= \$950$$

The store, however, requires an 8%, instead of a 5%, cash discount rate. Assuming that the billed cost of the invoice, at the higher cash discount rate, equals 100%, then:

$$\text{Loaded cost} = \frac{\text{Net cost}}{100\% - \text{loaded discount }\%}$$
$$= \frac{\$950}{100\% - 8\%}$$
$$= \frac{\$950}{.92}$$
$$= \$1,032.61$$

PRACTICE PROBLEMS—Anticipation and Loading

1. A vendor quotes the cost of an item at $30, with terms of 3/10 N30. If the buyer wants an 8% discount, however, what would be the "loaded" cost of each item?

_____
(Answer)

2. How much should be remitted the vendor on an invoice in the amount of $31,300, dated January 9, that carries terms of 2/10-90X, 12% anticipation permitted, if payment is made January 19?

_____
(Answer)

3. The Men's Suit buyer bought 20 suits at $69.75 each. The vendor allows no cash discount, but the buyer wants the suits billed at an 8% cash discount. What would be the billed amount of each suit under a loading arrangement?

_____
(Answer)

4. A store received an invoice dated March 8 for $350, which carried terms of 1/10-30X, N60, 12% anticipation permitted. How much would be remitted to the vendor if the invoice was paid March 17?

_____
(Answer)

5. If the anticipation rate offered by a vendor is 12%, how much should the store pay the vendor on an invoice for $1,000 dated June 10 and carrying terms of 5/10 N30 if the invoice was paid on June 12?

_____
(Answer)

Dating

The terms and dating indicated on a P.O. indicate how much and when to pay the vendor. *Dating,* in relation to terms of sale, refers to the due date, the length of time a vendor extends to the purchaser for payment of an invoice. The *discount date* refers to the last day of the cash discount period. The *net payment date* indicates when payment is due in order to maintain a favorable credit rating and avoid a possible late payment penalty.

When dating accompanies a cash discount, the first figure represents the percentage of discount that can be taken on a given invoice if payment is made within the time frame represented by the second, or dating, figure. For example, terms of 2/10 N30 on an invoice means that 2% can be deducted from the billed cost of that invoice if remittance to the vendor is made within 10 days following the date of the invoice. The net amount of the invoice is due if payment is made between the 11th and 30th day following the date of the invoice.

Dating practices vary widely from one industry to another, as well as within each industry. Often the nature of the goods influences the dating practices of a vendor. The Apparel industry, for example, offers a relatively high cash discount (8%) because of the high-risk and potentially high-markdown nature of the merchandise involved. This industry also offers a longer dating period than do many others (E.O.M.). The fact that the industry is largely made up of small firms which are frequently undercapitalized leads many to compete for business and improve their cash flow by extending favorable terms and dating.

Following are the principal types of dating.

C.O.D. (Cash on Delivery) Dating. This type of dating requires that payment of an invoice be made as delivery of the merchandise takes place. C.O.D. dating usually applies to purchasers who have poor or unproven credit ratings.

Problem:

Goods valued at $600 are purchased under C.O.D. dating terms by a newly opened fabric shop. What amount must be remitted to the vendor and when?

Solution:

Amount to be remitted = $600
Payment is due at time of delivery of goods

Regular (Normal or Ordinary) Dating. This is one of the most common types of dating. It is usually indicated by either the letter "N" or the word "Net," followed by a number that represents the number of days allowed (following the invoice date) to make payment without jeopardizing the purchaser's credit rating. For example, terms and dating of Net 30 means that the full amount of the invoice (no cash discount allowed) is due 30 days from the date of the invoice (which is implied to be the same date on which the merchandise is shipped).

Given terms and dating of 5/10 N30, the store may deduct 5% from the billed cost if the invoice is paid within 10 days following the invoice date. Or, if the store does not take advantage of the cash discount offer, the full amount of the invoice is due within 30 days following the date of the invoice. Vendors reserve the right to charge "carrying fees" or interest on the invoiced amount after the expiration of the net payment period.

It is important to note that in computing the last day on which cash discount may be taken or net payment made, the exact number of days in each month that is involved are used. It is also important to note that when terms involve a cash discount but no stated net payment days the *net payment date* is considered to be 20 days following the end of the discount period.

Problem:

How much should be remitted to the vendor for an invoice amounting to $500 dated November 16 and carrying terms of 4/10 Net 30 if:

1. the invoice was paid on November 26?
2. the invoice was paid on December 15?

Solution 1:

Invoice amount	= $500
Invoice date	= November 16
Terms and dating	= 4/10 N30
Cash discount	= $500 × 4%
	= $500 × .04
	= $20
Amount to be remitted November 26	= $500 − $20
	= $480

Solution 2:

Invoice amount	= $500
Invoice date	= November 16
Terms and dating	= 4/10 N30
Net payment due	= 30 − (November 30 − 16)
	= 30 − 14
	= December 16
Amount to be remitted December 15	= $500

E.O.M. (End-of-Month) Dating. This type of dating means that the cash discount period is computed from the *end of the month in which the invoice is dated* rather than from the date of the invoice itself. Given terms of 5/10 E.O.M., if the invoice is paid by the 10th day of the month following the one in which the invoice is dated, the store may deduct 5% from the billed cost of the invoice. Or, if the store elects not to take advantage of the cash discount offered, net payment is due 20 days after the expiration of the cash discount period.

It has become traditional in the trade, with respect to E.O.M. dating, to consider any invoice, dated on or after the 25th of any month, as being dated the first day of the following month. Arrangements of this kind, however, may vary among vendors.

E.O.M. dating allows retailers an extra period of time in which to sell their purchases, and, conceivably, to pay invoices out of monies received from sales to customers rather than having to be paid out of capital.

Problem:

An invoice for $1,000, dated March 17, carried terms of 8/10 E.O.M.

1. What is the last date for deducting the 8% cash discount?
2. What amount is due the vendor if the invoice is paid on that date?

Solution 1:

Invoice amount	= $1,000
Invoice date	= March 17
Terms and dating	= 8/10 E.O.M.
Last day of discount period	= 10 days after March 31
	= April 10

Solution 2:

Cash discount earned	= $1,000 × 8%
	= $1,000 × .08
	= $80
Payment due on April 10	= $1,000 − $80
	= $920

Had this invoice been dated March 27 instead of March 17, the last date for deducting cash discount would have been extended to May 10. Since an invoice dated between the 25th and last day of a month is considered to be dated the first day of the following month, the discount period would be 10 days following the last day of the month in which the invoice was considered dated, or April 1.

Extra Dating. This type of dating is also calculated from the date of the invoice, except that a specified number of *extra* days are granted for the taking of cash discount. For example, terms of 5/10 60X means that 5% cash discount can be taken if the invoice is paid 10 days plus an additional (extra) 60 days, or a total of 70 days following the date of the invoice. The full, or net, amount of the invoice is due 20 days after the expiration of the 70-day discount period, although this fact is often unstated. This type of dating is used to encourage retailers to bring in goods earlier than they might otherwise have done (because of lack of current O.T.B. or uncertainty as to extent of demand for the goods at an earlier date).

Problems:

An invoice dated May 16 has a billed cost of $1,800 and terms of 3/10 60X. Determine the:

1. final date for taking cash discount;
2. cash discount earned if the bill is paid August 14;
3. amount due if the bill is paid on July 20;
4. net payment date.

Solution 1:

May 31 – May 16	= 15 days
Month of June	= 30 days
July 1-25	= 25 days
Total (May 16-July 25)	= 70 days
Last day for cash discount	= July 25

Solution 2:

None: paid 20 days after end of the 70-day cash discount period
(July 31 – 25 + August 1-14).

Solution 3:

May 31 – May 16	= 15 days
Month of June	= 30 days
July 1-July 20	= 20 days
Total discount days taken	= 65 days
Billed cost	= $1,800
Cash discount earned	= $1,800 × 3%
	= $54
Amount due vendor	= $1,800 – $54
	= $1,746

Solution 4:

Last date for net payment	= 20 days after July 25
	= 20 – (July 31 – 25)
	= 20 – 6
	= 14
	= August 14

R.O.G. (Receipt of Goods) Dating.   Under this type of dating the discount period begins on the date the goods are received at the store (as evidenced by the date on the Receiving Apron) rather than the date of the invoice.

This type of dating was originally intended to serve as a financial aid to stores located a considerable distance from the market or their vendors' shipping points—who might receive invoices for merchandise a few days after shipment of those goods but who might not get delivery of the merchandise for a considerably longer time.

Originally intended mainly for heavy, bulky merchandise, such as furniture, major appliances, pianos, carpeting, and so on, which was largely transported by railroad freight or other fairly slow low-cost methods of transportation, today some of the larger stores in the United States are seeking these terms, if advantageous to them, for a wide range of soft goods, including apparel.

Problems:

An invoice for $1,000, dated April 4, carries terms of 5/10 R.O.G. If the goods covered by this invoice arrive at the store on May 7:

1. What is the last date for deducting cash discount?
2. How much should be remitted if payment is made on May 15?

Solution 1:

Last day for taking cash discount = Date of receipt of goods + 10 days
= May 7 + 10
= May 17

Solution 2:

Invoice amount	= $1,000
Invoice date	= April 4
Terms and dating	= 5/10 R.O.G.
Merchandise received	= May 7
Invoice paid	= May 15
Last day for taking cash discount	= May 7 + 10
	= May 17
Cash discount earned	= $1,000 × 5%
	= $50
Amount remitted to vendor	= $1,000 − $50
	= $950

Advance- or Post-Dating (Seasonal Discount).   In this type of dating, the *invoice date is advanced* so that additional time is allowed for payment to be made and for earning cash discount, with the length of the discount period being agreed upon by the vendor and buyer. This type of dating is often used by vendors to induce buyers to take in seasonal merchandise such as toys, Christmas decorations, "White Sale" goods, and so on, earlier than they might otherwise have been willing to do because of the savings involved. Vendors of this type of merchandise are willing to allow longer periods for payment of invoices if they can schedule their production more evenly throughout the year. This type of dating might also be extended by a vendor to a good regular customer who is temporarily in a disadvantageous cash flow position.

With this type of dating, net payment is not considered due until the last day of the month in which cash discount can be earned. After that date the invoice is considered overdue.

Problems:

A $1,000 invoice for merchandise shipped on June 10 is dated September 1 and carries terms of 5/10 N30.

1. What would be the amount of the cash discount earned if the invoice were paid on September 10?
2. What is the latest date on which this invoice could be paid without incurring a late penalty?

Solution 1:

Invoice date	= September 1
Invoice amount	= $1,000
Terms and dating	= 5/10 Net 30 (as of 9/1)
Invoice paid	= September 11
Last day for cash discount	= September 1 + 10 days
	= September 11
Cash discount earned	= $1,000 × 5%
	= $50

Solution 2:

Final day for net payment = Last day of month in which
cash discount expires
= September 30

Net Payment Date. This dating term refers to the date by which an invoice must be paid before it is considered overdue. The net payment date is determined by the type of dating that is agreed upon by both the retailer and vendor. Net payment dates for various types of dating are:

- *Regular dating:* the full amount of the invoice is due without penalty exactly 30 days from the date of the invoice;
- *E.O.M., R.O.G.,* and *extra dating:* the full amount of the invoice is due 20 days after the expiration of the cash discount period;
- *Advance- or post-dating:* the full amount of the invoice is due no later than the last day of the month in which the cash discount period expires.

PRACTICE PROBLEMS—Discounts and Dating

1. A bill for $81.00, dated February 26, bears terms of 8/10 E.O.M. and lists prepaid freight of $6.21.

   (a) In order to obtain the cash discount, what is the last
   day for payment of this bill?

   (a) _____
   (Answer)

(b) What amount should be remitted to the vendor at
that time?

(b) _____
(Answer)

2. Indicate in the spaces provided the final dates on which cash discount may be taken for invoices dated May 15. Merchandise is received in the store on June 2.

Terms	Last Day for Discount
(a) 8/10 N30	_____
(b) 2/10 E.O.M.	_____
(c) 2/10 60X	_____
(d) Net 30	_____
(e) 3/10 R.O.G.	_____

3. A department store receives an invoice dated October 12 in the amount of $6,750. How much must be paid on November 10 if terms are:

(a) 10/10 N30?

(a) _____
(Answer)

(b) 10/10 E.O.M.?

(b) _____
(Answer)

4. An invoice dated March 2 carries terms of 3/10 60X. When does the discount period expire? Explain.

5. A buyer purchased 75 lamps at a list price of $40 each. The trade discounts were 30%-20%-5%, with terms of 2/10 N30. The lamps were shipped and billed on October 18, and were received October 22. The bill was paid on October 31. What amount was paid?

_____
(Answer)

6. An invoice for $975 is dated September 10 and carries terms of 3/10 R.O.G. The goods arrive in the store on October 5.

(a) What is the last date that discount may be deducted?

(a) _____
(Answer)

(b) How much should be remitted if payment is made on that date?

(b) _____
(Answer)

Shipping Terms

Shipping terms, like discount and dating, are negotiated when purchases are being made, and constitute an important part of each Purchase Order. These have to do with whether (1) the vendor or the store is to pay transportation charges, and (2) at what point title to the merchandise will pass from the seller (the vendor) to the buyer (the store). If the store pays part or all of the transportation charges, the actual cost to the store of merchandise handled is increased by the amount of such charges. If the store assumes title to the merchandise before it actually reaches the store's premises and the merchandise is lost, stolen, or damaged in transit, the store, as owner of the merchandise, must file any claim for reimbursement with the carrier of the merchandise—*not* the vendor. Likewise, the store is legally responsible for payment of any invoice for merchandise to which the store has taken title.

Shipping terms vary from one industry to another and within the same industry. This is why they are said to be "negotiable." Some vendors pay all shipping charges within certain geographical boundaries. Some pay no charges under any circumstances. Some pay part of the charges, particularly to distant destinations. Vendors, however, are under governmental restraints in this respect; that is, the terms they offer to one customer they must offer to all. Buyers should remember, in negotiating shipping terms with a vendor, that transportation charges are a part of the cost of merchandise and therefore affect departmental markup. Also, the point at which the merchandise changes hands indicates who must file a claim in the event of damage or nondelivery. It is important, therefore, that the retailer negotiate for the most advantageous shipping terms, as a means of minimizing the cost of goods handled, as well as the risk of possible loss of the goods.

F.O.B. (Free on Board) Points. The most common types of shipping terms having to do with the point to which the vendor will pay the transportation charges and at which point title passes to the retailer are:

- **F.O.B. store, warehouse or service building.** Vendor pays all freight charges for getting the merchandise to the store or other designated destinations. Title passes to the retailer when the merchandise reaches its destination.
- **F.O.B. factory or shipping point.** Vendor pays all freight charges to the shipping point. Retailer pays all freight charges from the factory or shipping point to the store or its premises. Title passes to the retailer at the factory or shipping point, and, in turn, assumes all risks from that point.
- **F.O.B. consolidation point[2]** or port of destination or some city in transit mutually agreed upon. For example, New York vendors might sell to Hawaiian stores on the basis of F.O.B. Los Angeles, or Oakland, or San Francisco. The vendor pays the transportation charges to the consolidation point, city, or port of destination, and the retailer pays the transportation from the point to his/ her own premises. Unless otherwise agreed, risk of loss passes from vendor to retailer when goods arrive at a specified location in the designated city or consolidation point.

Stores that buy merchandise from vendors who sell with shipping terms of "F.O.B. factory" avoid the expense and risk of assuming title to the goods at the factory by negotiating for the shipping term "F.O.B. Store, Charges Reversed." With this arrangement, the store agrees to pay the transportation charges but does not assume title until the merchandise reaches the store.

Other Types of Shipping Terms (Domestic). In certain industries and under certain circumstances vendors extend special shipping terms to their retail store customers. The most common of these are:

Consignment. The vendor agrees to accept for return all merchandise not sold within a specified period of time after its receipt by the store. Title to consigned goods remain with the vendor while they are in the store.

Memorandum. Similar terms to that of consignment, with the exception that title to the merchandise passes to the retailer upon receipt of the goods.

Sale with a return privilege. The vendor agrees to accept for return the unsold portion of the purchased merchandise after a stated period of time. Title to the merchandise passes to the retailer upon receipt of the goods.

Shipping Terms Applying to Imports (C.I.F.–Cost, Insurance, Freight). Refers to imports where the vendor pays all transportation, insurance, and entry costs to the point listed after the C.I.F. and title passes to the retailer when the merchandise is shipped.

---

[2] Transportation terminal at which individual shipments intended for each addressee are sorted, consolidated, and delivered as one shipment, thereby greatly reducing transportation costs applying to individual shipments.

Purchase Order Terms

Preretailing. Assigning a retail price to each style listed on every purchase order at the time the order is written.

Purchase Markup Percentage. The markup percentage on the total order. The figure represents the total retail value of the order minus the total cost of the order divided by the total retail value.

Purchase Order. A legal contract between a store and a vendor to buy certain specified merchandise under certain specified conditions.

Discount Terms

Anticipation. An extra cash discount, if allowed by the vendor, for paying an invoice before the expiration of the regular cash discount period.

Cash Discount. A stated discount percentage off the billed cost of goods if payment of the invoice is made within a stipulated number of days following the date of the invoice.

C.O.D. (Cash on Delivery). The purchaser must pay for the merchandise at the time it is delivered. Usually required of purchasers with poor or unproven credit ratings.

Discount. A percentage reduction in the quoted and/or billed cost of merchandise if certain terms are met by the retailer.

Discount Date. The date by which payment of an invoice is due if the retailer wishes to take advantage of the cash discount offered.

Loading. The practice of intentionally increasing the cost price of purchases in order to attain a seemingly greater cash discount while still providing the wholesale price the vendor desires.

Quantity Discount. A percentage allowed off the billed cost of merchandise when a minimum stipulated quantity is purchased.

Seasonal Discount. An extra discount given by a vendor to a store that orders and/or takes delivery of merchandise in advance of the usual buying and/or delivery period. The purpose of this discount is to enable the vendor to maintain his/her operations during normally slack production periods.

Trade Discount. A percentage, or series of percentages, which reduce the list price of merchandise to cost price. Trade discounts are deducted from the billed cost before taking any cash discount offered.

Dating Terms

Advance Dating (Sometimes referred to as "As-of" Dating). A term of sale in which the invoice is dated some time later than the date on which the merchandise is shipped. The purpose is to extend the period of time in which cash discount is available.

Dating. The length of time a vendor extends to the purchaser for payment of an invoice. Unless otherwise stated the dating period starts the day following the date of the invoice—the day, it is implied, the merchandise was shipped.

E.O.M. (End-of-Month) Dating. Dating begins with the end of the month in which the invoice is dated. When an invoice is dated after the 25th of any month, it is a common industry practice to assume the invoice to be dated the first day of the following month and dating begins as of that date.

Extra Dating. A term of sale extending regular dating terms by an additional number of days.

Regular or Ordinary Dating. A term of sale which refers to the number of days following the date of the invoice allowed for payment in full.

R.O.G. (Receipt-of-Goods) Dating. A term of sale in which the discount period begins on the day the goods are received, rather than from the date of the invoice.

Shipping Terms

Consignment. The vendor agrees to accept for return all merchandise not sold in a specified period of time. Title to the goods remains with the vendor.

C.I.F. (Cost, Insurance, Freight). Refers to imports where the vendor pays all transportation, insurance, and entry charges to the point listed after the C.I.F. title when the merchandise is shipped.

Net Billed Cost. Net cost of merchandise after quantity, trade, and cash discounts have been deducted.

F.O.B. (Free on Board) Terms. Indicates the point to which the vendor will pay the transportation charges and at which point title passes to the purchaser. Typical F.O.B. terms are consolidation point; vendor's shipping point; store premises.

F.O.B. Consolidation Point. Vendor pays transportation charges and retains title to goods from shipping point to store's consolidation point. Purchaser assumes title to the goods and pays transportation charges on them from the consolidation point to the store.

F.O.B. Factory or Vendor's Shipping Point. Vendor pays all transportation charges to the factory or other shipping point. Retailer pays all transportation charges from the factory or other shipping point to the store. Title to the goods passes to the retailer at the factory or other shipping point.

F.O.B. Store. Vendor pays all freight charges to the store, or its warehouse or service building. Title passes to the retailer when the merchandise reaches the store or its premises.

Memorandum. Similar to consignment selling with the exception that title to the merchandise passes to the retailer upon receipt of the goods.

Sale with a Return Privilege. The vendor agrees to accept for return the unsold portion of the purchased merchandise. Title to the merchandise passes to the retailer upon receipt of the goods.

Shipping Terms. Indicate at what point title to merchandise changes hands (from vendor to store) and who is to pay the transportation costs.

Miscellaneous Terms of Sale

Vendor's Duns Number. Vendor's Duns number or other type of coded identification assigned by store to individual suppliers.

List Price. The gross billed (listed) price from which trade discounts are taken. Denotes the vendor's suggested retail price.

Net Payment Date. Final date on which an invoice must be paid before it is considered overdue and subject to penalty.

Net Price. The price after deduction of trade discounts. Also known as the *wholesale* or *vendor's selling price* and the *purchaser's cost* or *purchase price.*

Net Terms. A condition of sale in which cash discount is neither offered nor permitted.

Receiving Apron. A serially numbered, multi-part form prepared by a store's receiving clerk, on which is recorded all pertinent information to identify each shipment of merchandise and which may, on occasion, be used to check in merchandise. When attached to a covering invoice, it facilitates payment to the vendor and distribution of the purchase to the proper department.

Terms and Dating. Indicate the amount to be deducted from an invoice if payment is made within a specified period (when to pay and how much to pay).

REVIEW QUESTIONS—Purchase Orders and Terms of Sale

1. Define the following terms:

   (1) Cash discount

   (2) Trade discount

   (3) Anticipation

   (4) Net terms

2. Why is the Purchase Order considered such an important retail document?

3. Name at least three types of information relating to all shipments that should be recorded by the Order clerk on each P.O.

   (1)

   (2)

   (3)

4. Why is it important that each Purchase Order be written on the store's rather than the vendor's order form?

5. Name and briefly explain at least five types of information the buyer is required to fill in on most store Purchase Order forms?

(1)

(2)

(3)

(4)

(5)

6. Name at least three major factors, other than cost price, that need to be negotiated and clearly understood between buyer and vendor before the former places an order.

(1)

(2)

(3)

REVIEW PROBLEMS—Purchase Orders and Terms of Sale

1. A store received an invoice dated June 29 in the amount of $2,500. Goods covered by the invoice were received July 2. Indicate (a) the last date the invoice can be paid in order to get the discount and (b) the amount of the discount.

Terms	Last Day for Discount	Discount Amount
3/15 R.O.G.	_____	_____
8/10 N45	_____	_____
7/10 30X	_____	_____
6/15 E.O.M.	_____	_____

2. An invoice dated June 20 in the amount of $800 carried trade discounts of 20%-15%-5% and terms of 8/15 30X.

(a) By what date must this invoice be paid in order to earn the discount?

(a) _____
    (Answer)

(b) What amount should then be remitted to the vendor?

(b) _____
    (Answer)

3. If an invoice with 12% anticipation permitted were dated July 16 and paid July 25, which set of terms would be the most advantageous and by how much?

(a) 5/10 30X or 5/10 N30?

(a) _____
(Answer)

(b) Why?

4. If you were an owner-buyer for a fairly small specialty shop, would you always exercise the option to take anticipation when offered? Explain and defend your answer by indicating when anticipation is advantageous (a) to the buyer and when (b) to the vendor.

5. If you were a small independent dress manufacturer in a very competitive market, what terms of sale would you offer customers in order to stimulate your business?

6. An invoice for merchandise with a list price of $8,000 is dated October 28 and paid November 10. Terms are 3/10 E.O.M., F.O.B. store. Trade discounts are 40% and 10%, and anticipation of 12% is allowed.

   (a) What is the last day on which discount may be taken?

   (a) _____
   (Answer)

   (b) What is the last day for payment of the invoice without incurring a penalty?

   (b) _____
   (Answer)

   (c) What amount should be remitted on November 10?

   (c) _____
   (Answer)

7. A shoe buyer received a shipment of 50 pairs of shoes costing $18 the pair. The invoice is dated April 26 and terms are 6/10 E.O.M., F.O.B. factory. Anticipation is not permitted. Shipping charges of $92 are prepaid by the vendor.

   (a) What is the last date for taking discount?

   (a) _____
   (Answer)

   (b) If the invoice was paid on May 10, how much should be remitted to the vendor?

   (b) _____
   (Answer)

8. How much should be remitted on an invoice in the amount of $31,300 dated January 9 that carried terms of 2/10-90X, 12% anticipation permitted, if payment is made January 19?

   _____
   (Answer)

9. An invoice dated August 1 carries terms of 6/10 N30. The billed cost is $1,475.00

    (a) When must the invoice be paid in order to take advantage of the cash discount?

    (a) _____
          (Answer)

    (b) How much must be paid at that time?

    (b) _____
          (Answer)

10. An invoice for $81.00 dated February 26 bears terms of 8/10 E.O.M., F.O.B. factory. Prepaid inbound freight is billed at $6.21.

    (a) In order to obtain the cash discount, when is the last possible date on which the invoice must be paid?

    (a) _____
          (Answer)

    (b) If the invoice is paid on that date, what amount should be remitted to the vendor?

    (b) _____
          (Answer)

CHAPTER 6

MERCHANDISE PRICING
AND MARKUP

One of the objectives of every business enterprise is to operate at a profit level consistent with good, long-range business practices and ethics. An important factor in achieving maximum business profit is the price of the goods the firm offers for sale. Price is often the major reason behind customer patronage, or, in other words, why customers buy *where* they do. Price is also an important competitive weapon, particularly in highly competitive business situations where many products offered may be comparable, if not identical.

RETAIL PRICING: TERMINOLOGY POLICIES
AND PROCEDURES

In industrial organizations all decisions relating to the pricing of products is the responsibility of management. In retail organizations the actual pricing and repricing of all merchandise is the responsibility of individual departmental buyers or managers, while top management is responsible for formulating basic pricing policies that prevail throughout the store and the price structure within which the buyers operate.

With respect to pricing, it is important to remember that while the actual pricing and repricing of individual items of merchandise is an important responsibility of buyers and department managers, in the final analysis it is the sales volume—the proceeds from the sale of inventory—that must be great enough to cover not only the total cost of merchandise sold and all operating expenses, but provide a reward in the form of profit as well.

Pricing Terms

For a clear understanding of retail pricing it is important to understand the meaning of several widely used, price-related terms.

Price-Lining. The term *price-lining* refers to the practice of determining the various but limited number of retail prices at which a department's or a store's assortments will be offered for sale.

Price Line.   The term *price line* (or *price point*) refers to a specific price at which an *assortment* (several different types, styles, colors, sizes, etc.) of merchandise is *regularly* offered for sale. For example, if a Handbag Department offers, on a regular basis (not including special sale events), a selection of handbags in a variety of types, shapes, colors, materials, and sizes at $8, $10, $12, $15, $18, $22, $25, $30, and $35, each of these nine price points is referred to as a price line.

Price Range.   The term *price range* refers to the spread between the lowest and the highest price line carried in the store or department. For example, the price range in the Handbag Department mentioned above would be $8 to $35.

Price Zone.   The term *price zone* refers to a series of price lines or points that are relatively close to each other and that are likely to appeal to one particular segment of a store's or department's customers. The three most widely accepted retail price zones as indicated in the example above might be:

- promotional (low price zone), e.g., $8, $10, $12;
- volume (medium price zone), e.g., $15, $18, $22, 25;
- prestige (highest price zone), e.g., $30 and $35.

The Price Structure

What is referred to as the "price structure" of a store is determined by top management and is designed to attract the specific customer groups the store has chosen to serve. You will recall that one of the "rights" with respect to the merchandise offered customers by retailers is that it be offered at prices the customers are both willing and able to pay. *Price structuring* involves determining the price range at which each selling department will offer its merchandise and the price zone(s) to be featured in all selling departments throughout the store.

Major advantages of price lining are that it:

- simplifies consumer choice and facilitates selling;
- enables offering wide assortments at best selling price points;
- simplifies buying by limiting the range of wholesale costs;
- simplifies stock control;
- decreases marking costs and minimizes marking errors;
- reduces size of stock, resulting in favorable rate of turnover;
- decreases markdowns.

Establishing Price Lines.   Departmental buyers are responsible for establishing specific price lines within the range assigned each department by store management. Buyers are also responsible for the pricing and repricing of individual items that make up the merchandise assortment.

Retail price lines are determined mainly on the basis of wholesale costs and the markup percentage needed, as indicated on the seasonal merchandise plan for each department. Care should be taken, however, to see that there is enough spread between the various price lines so that customers can readily distinguish the differences in quality that exist (or should exist) in the merchandise offered at various price points in any one department's assortment.

Best-Selling Price Lines. Among each department's price lines there are always a limited number at which the greater share of total dollar and unit sales take place. These are referred to as *best-selling price lines.* Usually there are three, and usually they are to be found concentrated in the middle of the department's price range. It is at these price points that the greatest number of units of merchandise, in the greatest variety of types, styles, colors, and/or sizes, should be stocked. Determination of the quantities and varieties to be stocked at other price lines is based on the relative importance of each to the department's total volume.

Pricing Items. Once price lines have been established, buyers "buy into" those price lines. That is, they price merchandise at the established price line that comes closest to covering the wholesale price of the item, plus the initial markup percentage goal, plus taking into account any other considerations that may be relevant to assigning a retail price. Retail pricing should *never* be done on the basis of automatically applying the required markup percentage to the wholesale price of an item.

Basic Considerations in Pricing

Establishing price lines to be carried and assigning retail prices to all purchases require both skill and experience on the part of each buyer or department manager.

In addition to the wholesale cost of merchandise and the average markup required, the following factors should be given careful consideration in determining retail prices:

- the *quality of the merchandise,* e.g., does it have the quality that the store's customers expect for the retail price it needs to be marked?
- the *competitive stiuation,* e.g., at what price is the same or similar merchandise being sold in competitive stores within the home store's trading area?
- the *nature of the merchandise,* e.g., to what extent is it reasonable to expect that markdowns will have to be taken on the merchandise due to changing consumer taste, particularly for fashion goods, or its perishable or fragile nature, such as jewelry, millinery, cosmetics, fragrances, food, candy, and so on?
- *store policies,* e.g., does the store have a highly promotional image? That is, does it regularly feature "loss leaders" (low prices, low markup) to generate traffic in the store? Or does the store have a nonpromotional, prestige image, featuring exclusive, innovative merchandise? Or is it a store policy to meet any and all competitive prices?
- *handling costs,* e.g., would its handling involve high transportation costs? High security risks, such as exist with fine jewelry and furs? Special handling? Warehousing? Delivery?
- *selling expense,* e.g., would paying a commission over and above regular selling costs be required or must higher-salaried, professional sales personnel be required in order to sell the merchandise?
- *workroom costs,* e.g., are free alterations of the merchandise required in order to sell it, such as men's clothing?
- *turnover,* e.g., how frequently can this type of merchandise be expected to sell out and the stock replenished? Can it be reordered, and, if so, how quickly can reorders be delivered?
- *demand and supply,* e.g., is the market (replacement) value of this particular merchandise rising or falling?

BASIC PRICING FACTORS

The three basic factors involved in the pricing of goods are the following:

- *cost price* of each item;
- *retail price* assigned to each item;
- *markup* (abbreviated MU or simply M) which should be large enough to cover all necessary retail reductions[1] as well as all operating expenses necessary to sell the goods and provide a desired operating profit.

These three factors apply to the pricing of a single item, a group of items, or the entire stock of a department or a store.

Dollar Relationships

Given any two of the basic pricing factors, the third can easily be calculated. The following equations clearly indicate the interrelationship of the three pricing factors with retail always equalling 100.

- *Calculating $ Retail When $ Cost and $ Markup Are Known.*

Formula:

$$\$ \text{Retail} = \$ \text{Cost} + \$ \text{markup}$$

Problem:

If a retailer pays $6 for a scarf and needs a markup of $4, what should be the retail price of the scarf?

Solution:

$$\begin{aligned} \$ \text{Retail} &= \$ \text{Cost} + \$ \text{markup} \\ &= \$6 + \$4 \\ &= \$10 \end{aligned}$$

- *Calculating $ Markup When $ Retail and $ Cost Are Known*

Formula:

$$\$ \text{Markup} = \$ \text{Retail} - \$ \text{Cost}$$

Problem:

A retailer buys a scarf for $6 and decides to retail it for $10. What is the dollar markup on this item?

Solution:

$$\begin{aligned} \$ \text{Markup} &= \$ \text{Retail} - \$ \text{cost} \\ &= \$10 - \$6 \\ &= \$4 \end{aligned}$$

- *Calculating $ Cost When $ Retail and $ Markup Are Known*

Formula:

$$\$ \text{Cost} = \$ \text{Retail} - \$ \text{markup}$$

---

[1] *Retail reductions* is the inclusive trade term for markdowns, employee discounts, and stock shortages.

Problem:

What is the dollar cost of a scarf that retails for $10 and has a markup of $4?

Solution:

$$\$ \text{ Cost } = \$ \text{ Retail} - \$ \text{ Markup}$$
$$= \$10 - \$4$$
$$= \$6$$

Calculations Involving Percentage of Markup

While some stores merchandise on the basis of dollar retail, cost, and markup, by far the majority find that expressing these factors as percentages constitute a more valid concept, particularly for purposes of comparison and analysis of figures.

In percentage calculations, retail always equals 100%. For example, just as dollar retail equals dollar cost plus dollar markup, retail percentage or 100% equals the cost percentage plus the markup percentage.

• *Calculating Markup Percentage on the Basis of Retail Price.* Dollar markup can be converted to either a percentage of the retail price or a percentage of the cost price. Markup, as a percentage of the retail price, is more widely used today because most stores have adopted the Retail Method of inventory valuation (see Chapter 8). However, since some retailers, particularly the smaller ones, still use the older Cost Method, students should understand the theory and be able to calculate markup percentage on either base. But for purposes of all further discussion relating to markup in this text, the retail base is both implied and used, unless otherwise indicated.

The formula for calculating markup as a percentage of the retail price is merely a modification of the formula indicated above for calculating dollar markup, which is:

$$\$ \text{ Markup} = \$ \text{ Retail} - \$ \text{ cost}$$

To find what percentage the dollar markup is of the retail price, it is necessary to divide the dollar markup figure by the retail price.

Formula:

$$\text{Retail markup \%} = \frac{\$ \text{ Retail} - \$ \text{ cost}}{\$ \text{ Retail}}$$

$$= \frac{\$ \text{ Markup}}{\$ \text{ Retail}}$$

Problem:

What is the retail markup percentage on an item costing $6 and retailing for $10?

Solution:

$$\text{Retail markup \%} = \frac{\$ \text{ Retail} - \$ \text{ cost}}{\$ \text{ Retail}}$$

$$= \frac{\$10 - \$6}{\$10}$$

$$= \frac{\$4}{\$10}$$

$$= 40.0\%$$

135

- *Calculating Markup Percentage on the Basis of Cost Price.* The same basic formula is used in calculating markup as a percentage of the cost price *except* that the divisor is the cost price rather than the retail price.

Formula:

$$\text{Cost markup \%} = \frac{\$ \text{Retail} - \$ \text{cost}}{\$ \text{Cost}}$$

$$= \frac{\$ \text{Markup}}{\$ \text{Cost}}$$

Problem:

What is the markup percentage on the cost of an item with a wholesale cost of $6 and a retail price of $10?

Solution:

$$\text{Markup \% on cost} = \frac{\$ \text{Retail} - \$ \text{Cost}}{\$ \text{Cost}}$$

$$= \frac{\$ 10 - \$ 6}{\$ 6}$$

$$= \frac{\$ 4}{\$ 6}$$

$$= 66 \frac{2}{3}\%$$

The theory behind all calculations involving markup percentage is that the retail figure always equals 100%. And since retail = cost + markup, then cost = retail − markup, or 100% − retail markup %.

There are two additional formulas involving markup expressed as a percentage of the retail price with which it is essential that *all* retailers become familiar. These are:

$$\$ \text{Retail} = \frac{\$ \text{Cost}}{100\% - \text{RM \%}}$$

and

$$\$ \text{Cost} = \$ \text{Retail} \times (100\% - \text{RM \%})$$

The application of these formulas to daily buying and pricing situations are discussed beginning on page 140.

PRACTICE PROBLEMS—Markup in Dollars and Percentage

Group A:

Find the retail markup percentage for each of the following cost and retail figures:

	$ Cost	$ Retail	Retail M%		$ Cost	$ Retail	Retail M%
1.	$ 8.50	$13.00	_____	6.	$ 3.00	$ 5.00	_____
2.	84.00 dz.	11.95 ea.	_____	7.	126.00	200.00	_____
3.	72.00 dz.	9.95 ea.	_____	8.	9.60 dz.	1.50 ea.	_____
4.	45.00 dz.	6.25 ea.	_____	9.	36.00 dz.	6.00 ea.	_____
5.	24.00	40.00	_____	10.	6.25	9.90	_____

Group B:

Find both the dollar and retail markup percentage from the following cost and retail prices.

	$ Cost	$ Retail	$ M	RM %
1.	$ 7.75	$ 13.00	_____	_____
2.	14.75	25.00	_____	_____
3.	42.00 dz.	6.00 ea.	_____	_____
4.	21.50 dz.	3.00 ea.	_____	_____
5.	6.25	9.95	_____	_____
6.	10.00	15.00	_____	_____
7.	15.00	20.00	_____	_____
8.	21.00	35.00	_____	_____
9.	65.00	125.00	_____	_____
10.	57.00 dz.	7.95 ea.	_____	_____

Group C:

Find minimum retail at which goods could be marked in order to obtain the indicated markup percentage:

	$ Cost	RM%	$ Retail		$ Cost	RM%	$ Retail
1.	$15.00	40.0	_____	6.	$ 15.00 dz.	42.0	_____
2.	25.00	48.0	_____	7.	12.75	40.2	_____
3.	42.50	45.0	_____	8.	2.75	50.0	_____
4.	12.75	50.0	_____	9.	27.00 dz.	48.0	_____
5.	75.00	47.5	_____	10.	125.00	45.0	_____

Group D:

Find the maximum cost at which goods should be bought in order to obtain the indicated retail markup percentage:

	$ Retail	RM%	$ Cost		$ Retail	RM%	$ Cost
1.	$120.00	45.0	_____	3.	29.95	42.5	_____
2.	75.00	50.0	_____	4.	3.98	42.0	_____

5.	18.95	44.0	_____	8.	6.50	39.8	_____
6.	$100.00	40.0	_____	9.	69.95	48.0	_____
7.	1.95	41.3	_____	10.	45.00	47.5	_____

TYPES OF MARKUP

Markup may expressed in dollars or as a percentage of sales, or both. The three types of markup most frequently referred to in merchandising mathematics are: initial, cumulative, and maintained markup. The first two are based on purchases, while the third is based on sales.

Initial Markup

The term *initial markup,* or purchase markup, refers to the dollar difference between the delivered cost of purchases and the retail prices at which those purchases were marked when first brought in to stock. *Delivered cost* is defined as the billed cost of merchandise (the cost as it appears on the vendor's invoice), plus any transportation costs incurred in getting the merchandise to the store.

Initial markup, as a percentage of net sales, is an important goal figure included by most retailers in their seasonal merchandise plans. Initial markup is an *averaged* figure, representing the difference between the billed cost of purchases made throughout a given period and the retail prices placed on those purchases when they are first received into stock. It represents the amount that must be obtained from sales in order to cover estimated operating expenses, retail reductions (the trade term for markdowns, employee discounts, and stock shortages), workroom costs, if applicable, and desired operating profit during a given period.

Formula (for calculating Initial Retail Markup percentage):

$$\text{Initial markup} \% = \frac{\text{Expenses} + \text{profit} + \text{workroom costs} + \text{markdowns} + \text{employee discounts} + \text{stock shortages}}{\text{Net sales} + \text{markdowns} + \text{employee discounts} + \text{stock shortages}[2]}$$

Problem:

The owner of a Maternity shop made the following estimates for the upcoming fall season:

Sales	$60,000
Retail reductions	3,000
Operating expenses	18,750
Profit goal	6,000
Workroom costs	840

From these estimates, what average initial markup will she need to get on purchases for the season?

---

[2] It is necessary to add retail reductions to net sales in order to determine the total value of all goods when they were first put into stock.

Solution:

$$\text{Needed markup \%} = \frac{\begin{array}{c}\text{Operating expenses + profit}\\ \text{+ retail reductions + workroom costs}\end{array}}{\text{Net sales + retail reductions}}$$

$$= \frac{\begin{array}{c}\$18,750 + \$6,000\\ + \$3,000 + \$840\end{array}}{\$60,000 + \$3,000}$$

$$= \frac{\$28,590}{\$63,000}$$

$$= 45.38\%$$

Cumulative Markup

The term *cumulative markup* refers to the dollar difference between the total delivered cost and the total retail of all merchandise handled during a given period. Total merchandise handled, you will recall from Chapter 3, represents the beginning inventory plus net purchases and net transfers in that occur during any given period. It is an *average* figure, representing as it does the average markup on the beginning inventory (made up of merchandise with varying markups because of prior retail reductions), plus new purchases with varying markups because of the necessity to mark goods at already established price lines.

Cumulative markup percentage at retail is calculated as follows:

Formula:

$$\text{Cumulative retail markup \%} = \frac{\begin{array}{c}\text{\$ Retail of total merchandise handled}\\ - \text{\$ cost of total merchandise handled}\end{array}}{\text{\$ Retail of total merchandise handled}}$$

Problem:

From the following figures, calculate the cumulative markup percentage for a Stationery Department for the month of October.

	Cost	Retail
October 1 inventory	$14,500	$27,300
Transportation costs	500	
Net purchases and transfers in	9,100	16,600

Solution:

$$\text{Cumulative markup \%} = \frac{\begin{array}{c}\text{\$ Retail of total merchandise handled}\\ - \text{\$ cost of total merchandise handled}\end{array}}{\text{\$ Retail of total merchandise handled}}$$

$$= \frac{\begin{array}{c}(\$27,300 + \$16,600)\\ - (\$14,500 + \$500 + \$9,100)\end{array}}{\$27,300 + \$16,600}$$

$$= \frac{\$43,900 - \$24,100}{\$43,900}$$

$$= \frac{\$19,800}{\$43,900}$$

$$= 45.1\%$$

Maintained Markup

The term *maintained markup* refers to the difference between the actual price at which goods are sold and the gross cost of those goods (see Chapter 3). Maintained markup is a "gross" figure because though it takes markdowns, employee discounts, and stock shortages (retail reductions) into account, it does not include cash discounts earned or workroom costs.

Maintained markup percentage is considered a key figure in estimating operating profit and evaluating merchandising operations. Like initial markup percentage, maintained markup percentage is calculated on a retail base. These two types of markup, however, should not be confused because they are not percentages of the same thing. Initial markup relates to retail prices placed on new purchases, while maintained markup relates to the retail price at which goods are actually sold.

Formula:

$$\text{Maintained markup \%} = \text{Initial markup \%} - (\text{total retail reductions \%} \times [100\% - \text{initial markup \%}])$$

Problem:

What would be a department's maintained markup percentage if the initial markup were 48.5% and retail reductions 15.5%?

Solution:

$$\text{Maintained markup \%} = \text{Initial markup \%} - (\text{retail reductions \%} \times [100\% - \text{initial markup \%}])$$
$$= 48.5\% - (15.5\% \times 51.5\%)$$
$$= 48.5\% - 8.0\%$$
$$= 40.5\%$$

BASIC PRICING FORMULAS

Retailers are faced many times each day with numerous decisions relating to the buying and pricing of goods for resale. They know that the initial markup percentage goal figure is intended as an *average* for the period involved. They know that in order to achieve maximum profits, both markup and sales volume must be maximized, but not beyond the point at which the number of sales transactions or the average sale figure are adversely affected. They also know that given any two of the three figures—retail, cost, and markup %—the third can easily be found.

Calculating Markup Percentage
When $ Cost and $ Retail Are Known

• *Calculating Markup Percentage on a Single Item.* The following example illustrates how to calculate the markup percentage on a single item.

Formula:

$$\text{Retail markup \%} = \frac{\$\text{ Retail} - \$\text{ Cost}}{\$\text{ Retail}}$$

Problem:

What is the retail markup percentage on an item that costs $1.20 and is retailed at $2.00?

Solution:

$$\text{Retail markup \%} = \frac{\$ \text{ Retail} - \$ \text{ Cost}}{\$ \text{ Retail}}$$

$$= \frac{\$2.00 - \$1.20}{\$2.00}$$

$$= \frac{\$0.80}{\$2.00}$$

$$= 40.0\%$$

• *Calculating Markup Percentage on a Group of Items with Varying Costs and/or Retails.* Buyers frequently order several different items on a single purchase order, with each item having a different cost and retail price. In addition to the total cost and total retail of each item, most purchase orders require calculation of the total dollar cost and total dollar retail of each order and the markup calculated on the entire purchase, which is regarded as a single transaction.

Formula:

$$\text{Retail markup \%} = \frac{\$ \text{ Retail} - \$ \text{ Cost}}{\$ \text{ Retail}}$$

Problem:

A buyer ordered 10 raincoats at a cost of $37.75 each to retail at $75.00 each, and 8 raincoats at a cost of $49.75 each to retail at $100 each. What is the markup percentage on this purchase?

Solution:

$$\begin{aligned}
\text{Total cost} &= (\$37.75 \times 10) + (\$49.75 \times 8) \\
&= \$377.50 + \$398.00 \\
&= \$775.50
\end{aligned}$$

$$\begin{aligned}
\text{Total retail} &= (\$75 \times 10) + (\$100 \times 8) \\
&= \$750 + \$800 \\
&= \$1,550
\end{aligned}$$

$$\begin{aligned}
\$ \text{ Retail} &= \frac{\$ \text{ Markup}}{\$ \text{ Retail}} \\
&= \frac{\$1,550 - \$775.50}{\$1,550} \\
&= \frac{\$774.50}{\$1,550} \\
&= 50.0\%
\end{aligned}$$

Calculating $ Retail When $ Cost and Desired Markup % Percentage Are Known

In wholesale markets goods may be priced individually or in multiple quantities, that is singly, by the dozen, or by the gross. Retail buyers, however, "think in terms of retail."

Before ordering merchandise, they must be convinced that their customers would be willing to pay for each item the retail price that would have to be placed on it considering its cost price, the necessary departmental markup, and all other pricing considerations.

If the quoted cost price is for multiple units, buyers usually convert it to individual unit cost when considering making a purchase. The unit retail price is then calculated on the basis of unit cost price and the desired markup percentage as follows:

Formula:

$$\$ \text{Retail} = \frac{\$ \text{Cost}}{(100\% - RM\,\%)^3}$$

Problem:

Women's driving gloves are offered to a buyer at a cost of $48 a dozen. If the buyer needs to get a 45% markup, what would be the minimum price at which each pair of these gloves should be retailed?

Solution:

$$\$ 48 \text{ dozen} = \$4 \text{ pair}$$

$$\$ \text{Retail} = \frac{\$ \text{Cost}}{100\% - RM\,\%}$$

$$= \frac{\$4}{55.0\%} \quad \text{or} \quad \frac{\$4}{.55}$$

$$= \$7.27$$

Alternative Solution:

$$\$ C = \$4$$

$$\% C = 100\% - 45\%$$

$$= 55.1\%$$

$$x = \$ R$$

$$\frac{\$4}{x} = \frac{55}{100}$$

$$55x = \$400$$

$$x = \frac{\$400}{55}$$

$$= \$7.27$$

Calculating $ Cost When $ Retail and Desired Markup Percentages Are Known

In buying into the retail price lines already established in their departments, buyers must be able to determine the maximum wholesale price they can afford to pay for each item they purchase in order to achieve their initial markup percentage goal for the season.

Formula:

$$\$ \text{Cost} = \$ \text{Retail} \times (100\% - RM\%)$$

---

[3] Usually referred to as the cost complement of the retail markup percent.

Problem:

A Sportswear buyer plans to buy a group of skirts to retail at $20 for a special event and needs to get a 48.0% markup. What is the most she can pay for each skirt?

Solution:

$$\$ \text{Cost} = \$ \text{Retail} \times (100\% - \text{RM} \%)$$
$$= \$20 \times 52.0\%$$
$$= \$20 \times .52$$
$$= \$10.40$$

Alternative Solution:

$$\$ \text{MU} = \$ R \times \text{RM} \%$$
$$= \$20 \times .48$$
$$= \$9.60$$

$$\$ C = \$ R - \$ \text{MU}$$
$$= \$20 - \$9.60$$
$$= \$10.40$$

PRACTICE PROBLEMS—Markup: Finding Third
Price-Related Figure When Two Are Known

1. If the retail price of a piece of luggage was $35.00, which represented a 40% markup, what was its cost?

_____

(Answer)

2. If the cost price of an article is $4.20 and the markup represents 40%, what is the retail price?

_____

(Answer)

143

3. A Fashion Accessories buyer purchased 1 dozen scarfs at $22.50 a dozen, which she intends to retail at $3 each. On the same order she bought another 1 dozen scarfs at $29.50 a dozen, which she intends to retail at $4 each. What is the markup percentage on this order?

_____
(Answer)

4. Determine the markup % on the following order:

Amount	Cost	Retail
24 pcs.	$15.75 doz.	$2.00 ea.
14 pcs.	22.50 doz.	3.00 ea.
18 pcs.	28.50 doz.	4.00 ea.

_____
(Answer)

5. At a 48.5% markup, what would be the minimum retail price of a dress that cost $39.75?

_____
(Answer)

6. A buyer purchases an item costing $54.00 a dozen, which he retails at $7.95 each. What markup percentage does this represent?

—————
(Answer)

7. If the $80 retail price of an item represents a 37.5% markup, how much did it cost?

—————
(Answer)

8. If a Men's Furnishings buyer bought 12 ties costing $78 a dozen and marked them up 35%, what was the retail price of each tie?

—————
(Answer)

9. A Junior Sportswear buyer bought 40 dozen T-shirts at $36 a dozen, 20 dozen at $33 a dozen, and 5 dozen at $39 a dozen. If he marked them all at the same retail price of $4.99, what was his markup percentage on the entire purchase?

_____
(Answer)

10. A buyer buys a dozen handbags at $84 a dozen and retails them at $14 each. What is the markup percentage on this purchase?

_____
(Answer)

AVERAGING MARKUP

It was noted earlier in the chapter that cumulative markup is the *average* markup obtained on the total merchandise handled during a given period. But average markup does not apply only to the calculation of cumulative markup. Average markup also applies to the markup on an entire stock of goods, to single purchases, or to a group of purchases.

Buyers are continually engaged in writing orders for merchandise and therefore must be continually involved in averaging markups as they mark their purchases into established price lines, for the following reasons:

- the wide variations and fluctuations that exist in the cost prices of similar types of merchandise that are handled in any one department or store would result in widely varying retail prices were initial markup percentage to be applied uniformly to each item purchased;
- the higher handling costs, promotional expenses, and markdowns necessitated by the highly volatile and/or fragile nature of some types of merchandise require higher-than-goal markup on purchases of such goods;

- the necessity to price goods at one of several customary but limited number of price points within an established price range results in widely varying markups because of widely varying cost prices;
- most stores periodically hold one or more types of annual sales promotional events in which each selling department is required to participate. Buyers or department managers providing lower-priced merchandise for such events must eventually balance the lower markup goods they are required to buy for such occasions with higher markup goods for regular stock in order to achieve the planned average markup goal.

The purpose of averaging markup is to so balance below-goal markups on some purchases with above-goal markups on others that the planned markup necessary for a profitable operation may be achieved. The term *average markup* refers to the average markup obtained on two or more separate purchases with different cost and/or retail prices found by totaling the cost and retail values of those purchases and from those figures calculating an average markup percentage. It is important to note that average markup *cannot* be obtained by averaging the markup on individual items constituting a total purchase. *Percentages cannot be averaged.*

The three basic markup (or pricing) formulas used for determining markup percentages involving single costs and single retails are also used in calculating average markup on purchases involving multiple costs and/or multiple retails. According to most retailing authorities, this type of problem can be solved by either one of two rather complicated methods—the ratio method or the algebraic method. The author has found the following format far simpler to use in solving averaging problems.

	Cost		Retail			Formula
Amount	*Each*	*Total*	*Each*	*Total*	*M %*	*Used*

The figures provided in the statement of the problem should be entered in the space below the appropriate heading and a question mark (?) inserted in the space provided for the answer being sought. It has also been found helpful to indicate alongside this format a space for noting the formula used in determining the cost, retail, or markup figure needed in solving the problem. This format can be used for solving all averaging problems, regardless of whether the answer involves cost, retail, or markup.

Averaging Markup When Retail Price and Planned Markup Percentage are Known

In order to achieve a planned average markup goal, buyers must be able to determine the markup percentage they should obtain on current or future purchases in order to balance out the markup they have achieved to date.

To solve this type of problem, use the above format and proceed as follows.

1. Calculate the total retail value of the purchase(s) under consideration.
2. Calculate the total dollar cost of the purchase(s), a cost figure that may not be exceeded if the desired markup goal is to be achieved.
3. From these totals subtract the cost and retail value of each subsequent purchase as it is made.
4. Calculate the markup percentage needed on the balance of purchases to be made, as indicated by the dollar cost and retail remainder figures.

Following is an example of how the format indicated above can be used in solving a problem that involves finding the markup needed on the *balance* of purchases when retail price and planned markup percentage are known.

Problem:

A Leisurewear buyer needs 500 robes to retail at $28 each for a storewide promotion and must achieve a 46% markup on all purchases for the event. If she purchases 150 robes at $16.75 each, what markup percentage must she get on the balance of the purchases if she is to obtain the desired markup percentage?

Solution:

Using the format indicated above, first enter in the proper spaces all information given in the general statement of the problem. Next indicate, with a question mark, the specific problem that is to be solved. At this point the solution format will look like this:

	Cost		Retail			
Amount	Each	Total	Each	Total	M %	Formula
500			$28.00		46.0	
150	$16.75		28.00			
350					?	

In order to arrive at a final solution to the problem, procede with and record your calculations as directed.

	Cost		Retail			
Amount	Each	Total	Each	Total	M %	Formula
(1) 500		(2) $7,560.00	(1) $28.00	(1) $14,000.00	46.0	(2) $ C = $ R $\times$ CCRM %
						= $14,000 $\times$ .54
						= $7,560
(3) 150	(3) $16.75	(3) 2,512.50	(4) $28.00	(4) 4,200.00		
(5) 350		(6) $5,047.50		(7) $ 9,800.00	(8) 48.5	(8) M % = $\dfrac{\$ R - \$ C}{\$ R}$
						= $9,800 −
						5,047.50
						= 48.5%

Step 1: Calculate total retail of 500 pieces at $28.00 each:

$$\text{Total retail} = 500 \times \$28$$
$$= \$14,000$$

Step 2: Calculate total cost when retail and M % are known:

$$\$ \text{Cost} = \text{Retail} \times (100\% - \text{RM} \%)$$
$$= \$14,000 \times .54$$
$$= \$7,560$$

Step 3: Calculate total cost of 150 pieces at $16.75 each:

$$\text{Cost} = 150 \times \$16.75$$
$$= \$2,512.50$$

Step 4: Calculate total retail of 150 pieces at $28 each:

$$\text{Retail} = 150 \times \$28$$
$$= \$4,200.00$$

Step 5: Subtract from 500 pieces needed the order placed for 150 pieces.

$$\text{Balance} = 500 - 150$$
$$= 350$$

Step 6: Subtract from total cost of 500 pieces at $7,560, the cost of 150 pieces purchased at $2,512.50 in order to obtain the amount that can be spent to purchase the balance needed of 350 pieces.

$$\text{Balance of cost} = \$7,560 - \$2,512.50$$
$$= \$5,047.50$$

Step 7: Subtract from total retail of $14,000 the retail of the 150 pieces purchased to obtain the total retail of the remaining 350 pieces to be purchased.

$$\text{Balance needed at retail} = \$14,000 - \$4,200$$
$$= \$9,800$$

Step 8: Calculate markup percentage needed on balance of purchases when the cost balance is $5,047.50 and the retail balance is $9,800.

$$\text{Retail markup \%} = \frac{\$\text{ Retail} - \$\text{ cost}}{\$\text{ Retail}}$$
$$= \frac{\$9,800 - \$5,047.50}{\$9,800}$$
$$= \frac{\$4,752.50}{\$9,800.00}$$
$$= 48.5\%$$

PRACTICE PROBLEMS—Averaging Markup Percentage
When Cost and Retail Prices Are Known

1. The Men's Furnishings buyer intends to buy $300 worth of neckties at retail for a special sales event. His first order is for 38 neckties at $22.50 a dozen. He plans to retail these for $2.79. What markup should he strive to obtain on the balance of his purchases if the average markup goal is 45%?

_____
(Answer)

2. A Fabrics buyer had a stock on hand of $8,000 at retail, which represented a cost of $5,500. He purchases additional fabrics for $11,000 at cost which he intends to retail at $19,000. If he needs an additional $7,000 worth of merchandise at retail, at what markup percentage must he buy the goods if he is to achieve an average markup of 42%?

_____
(Answer)

3. A buyer needs $15,000 worth of merchandise at retail for a special event next month. The first purchase is for $3,000 at cost to be retailed at $5,000. At what markup percentage must the buyer purchase the balance of the goods he needs for the event if he is to achieve an average markup of 42%?

_____
(Answer)

4. A Lamp buyer needs $10,000 worth of goods at retail and a markup of 42%. His first purchase is for 300 lamps which cost $7 each and which he retails at $13.00 each. What markup must the buyer obtain on the remainder of his purchases in order to attain the required average of 42%?

_____
(Answer)

5. A Coat buyer plans to buy $5,000 worth of coats at retail for the store's Anniversary Sale at a planned markup of 49%. His first purchase is 50 coats costing $31.75 each, which he plans to retail at $55 each. What markup percentage should the buyer obtain on the balance of his purchases if he is to attain his planned markup goal of 49%?

_____
(Answer)

Averaging Costs When Retail Price and Planned Markup Percentage Are Known

An averaging problem that involves a single retail price and two cost prices is a common merchandising occurrence. This is basically the situation that is involved when buying merchandise at two different but fairly close cost prices and marking them both into a single established retail price line. To fully understand this concept it is important to remember that the buyer, in trying to proportion the varying costs, is primarily concerned with *aggregate* markup rather than individual markup.

Here again, two methods have been advanced for solving this type of averaging —the ratio one and the algebraic one. But the method suggested by this author is believed to be much simpler to understand as well as to calculate.

Problem:

A buyer plans to buy 300 umbrellas to retail at $8.00 each. The departmental markup goal is 45.0%. The first order placed is for 100 umbrellas at a cost of $4.75 each. What is the most the buyer can pay for each of the 200 umbrellas that still need to be purchased?

Solution:

First enter in the proper spaces all information given in the general statement of the problem. Next indicate, with a question mark, the specific problem that needs solving. Then proceed as directed.

Amount	Cost Each	Cost Total	Retail Each	Retail Total	M %	Formula
(1) 300		(2) $1,320.00	(1) $8.00	(1) $2,400	45.0	(2) $ C = $ R X CCRM %
(3) 100	(3) $4.75	(3) — 475.00				= $2,400 X .55
(4) 200		(4) $ 845.00				= $1,320.00
	(5) $4.225 or $4.23					(5) $845 ÷ 200 =
						$4.225 or $4.23

Step 1:   Calculate the total retail of 300 umbrellas at $8 each:

$$\text{Total retail} = 300 \times \$8$$
$$= \$2,400$$

Step 2:   Calculate the total cost when total retail and RM % are known:

$$\text{Total cost} = \text{Total retail} \times (100\% - RM\%)$$
$$= \$2,400 \times 55.0\%$$
$$= \$2,400 \times .55$$
$$= \$1,320$$

Step 3:   Calculate the total cost of 100 umbrellas at $4.75 each:

$$\text{Total cost} = 100 \times \$4.75$$
$$= \$475.00$$

Step 4:   Calculate the total cost of 200 remaining umbrellas to buy:

$$
\begin{array}{lr}
\text{Cost of 300 umbrellas} = & \$1,320.00 \\
\text{Cost of 100 umbrellas} \quad - & 475.00 \\
\text{Cost of remaining 200} = & \$ \ \ 845.00 \\
\end{array}
$$

Step 5:   Calculate maximum cost of each of the 200 umbrellas yet to be purchased:

$$\text{Cost of each} = \$845.00 \div 200$$

$$= \$4.225 \ \text{ or } \ \$4.23$$

PRACTICE PROBLEMS—Averaging Costs When Retail
Price and Markup Percentage Are Known

1. The T-shirt buyer plans to purchase 600 T-shirts to retail for $4.79 each and to achieve an average markup of 40% on the purchase. If she places the first order for 100 at a cost of $3.00 each, what is the average price she can pay for each of the remaining T-shirts she needs?

_____
(Answer)

2. The Shoe buyer needs 300 pairs of shoes to retail at $13.95 a pair. The markup in his department is 42%. His first purchase consists of 125 pairs at $8.75 and 60 pairs at $7.75. What is the most he can pay for each of the remaining pairs he must buy if he is to attain his departmental markup?

                                                                            _____
                               (Answer)

3. A small specialty chain store owner operates on a 48% markup. He needs 120 skirts to retail at $11.00 each and 80 jackets to retail at $12.00 each. If he pays $6.25 for each jacket, how much can he afford to pay for each skirt if he is to achieve his planned markup percentage on the entire purchase?

                                                                            _____
                               (Answer)

4. A Boutique buyer is planning a special cashmere sale. Her first purchase is for 5 dozen cashmere sweaters at a cost of $17.75 each, which she retails at $32.00 each. She also needs 100 cashmere mufflers which she plans to retail at $12.00 each. If the required markup is 50%, how much can she afford to pay for each muffler?

                                                                            _____
                               (Answer)

5. The Glove buyer plans to buy 400 pairs of gloves for a special $5.00 sale at an average markup of 42%. Her first purchase consists of 100 pairs of gloves at a cost of $3.50 the pair.

(a) What is the most she can pay for the balance of her purchases if she is to achieve her markup goal?

(a) _____
(Answer)

(b) What will the average cost per pair be on the balance of her purchases?

(b) _____
(Answer)

Averaging Retail When Cost Price(s) and Needed Markup Percentage Are Known

The averaging process may also be applied to problems that involve determining an *average retail price* which would yield a desired markup percent when applied to purchases made at two or more different cost prices. Here again the buyer is concerned with total or *aggregate* markup—not individual item markup.

Problem:

A Sportswear buyer purchased a specially-priced group of slacks at the following prices for her store's Anniversary Sale: 100 pairs at $14.75 each, regularly $16.75; 50 pairs at $16.75 each, regularly $18.75; and 25 pairs at $18.75 each, regularly $20.75. If she wants to retail them all at the same price and needs to get a 40% markup, what would be the minimum retail price of each pair if she is to achieve the desired markup?

Solution:

First enter in the proper spaces all information given in the general statement of the problem. Next indicate with a question mark the specific problem that needs solving. Then proceed as directed.

	Cost		Retail			
Amount	Each	Total	Each	Total	M %	Formula
100 pr.	$14.75	$1,475.00				
50 pr.	16.75	837.50				
25 pr.	18.75	468.75				
(3) 175 pr.		(1) $2,781.25	(3) $26.49	(2) $4,635.42	40.0	(2) $ R = $\dfrac{\$ C}{CCRM \%}$

$$= \frac{\$2,781.25}{.60}$$

$$= \$4,635.42$$

$$(3) \ \$ R \ each = \frac{\$4,635.42}{175}$$

$$= \$26.49$$

Step 1: Calculate the total cost of the 175 pairs of slacks:

$$
\begin{aligned}
100 \text{ pr. at } \$14.75 &= \$1,475.00 \\
50 \text{ pr. at } \$16.75 &= 837.50 \\
25 \text{ pr. at } \$18.75 &= 468.75 \\
\text{Total cost } 175 \text{ pr.} &= \$2,781.25
\end{aligned}
$$

Step 2: Calculate the total retail price of 175 pairs:

$$\$ R = \frac{\text{Cost}}{(100\% - RM \%)}$$

$$= \frac{\$2,781.25}{60\%}$$

$$= \frac{\$2,781.25}{.60}$$

$$= \$4,635.42$$

Step 3: Calculate retail price of each pair:

$$175 \text{ pr.} = \$4,635.42$$

$$1 \text{ pr.} = \frac{\$4,635.42}{175}$$

$$= \$26.49$$

PRACTICE PROBLEMS—Averaging Retail When Cost Price and Markup Percentage Are Known

1. A Toy buyer made a special purchase of 10 dozen toy animals at $8.75 a dozen, 28 dozen toy soldiers at $7.25 a dozen, and two dozen toy trucks at $8.50 a dozen.

   (a) At a 41% average markup to be obtained on the order: what would be the lowest retail price of each toy if they were all to be retailed at the same price?

   (a) _____
   (Answer)

(b) If price lines to be featured for this sales event were to be 99¢, $1.19, and $1.39, into which price line do you think the above toys should be marked? Why?

(b) _____
(Answer)

2. The Men's Sportswear buyer purchased 20 tweed jackets at $24.75 each and 20 checked jackets at $39.75 each. His department works on an average markup of 48%.

(a) If he retails the tweed jackets at $49.95, what should be the lowest retail price each checked jacket should be marked?

(a) _____
(Answer)

(b) If the department featured regular price lines of $49.95, $59.95, $69.95, and $75, in your opinion into which price line should the checked jackets be marked?

(b) _____
(Answer)

3. The Jeans buyer buys a "job lot" of slacks to be retailed all at the same price. Planned markup is 45%. She pays $6.25 each for 100 jeans and $5.75 each for 200 jeans. What should be the minimum retail price of each pair of jeans if she is to attain her planned markup?

_____
(Answer)

4. A Sportswear buyer purchases a closeout at the end of the season of 40 tweed jackets at $17.75 each, 75 blazers at $19.75 each, and 30 cashmere jackets at $28.75 each. What should be the average retail price of each jacket if the buyer is to retail them all at the same price and still achieve a 50% markup on the order?

_____
(Answer)

5. A Handbag manufacturer at the end of the spring season offered a retailer the following merchandise: 50 at $16.75 each, 75 at $12.75 each, and 40 at $14.75 each. What would be the average retail price of all 165 handbags if the buyer decided to buy the lot, retail them all at the same price, and obtain a 49% markup?

_____
(Answer)

SUMMARY OF KEY TERMS

Average Markup. Refers to the markup achieved on total cost and retail values of a number of purchases involving multiple cost and/or retail prices.

Best-Selling Price Lines. Those price points at which the greater share of total dollar and unit sales take place.

Cumulative Markup. The dollar difference between the total delivered cost and the total retail of all merchandise handled during a given period.

Delivered Cost. Billed cost of merchandise as it appears on the vendor's invoice, plus transportation costs in getting the goods to the store.

Initial Markup. Refers to the dollar difference between the delivered cost of purchases and the retail prices at which those purchases were marked when first received into stock.

Maintained Markup. The difference between the actual price at which goods are sold and the gross cost of those goods, taking into consideration markdowns, employee discounts, and stock shortages.

Markup Percentage. Markup expressed as a percentage of the cost price or the retail price.

Price Line. Refers to a specific price point at which an *assortment* of merchandise is regularly offered for sale.

Price Lining. Refers to the practice of establishing a series of retail prices at which an assortment of goods will be offered for sale.

Price Range. Refers to the spread between the lowest and highest price line carried in a store or department.

Price Structure. The price range at which each selling department will offer its merchandise and the price zone(s) to be featured throughout the store. Determined by store management.

Price Zone. Refers to a series of adjacent price lines that are likely to have special appeal to one particular segment of a store's customers.

REVIEW QUESTIONS

1. The practice of establishing a series of retail prices at which an assortment of merchandise will be offered for sale is referred to as _____ _____.

2. The spread between the lowest and highest price lines carried in a store or department is referred to as the _____ _____.

3. A series of adjacent price points that are likely to have special appeal to one particular segment of a store's customers is referred to as _____ _____.

4. A price point at which an assortment of merchandise is regularly carried is referred to as a _____ _____.

5. Indicate and briefly explain three basic considerations that influence the setting of retail prices.

   (1)

   (2)

   (3)

6. Indicate at least two advantages of price lining.

   (1)

   (2)

7. Name the three basic factors involved in pricing goods.

   (1)

   (2)

   (3)

8. The difference between the delivered cost of purchases and the retail prices at which those purchases are marked when first brought into stock is referred to as _____ _____.

9. The difference between the total cost and total retail of all merchandise handled during a given period is referred to as _____ _____.

10. The difference between the actual price at which goods are sold and the gross cost of those goods is referred to as _____ _____.

REVIEW PROBLEMS—Markup: Regular and Averaging

1. For each of the following sets of figures, complete the dollar markup and retail markup percentage (corrected to second place past the decimal):

	Retail	Cost	$ RM	RM %
a.	$ 5.00	$ 3.00	_____	_____
b.	200.00	126.00	_____	_____
c.	700.00	400.00	_____	_____
d.	1.50 ea.	9.60 dz.	_____	_____
e.	7.95 ea.	57.00 dz.	_____	_____

2. For each of the following sets of figures, calculate the minimum dollar retail:

	Cost	RM %	Retail
a.	$ 15.00	40.00	_____
b.	25.00	33.33	_____
c.	15.00 dz.	42.00	_____
d.	106.25 dz.	45.00	_____
e.	42.50	41.00	_____

3. For each of the following sets of figures, calculate the cost in dollars and cents:

	Retail	RM %	Cost
a.	$100.00	40.00	_____
b.	18.95	44.00	_____
c.	90.00	33.33	_____
d.	75.00	50.00	_____
e.	3.98	42.22	_____

4. This is a two-part problem:

    (a) Calculate the figures to go in each of the spaces provided below.

	Cost	Retail	RM %
Beginning inventory	$15,000	$_____	40.0
Purchases, February	10,500	_____	41.0
Purchases, March	12,000	17,000	_____
Purchases, April	_____	20,000	32.0

(b) Determine the cumulative markup percentage for
the three month period.

(b) _____
(Answer)

5. A Dress Department manager received 65 dresses at a cost of $10 each. Fifty were sold at $17 each, and the balance were sold at $12 each. What was the maintained markup percentage on this purchase?

_____
(Answer)

6. A buyer ordered 10 coats costing $59.75 each to retail at $100 each, 8 coats costing $69.75 each to retail at $125 each, and 6 coats costing $79.75 each to retail at $150 each. Calculate the markup percentage on the whole purchase.

_____
(Answer)

7. A buyer buys 42 blouses costing $45.00 a dozen. If the departmental markup is 40%, what would be the minimum retail price at which each blouse should be marked?

_____
(Answer)

8. Men's shirts which cost $24.50 a dozen require a markup of 46.5%. Find the retail price that should be placed on each shirt.

_____
(Answer)

9. If a suit that cost $67.50 has a markup of 62.5%, what would be the minimum retail price it should be marked?

_____
(Answer)

10. A buyer purchased the following:

500 jackets costing $16 each to sell at $30 each
700 pairs of slacks costing $9 each to sell at $15 each
300 skirts costing $12 each to sell at $22 each

(a) What is the initial markup on this order?

(a) _____
(Answer)

(b) What markup percentage is maintained if all goods are sold at the original retail, except 200 pairs of slacks which were cleared out at 30% off, and 100 jackets which were cleared out at $22?

(b) _____
(Answer)

11. A Men's Sportswear buyer needed to buy 275 men's golf hats to retail at $10 on which he wishes to achieve an average markup of 45%. His first purchase was for 125 hats at a cost of $6 each. What markup must he get on the balance of his purchases if he is to achieve his average markup?

_____
(Answer)

12. A buyer purchases a lot of 200 handbags at a cost of $4.80 each. She retails 120 of them at $8.50 each. What is the minimum retail price she must place on the remainder of the handbags in order to achieve an average markup of 45%?

_____
(Answer)

13. A buyer purchases the following blouses at cost: 40 at $4.45 each; 36 at $4.75 each; and 38 at $3.75 each. If she wishes to retail them all at the same price, what would be the minimum retail price of each if she needs to get a 46.5% markup on the entire purchase?

_____
(Answer)

14. A Jewelry buyer buys a lot of 50 watches at $27.50 each. When retailing them she decides to mark (a) 20 at $39.95; (b) 20 at $45; and (c) 10 at $50. What markup percentage would she get at each of these prices?

(a) _____
       (Answer)

(b) _____
       (Answer)

(c) _____
       (Answer)

15. A Men's Furnishings buyer purchased 4 dozen men's wool scarfs at $48.00 a dozen. If he is required to obtain an average markup of 48%, what would be the minimum retail price he should put on each scarf?

_____
   (Answer)

CHAPTER 7

REPRICING MERCHANDISE: markdowns, additional markups, and employee discounts

Rarely is a stock of goods sold in its entirety at the retail prices placed on the various items when they are first brought in to stock. Price adjustments that either increase or decrease the original retail price are frequently being made during the period in which the merchandise remains in stock. These changes must be properly reported to the store's Accounting office if an accurate Book Inventory figure (see Chapter 9) is to be maintained. These are also an important factor in planning initial (or purchase) markup (see Chapter 6), and they must be constantly controlled if an operating profit is to be achieved.

Most retailers use a special form called a Price Change Report for recording the following adjustments in the retail price of stock on hand:

- markdowns—decreases in presently marked prices;
- markdown cancellations—increases in the price of merchandise previously marked down;
- additional markup—increases in the price placed on merchandise when it was first placed in stock;
- markup cancellation—reduction in additional markup taken on merchandise after it originally came in to stock and a retail price placed on it.

While forms used for recording such increases or decreases in the retail value of the stock on hand are not standardized, the following information is required on most of them:

1. type of price adjustment being made;
2. department number;
3. effective date of price change;
4. vendor's Duns number or assigned house number;
5. season letter or code;

167

6. classification of merchandise;
7. style number;
8. present unit price;
9. new price to be marked;
10. difference between present and new price per unit;
11. count of units to be repriced;
12. description of merchandise;
13. retail amount of each entry;
14. total price adjustment as recorded on each form;
15. authorizing signatures;
16. number of price change sheet.

Some price change reporting forms also require that the reason or reasons for each price adjustment be indicated. Reasons might include: promotional remainders; special sale from stock; shopworn, soiled, or damaged; stolen; and so on.

Electronic data processing has made it possible to take markdowns at the point of sale rather than manually listing them on price change sheets and showing the markdown on each item's price ticket. Identifying information with regard to each marked-down item, less the percentage of markdown, is fed into the computer's memory bank through the electronic cash register as each sale is being made and automatically totaled. Thus, much time and paperwork is saved, while improving accuracy in handling the figures.

The original pricing of merchandise was the subject of Chapter 6. The repricing of merchandise, such as markdowns, markdown cancellations, additional markups, markup cancellations, and employee discounts, is the subject of this chapter. Stock shortages are discussed in Chapter 9.

MARKDOWNS

The most common type of price adjustment is called a *markdown*. This is the trade term for the downward revision in the retail price at which an item or group of items is currently marked.

Markdowns are of great concern to retailers because they represent reductions in the spread between the actual cost of merchandise and the retail prices at which the merchandise is finally sold—in other words, a reduction in maintained markup—the markup actually realized from the sale of goods. Lower markup results in lowered gross margin and subsequently in potential operating profit—the "bottom line." Large markdowns may cause some stores to fall short of realizing their planned markup. In others, failure to take needed markdowns may cause net sales to fall short of plan. For all these reasons, markdowns, although necessary in the ordinary, day-to-day conduct of a retail business, must be carefully watched and controlled.

Purpose of Markdowns

A markdown is, in effect, the retailer's way of correcting the price of an item so that the price reflects more accurately the actual, current value of that item. In this connection, it is important to remember that the actual value of an item is the value the *customer* places on that item—how much he or she is willing to pay for it—*not* what it cost. In that context, the price a customer will pay for an item has no relation to the actual cost price of the item, or what the retailer paid for it.

Markdowns (abbreviated M.D.) are not necessarily a "curse." Rather they need to be considered a "cure"—a merchandising tool that can be used to good advantage if the merchandiser utilizes markdowns as the means of ridding stocks of slow sellers and uses the money from their sale to buy faster sellers.

The major reasons for taking markdowns are to:

- clear stocks of odds and ends and shopworn merchandise;
- create additional open-to-buy for the purchase of new, fresh merchandise to "liven up" the stock;
- attract more customers to the store by offering them bargains;
- stimulate the sale of merchandise to which customers are not responding satisfactorily;
- meet lower competitive prices for the same merchandise.

Markdown Calculations

Markdowns are expressed in dollars, or as a percentage of sales, or both. Markdowns have an adverse effect on gross margin, because they reduce the selling price of merchandise and therefore maintained markup (the difference between the gross cost of merchandise sold and the retail prices at which it was sold).

Dollar Markdowns. The dollar markdown of a single item is the dollar-and-cents difference between the price at which the item is presently marked and the new, lower price to which it is being marked. To find the total dollar markdown, multiply the unit dollar markdown by the number of units to which the markdown applies. Form 7-1 is an example of markdowns taken in one department for a storewide sales event.

FORM 7-1 PRICE CHANGE FORM: MARKDOWN

Formulas:

$$\$ \text{ Unit markdown } = \text{Present retail price } - \text{ new lower retail price}$$

$$\text{Total } \$ \text{ markdown } = \$ \text{ Unit markdown} \times \text{ number of units being marked down}$$

Problem:

If a Book buyer reduced a group of 40 books from $10 to $6.99 for a special two-day sale, what was the amount of the dollar markdown taken?

Solution:

$$\$ \text{ Unit markdown } = \text{Present unit retail } - \text{ new unit retail}$$
$$= \$10.00 - \$6.99$$
$$= \$3.01$$

$$\text{Total } \$ \text{ markdown } = \$ \text{ unit markdown} \times \text{ number of units being marked down}$$
$$= \$3.01 \times 40$$
$$= \$120.40$$

Markdown Percentage. For planning and control purposes, dollar markdowns are usually converted into percentages. These may be expressed either as (a) a percentage of net sales for a given period; or (b) as a percentage off the original retail price. The following formula is used when markdowns are expressed as a *percentage of net sales for a given period.:*

Formula:

$$\text{Markdown } \% = \frac{\$ \text{ Markdowns taken in a given period}}{\$ \text{ Net sales for the same period}}$$

Problem:

If a store's net sales for December were $10,000 and markdowns taken during that month amounted to $550, what was the December markdown percentage?

Solution:

$$\text{Markdown } \% = \frac{\$ \text{ Markdowns for month}}{\$ \text{ Net sales for month}}$$

$$= \frac{\$550}{\$10,000}$$

$$= 5.5\%$$

Figures representing the percentages by which items are reduced from their original price are often used in advertising price reductions to the public. In such cases markdowns are expressed as a *percentage off the original retail price* rather than as a percentage of sales.

Formula:

$$\text{Markdown } \% = \frac{\$ \text{ Markdown}}{\text{Original } \$ \text{ retail price}}$$

Problem:

If an item retailing originally at $50 were marked down to $40, what was the markdown percentage?

Solution:

$$\text{Markdown \%} = \frac{\$ \text{ Markdown}}{\text{Original \$ retail price}}$$

$$= \frac{\$50 - \$40}{\$50}$$

$$= \frac{\$10}{\$50}$$

$$= 20.0\%$$

The next problem illustrates how markdowns can be expressed as *a percentage of total sales of an item or group of items.*

Problem:

A Giftware buyer purchased 100 sets of glasses at $5.50 a set and retailed them at $10 a set for a special sales event. Seventy-five sets were sold during the sale period. After the sale was over the buyer reduced the remaining 25 sets to $7.00, at which price 20 sets were sold. In order to close out this item, the buyer reduced the price of the remaining sets to $5 each and all were sold at that price. What was the markdown percentage of this purchase?

Solution:

$$\text{Markdown \%} = \frac{\text{Total \$ markdowns taken}}{\text{Total \$ net sales of item(s)}}$$

1st markdown $= (\$10 - \$7) \times 25$
$= \$3 \times 25$
$= \$75$

2nd markdown $= (\$7 - \$5) \times 5$
$= \$2 \times 5$
$= \$10$

Total M.D.s taken $= \$75 + \$10$
$= \$85$

Total net sales $= (75 \times \$10) + (20 \times \$7) + (5 \times \$5)$
$= \$750 + \$140 + \$25$
$= \$915$

$$\text{Markdown \%} = \frac{\$85}{\$915}$$

$$= 9.29\%$$

Causes of Markdowns

By analyzing the causes of markdowns, the retailer can make an effort to minimize them.

The most common causes of markdowns, although not necessarily listed in order of their importance are:

- buying errors;
- pricing errors;
- selling errors;
- special sales from regular stock;
- broken assortments, remnants, etc.;
- remainders of special purchases.

Buying Errors.   Failure to analyze trends in customer demand and/or make appropriate buying plans will inevitably result in having to take large merchandise markdowns.

Typical buying errors are:

- *Overbuying*
  - in relation to actual demand;
  - in relation to stock on hand and on order;
  - failure to test merchandise before ordering it in depth.
- *Buying wrong sizes*
  - size distribution of purchases unbalanced to actual rate of sales made;
  - accepting merchandise from vendors sized contrary to order.
- *Buying poor styles, qualities, materials, colors*
- *Poor timing*
  - in taking of markdowns;
  - in scheduling delivery of orders;
  - in receiving merchandise after cancellation date.

Pricing Errors.   Merchandising has been defined as having the *right* merchandise at the *right* time, in the *right* quantitites, in the *right* place, and at prices customers are both willing and able to pay.

Major pricing errors that lead to markdowns are:

- setting the initial retail price too high;
- not being competitive in price for same goods;
- failure to lower retail prices in a falling market;
- deferring the taking of price reductions too long;
- calculated risks involved in carrying too many "prestige" items.

Selling Errors.   Another cause of markdowns arises from selling errors. Major selling errors that lead to markdowns are:

- failure to show and display merchandise properly;
- careless handling of merchandise, resulting in soiled and damaged goods;
- uninformed sales personnel;
- high-pressure or careless selling techniques that inevitably lead to high customer returns and eventual markdowns.

Special Sales from Regular Stock.   Stores regularly hold special sales to commemorate their founding, special holidays, and local community or other special events. For these occasions they frequently reduce merchandise from their regular stock for a one, two, or three-day event. They may also take advantage of such special sales to mark down and clear their stocks of the following items:

Broken Assortments and Remnants, such as:

- remainders of current season's styles and colors not being reordered;
- remainders of old season merchandise;
- remnants of piece goods, carpeting and so on.

Remainders of Special Purchases.   Merchandise that cannot be reordered or worked into regular stock.

Timing of Markdowns

Top management of each retail organization determines the firm's policy with regard to the taking of markdowns. Basically there are two choices available: taking them "early" (when their rate of sale begins to slow down) or taking them "late" (usually at the end of each major selling season or semiannually).

Early Markdowns. Early markdowns refer to the policy of taking markdowns on individual styles after they have remained in stock a predetermined length of time or as soon as their rate of sale begins to slow down.

Most department stores, popular-priced specialty stores, and large general merchandise chains follow a policy of taking early markdowns. In those stores marked-down merchandise is usually displayed separately from the regular price goods, often on "clearance" racks or in a special section of a department's selling floor.

Major advantages of taking early markdowns are:

- improve stock turnover rate;
- smaller price reductions are usually needed to move merchandise while there is still interest in and use for the goods involved;
- odds and ends and slow-moving stock can be quickly disposed of rather than being left to clutter up and depreciate the value of faster-moving stock;
- enhances goodwill by providing customers with "bargains" before the end of the normal selling season.

Late Markdowns. "Late" markdowns are those that are only taken semiannually or at the end of a selling season, with very few markdowns being taken in between. High-fashion specialty stores and small stores or shops usually adopt a late-markdown policy. Unlike large department stores and popular-priced specialty stores, the stock of small stores, as well as high-fashion specialty shops, is usually limited, consisting mainly of only a few pieces of each style stocked. So the criteria for identifying and taking early markdowns does not apply in the case of high-fashion and/or small stores. Also, customers of such stores are usually more interested in new and innovative styling, fine workmanship, and top quality than in "bargains." Furthermore, these types of stores as a rule attract only limited traffic, whereas a high degree of traffic is necessary to move out markdowns.

Stores that elect a late-markdown policy either leave slow-sellers and stock remnants in their regular floor stock or accumulate such merchandise in a stockroom until the end of a major selling season, at which time they hold well-advertised, special markdown sales.

Major advantages in taking late markdowns are:

- the store can maintain an exclusive image throughout most of the year;
- customers attracted to these types of stores are likely to become suspicious of the store's regular prices if markdowns are taken and regularly displayed on the selling floor;
- if stores with limited stock were to take early markdowns, this would seriously deplete their regular-priced merchandise;
- end-of-season markdowns can be advertised as an event that is looked forward to by bargain seekers and those who appreciate fine quality and unusual styling but cannot afford the store's regular prices.

End-of-the-Month (E.O.M.) Clearances. Some stores attempt a compromise between early and late markdowns by holding monthly clearance sales, usually on the last day or the last weekend of every month. This has met with varying degrees of success, depending on the store's image and clientele. Also, not all types of merchandise or seasons of the year are suitable for either the regular monthly taking or promoting of markdowns.

Seasonal Markdowns. There is a growing trend for retailers of all types of merchandise to take markdowns on seasonal goods just prior to the close of the normal selling season instead of waiting until the season is over. Examples abound, such as the markdowns taken on holiday wearing apparel and accessories, toys, Christmas cards, and decorations just prior to Christmas.

Amount of Markdown to Be Taken

It is difficult to generalize on the "right" dollar amount of the markdown to be taken on various types of merchandise because the "right" price depends on many factors, such as:

- the reason for taking a reduction (need to quickly convert stock into cash? regular end-of-month, end-of-season, or semiannual clearance? special, limited-time sale from stock?);
- the nature of the merchandise (high fashion? mass fashion? damaged or soiled? staple goods? odds-and-ends?);
- timing of the markdowns in relation to the normal selling season (end-of-season? peak-of-season? early in season?);
- the quantity on hand (odds-and-ends? large quantity of a single style? few pieces of a style?);
- original markup (high? low? regular?).

As far as percentage reductions go, fashion goods are usually reduced 30% to 50%, with the larger percentage taken on the higher-priced goods. On the other hand, a 10% reduction in the price of staple merchandise may be enough to achieve a considerable acceleration in the rate of sale of this type of item.

The purpose of markdowns, as previously stated, is to sell the merchandise quickly. In order to achieve this purpose, the following rules with regard to the amount of markdown taken should be carefully considered and applied:

- The first markdown should be sharp enough to move out most or at least a large part of the goods. Small markdowns are usually ineffective, and having to take a succession of them in order to move out the goods may actually increase the total amount of markdown dollars involved.
- Markdowns should be great enough to attract customers who would or could not pay the original price.
- Markdowns should not be so large as to invite skepticism of actual value involved.

MARKDOWN CANCELLATIONS

The sum of all reductions in retail prices are referred to as gross markdowns. Raising the price of a previously marked down item (or group of items) back up to or toward a former retail price is known as a *markdown cancellation.* During any given accounting period, markdown cancellations are subtracted from gross markdowns to determine a net markdown figure for that period.

A previously stated, many stores use a multipurpose price change form for the recording of markdown cancellations.

The same procedures apply to the recording of markdown cancellations as for markdowns except that the merchandise is being *marked up* from a lower to a higher price instead of *down* from a higher to a lower price. In the case of cancellations, the "present price" refers to the marked-down price, while the "price to be marked" indicates the higher price to which the *previously marked down merchandise* is being raised. Furthermore, when recording markdown cancellations, the serial number of the price change form on which the merchandise was originally marked down should be noted on the form on which the cancellation is being taken. It is interesting to note that in the case of one store using this particular type of price change report for four types of price changes, markdown cancellations must be indicated in red. The purpose of this requirement is, of course, to clearly differentiate markdown cancellations from other types of price changes. Form 7-2 is an example of a markdown cancellation in which 15 Orlon sweaters previously marked down to $4.99 are being marked up to $7.99.

Formula:

Net $ markdowns = $ Gross markdowns − $ markdown cancellations

Problem:

A Coat buyer reduced 36 untrimmed cloth coats for a special two-day sale from $150 to $119.99. Twenty-eight of the coats were sold during the sale. The day after the sale was over the remaining eight coats were returned to their original retail price. Determine:

(a) the amount of the gross markdown

(b) the amount of the markdown cancellation

(c) the amount of the net markdown

FORM 7-2 MARKDOWN CANCELLATION

Solution 1:

(a) Gross Markdown   = (Former price − markdown price) × number of pieces
         = ($150 − $119.99) × 36
         = $30.01 × 36
         = $1,080.36

Solution 2:

(b) Markdown Cancellation = (New price − former price) × number of pieces
         = ($150 − $119.99) × 8
         = $30.01 × 8
         = $240.08

Solution 3:

(c) Net Markdown   = Gross markdown − markdown cancellation
         = $1,080.36 − $240.08
         = $840.28

PRACTICE PROBLEMS—Markdowns and Markdown Cancellations

1. A buyer reduces four chairs from $119 to $88 each.

  (a) What is the amount of the dollar markdown?   (a) _____
                       (Answer)

  (b) What is the markdown as a percentage of the original price?   (b) _____
                       (Answer)

2. A Drapery buyer took markdowns during January of $1,460. If January sales amounted to $19,000, what was the markdown percentage for the month?

                       _____
                       (Answer)

3. A buyer reduced 38 sweaters from $40 to $29 each for a special two-day sale. During the sale 31 sweaters were sold and the remainder returned to their original price after the sale.

  (a) What was the original markdown in dollars?   (a) _____
                       (Answer)

  (b) What was the markdown cancellation in dollars?   (b) _____
                       (Answer)

(c) What was the net markdown taken?

(c) _____
(Answer)

4. The merchandise plan for a dress department indicated planned sales of $260,000 and planned markdowns of 9.2%.

(a) What was the planned dollar amount of markdowns?

(a) _____
(Answer)

(b) If actual markdowns taken amounted to $25,400, how did the actual percentage compare with plan, and by how much?

(b) _____
(Answer)

5. A Camera Shop buyer had 100 imported cameras in stock at $39.95. He reduced them to $20 for a special sales event and sold 60 at the reduced price. After the sale, he marked up the remaining 40 to $29.95 and sold them all at this price.

(a) What was his net markdown in dollars?

(a) _____
(Answer)

(b) What was the markdown percentage resulting from these transactions?

(b) _____
(Answer)

ADDITIONAL MARKUP

Sometimes it becomes necessary to adjust upward the price at which the merchandise is already priced and in stock.

When merchandise that is already in stock is considered as being priced too low and the buyer decides that (1) it should be marked higher than the traditional markup percent, or (2) there is an increase in wholesale costs or market value, or (3) when identical merchandise is being sold at a higher price by the competition, an *additional markup* may be taken to increase the retail (selling) price. Additional markup is taken always *after* and *in addition* to the original markup that was taken when the merchandise was first received into stock. Additional markup affects only the *retail* value of the merchandise (the cost is not involved because it already has been noted in the accounting records). Additional markup therefore represents an increase in the department's cumulative markup (the markup on total merchandise handled).

Additional markup is not a common type of adjustment in the retail value of inventory on hand. But when such an adjustment becomes necessary, it, too, can be recorded on a multipurpose price change form. Form 7-3 is an example of repricing 27 blouses that are being marked up from $11.99 to $13.00 each.

CANCELLATION OF ADDITIONAL MARKUP

In some cases it may be necessary to reduce the retail price of merchandise on which additional markup has previously been taken because (1) the competition is selling the same merchandise at a lower price, or (2) the merchandise is not selling at the additional markup price. This type of downward adjustment in the retail price of merchandise, however, is used *only* to offset a prior additional markup. It is used mainly to adjust the markup on a merchandise purchase in accordance with the buyer's original pricing intent or to reflect changing market conditions. It should *never* be used to manipulate inventory values. The effect is exactly the same as with a markdown cancellation—gross additional markups minus additional markup cancellations equal net additional markup.

FORM 7-3 ADDITIONAL MARKUP

Like markdown cancellations, markup cancellations may be recorded on multipurpose price change forms (see Form 7-4) and

- must show the price change form number of the additional markup being canceled in whole or in part;
- may never exceed the amount of such additional markups;
- usually must be taken within 90 days of the original additional markup.

EMPLOYEE DISCOUNTS

It is common practice for retail stores to grant a reduction in the retail price of merchandise to their employees and often to dependents of those employees as well. This type of reduction in price is known as an *Employee Discount* and is usually stated as a percentage off the marked retail price of merchandise. For example, if a store allows a 20% employee discount, an employee pays 20% less than the marked retail price for their purchases in the store.

The percentage of discount allowed full and part-time employees, as well as regular and temporary employees, varies from store to store. Often a larger discount is granted on apparel and accessories suitable for wear to work than the percentage granted on household, gift, or "big ticket" items.

There is no special form used for recording discounts allowed employees and other favored customer groups. Instead, such transactions are recorded on the store's regular saleschecks, regardless of whether it is a cash or a charge sale, or rung up on an electronic register indicating the amount of the discount.

							UNIT PRICE						RETAIL AMOUNT	

Smith & Welsh

MC

ORIGINAL WITH MERCHANDISE TO MARKING DEPT. OR DIRECT TO STATISTICAL IF MERCHANDISE MARKED BY DEPARTMENT.

PRICE CHANGE REPORT

Copy # Which Corresponds To Type Price Change into MC Block at Extreme Bottom of This Form.

1	MARK UP	To Increase Selling Price From Original Retail	
2	MARK DOWN	To Decrease Present Retail	
3	MARK DOWN CANCELLATION	To Cancel Previous MD. #(S)	
4	MARK UP CANCELLATION	To Cancel Previous MU #(S) 049645 *	

DIV'N # 5 | 9   DEPT. # 1 8 9   BR. DEPT. # —

DATE PRICE CHANGE EFFECTIVE 8/21/79

Give below period # in which price change to be used and explanation, as Nov. Clover, etc. VII

VENDOR NUMBER								SEASON LETTER	CLASSI-FICA-TION	REFERENCE NO.	PRESENT PRICE	PRICE TO BE MARKED	DIFF.	BUY COUNT	MARK COUNT	DESCRIPTION OF MERCHANDISE	DOLLARS	CENTS
0	0	8	1	2	9	5	9	T	2	181	13.00	11.99	1.01	4	4	Blouses	4 0	4

DEPT. MGR. SIGNATURE *Jane Doe*   DATE 8/21/79   TOTAL → 4 0 4

D. M. M. OR BR. MGR. SIG. *John Mann*   DATE 8/21/79   MARKING DIV'N. *June Evans*   DATE 8/22/79   See Inside Cover for Specific Rules Regarding Price Changes.

THIS PRICE CHANGE REPORT CANNOT BE PROCESSED UNLESS ALL BLOCKS AT TOP AND BOTTOM ARE FILLED IN CORRECTLY.

DO NOT GUESS - REFER TO COVER IF NECESSARY

MC 8 5   DEPT. # 4 1 8 9   HASH TOTAL 1 0 4 1   FOR ACCOUNTING USE ONLY 4 0 4

*Previous Markup sheet number.   RED MUST be used for MU Cancellations   049646

FORM 7-4 ADDITIONAL MARKUP CANCELLATION

The procedure is to record for each such transaction the following information:

- employee name and store identification number;
- appropriate description of each item of merchandise being purchased;
- the marked retail price of each item;
- the percentage and dollar amount of discount allowed;
- the net cost to the purchaser;
- sales tax (if any) is calculated on the discounted price of the goods.

Since under the manual system the store's Sales Audit department receives a copy of all saleschecks, the amount of discount allowed on employee and other favored-customer-group purchases can be tabulated by departments, the information forwarded to the Statistical department, and the selling department's book inventory adjusted downward by an identical amount.

Problem:

Assume that Miller's Menswear Shop allows its employees a 20% discount on their purchases. If Jack Smith, a salesman, purchased a shirt marked $10, how much would he actually pay for the shirt and how would the sale be recorded?

Solution:

1 shirt, class C, size 15½-32, white	$10.00
Employee No. 144, less 20%	− 2.00
Net amount	$ 8.00
Sales tax, 5%	+ .40
Paid in cash	$ 8.40

Were an employee discount sale to be written or rung up solely in the basis of the net amount of the sale, an inventory shortage equal to the amount of the discount would have been created.

Many retailers also grant a percentage discount off the marked price of purchases made by certain "favored" groups of customers, such as the clergy, charitable organizations, the diplomatic and consular corps, and so on. The rate of discount extended in such cases is usually less than that granted to employees—generally about 10%. As in the case of employee discounts, a record must be made of each such discounted transaction so that the retail value of the selling department's book inventory can be properly adjusted and an inventory shortage forestalled.

Employee and favored-customer discounts reduce maintained markup and gross margin because they reduce the spread between the cost of the merchandise and the retail price at which that merchandise is actually sold—just as markdowns do.

PRACTICE PROBLEMS—Additional Markup,
Cancellation of Additional Markup,
Employee Discounts

1. A week after a buyer had received a shipment of 24 decorative pillows and had then marked $8.95 each, she discovered that a competitor was selling identical pillows at $9.95 each. If the buyer decided to remark her merchandise to $9.95:

   (a) What is the price change called? (a) _____

   (Answer)

(b) Illustrate the procedure that would be involved in the price change.

2. Several days after a group of 14 photograph albums were received into stock, it was discovered that they had been erroneously marked $6.50 each instead of $5.00 each. Explain the procedure involved in correcting this error.

3. Explain the basic difference between markup and additional markup.

4. If a store allowed its employees a 25% discount on all merchandise purchased, what would an employee pay for a pair of shoes that retails for $28?

_____
(Answer)

5. If the state in which the store above was located had a 4% sales tax, what would the employee actually pay for this pair of shoes?

_____
(Answer)

6. The Ladies' Aid Society of a local church bought 50 yards of fabric retailing at $1.89 a yard, which they intended to make up as curtains for their Fellowship Room. If the store allowed a 10% discount on all purchases by charitable or nonprofit groups, how much did the group pay for this purchase?

_____
(Answer)

7. Do you think a sales tax would be charged on this purchase? Defend your answer.

SUMMARY OF KEY TERMS

Additional Markup. An increase in the retail price of in-stock merchandise above that at which it was marked when it was received.

Cancellation of Additional Markup. A reduction in the retail price to offset a prior additional markup.

Dollar Markdown. The difference between the new lower price to which merchandise is marked and its former retail price.

Early Markdowns. Refers to the policy of taking markdowns on merchandise as soon as its rate of sale starts to decline, or, in some cases, after the merchandise has been in stock a specified period of time.

Employee Discount. A percentage discount off the marked price of merchandise allowed by most stores to their employees and the latter's dependents.

Favored-Customer Discount. A percentage discount allowed off the marked price of merchandise purchased by charitable and/or nonprofit organizations.

House Number. An identifying number code assigned by a store to each of its various vendors. This vendor or "house" number appears on most price tickets in order to indicate the source of the merchandise.

Late Markdowns. Refers to the policy of taking markdowns semiannually or after the end of a selling season.

Markdown. A downward revision in the retail price at which an item or group of items is currently marked.

Markdown Cancellation. An upward price adjustment on merchandise that had previously been marked down.

Price Adjustment. Adjustments that either increase or decrease the retail price at which merchandise is presently marked.

REVIEW QUESTIONS—Repricing Merchandise

1. What kind of price change should be written in each of the following situations?

   (a) 150 suits were purchased at the same cost, but 25 of them looked like better values, so the department manager decided to raise their retail price $10.00 each.

   _____

   (b) One month later the 25 suits were still on hand, so the department manager decided to lower the retail by $5.00 each.

   _____

   (c) Four hundred pairs of slippers were purchased for a sale and retailed at $7.99 rather than the regular $8.95. After the sale, the 200 remaining pairs were marked at $8.95.

   _____

   (d) A Coat buyer had 25 slow sellers in the $99.95 price line and reduced them to $89.95.

   _____

   (e) Out of 1,500 towels reduced from $2.95 to $2.49 for a sale, 500 remained when the sale was over and were marked back up to the original price.

   _____

2. Markdowns are expressed as a percent of _____ or _____.

3. Give four major reasons for taking markdowns.

   (1)

   (2)

   (3)

   (4)

4. Name three common causes of markdowns and give two examples of each.

(1)

    (a)

    (b)

(2)

    (a)

    (b)

(3)

    (a)

    (b)

REVIEW PROBLEMS—Repricing Merchandise

1. Compute the markdown percentage from the following figures:

Markdowns	$ 15,000
Markdowns cancellations	5,000
Gross sales	220,000
Customer returns	20,000

_____
(Answer)

2. Gross volume in the Hosiery Department last week was $97,000. Employee discounts and customer returns were each $700. Markdowns for the week amounted to $6,300. What was the markdown percentage for last week?

_____
(Answer)

3. The following merchandise was purchased by a salesgirl at Martin's where employees get a 20% discount on merchandise that can be worn during store hours and a 10% discount on any other merchandise purchases. What was the total cost to the employee of this purchase?

2 slips	@ $6.98 each
3 pantyhose	@ $3.00 each
2 pajamas	@ $7.98 each

_____
(Answer)

4. A buyer reduced 95 coats from $100 to $69 for a one-day special sales event. After the event the remaining 58 coats were remarked to the original price.

(a) What was the dollar amount of the markdown cancellation?   (a) _____
                                                                     (Answer)

(b) What was the dollar amount of the net markdowns?   (b) _____
                                                             (Answer)

5. A buyer authorized the following markdowns during September:

> 80 blouses from $9.00 to $5.99
> 115 blouses from $8.00 to $5.99
> 85 blouses from $7.00 to $4.99

Sales volume in the department for the month was $40,000. What was the markdown percentage for September?

_____
(Answer)

6. Markdowns amounted to 3.5% in August. The dollar amount was $8,750. What were the August net sales?

_____
(Answer)

7. The Housewares buyer marked down 112 of the $9.98 wastepaper baskets in stock to $6.99 for a special sale. After the sale the 37 remaining baskets were returned to their original price. What was the dollar net markdown?

_____
(Answer)

8. A buyer purchased 90 lightweight jackets at $15.50 each and retailed them at $30. Three weeks later her unit control records showed that only one-fifth of the jacket had been sold so she decided to reduce the price. What would be the lowest retail price to which she could mark the remaining jackets and still achieve an average markup of 42%?

_____
(Answer)

9. The slacks sales volume in the Boys' Department last month was $9,670. Early in the month the buyer authorized markdowns of 156 pairs of corduroy slacks from $7.98 to $4.99. Later, however, 57 pairs of these slacks were remarked to their original price. What was the markdown percentage for slacks last month?

_____
(Answer)

10. Employee discounts in December amounted to 4.25% or $19,550. What were the net sales in December?

_____
(Answer)

CHAPTER 8

INVENTORY CONTROL:
devices and procedures

"Inventory," as indicated in Chapter 3, is the trade term for stock on hand, the composite of all the individual units of merchandise a merchant has purchased from a variety of vendors and assembled in convenient locations for the purpose of profitable resale to ultimate consumers.

Retail inventories tend to be subject to more rapid obsolescence and more vulnerable to theft both from within and without the organization than are the inventories of most other types of business firms. For these reasons acquiring and maintaining retail inventories involve considerable financial risk and therefore must be closely controlled and subject to continual evaluation if a reasonable profit from sales of that inventory is to result.

CHARACTERISTICS OF RETAIL INVENTORIES

Retail inventories have certain distinctive characteristics that because of their nature require closer controls than do the inventories of other types of business inventories. For example, they:

- represent by far the *major portion of each retail firm's total assets,* as compared to its other business assets, such as real estate, fixtures, equipment, and so on;
- *fluctuate widely in value* from month to month and season to season, depending on the extent of customer demand for each of the various types of merchandise involved (some have been known to vary as much as 30% up or down from the average inventory value for the year);
- are subject to *constant change in composition* (new items are constantly being added and old ones dropped) because of continuous technological advances and changing consumer demand due to changing tastes and life styles;

189

- are *extremely diversified,* being made up of hundreds to thousands of different stockkeeping units, each with marked differences in relation to all other items, especially with regard to type, markup, and rate of sale. (This is the basic reason why merchandise is usually segregated into departments for purposes of better control of stock in relation to sales, as well as quicker identification of specific centers of consumer demand.);
- are *predominately perishable and short-lived* (true not only of obviously fashion-influenced items but also of many types of staple goods that significantly deteriorate in value over a period of time or become obsolete as newer versions of the item come on the market), and for this reason merchandise markdowns become a major offset to retail profit and require close control;
- are *more vulnerable to theft* by shoplifters, as well as *pilferage by employees* than are the inventories of other types of business firms. (Adequate safeguards against shoplifting and pilferage are difficult and expensive to maintain because of the nature of the merchandise and the fact that it is usually stored and displayed in locations to which both the general public and employees have easy to fairly easy access.)

In view of these and other distinctive characteristics of retail inventories, their control presents a major problem to most retailers.

IMPORTANCE OF INVENTORY CONTROL AND VALUATION

Because of the high degree of risk involved in the acquisition and adequacy of retail inventories it is of utmost importance that both the dollar value and the composition of stocks be closely controlled at all times in relation to sales if a desired profit is to result.

Objectives of Inventory Control

The major objectives of retail inventory control are:

- to maintain an inventory that is at all times neither too large nor too small in relation to customer demand;
- to time the delivery of purchases so that merchandise is available for sale neither too early nor too late in relation to demand;
- to keep purchases in line with the firm's ability to pay for them; and
- to have sufficient funds available at all times for the purchase of new or reorder goods as these may be needed.

Activities Involved

Inventory control involves the following activities:

- assigning a retail price to each item at the time it is first received into stock;
- maintaining current, accurate records of the cost and retail values of the inventory on hand at the beginning of each accounting period, as well as additions to that inventory as these occur throughout the period;
- repricing various items of stock on hand as such price changes are deemed necessary;

- counting the on-hand inventory at regular intervals during each 12-month period, or at least at the end of each accounting year;
- conducting continuous evaluation of stock on hand and on order in relation to both planned and actual sales and stock figures.

Valuation of the Closing Inventory

It is important to remember that, as indicated in Chapter 6, the retail price placed on merchandise involves consideration of a number of factors other than just the price at which the goods were purchased and/or the initial or purchase markup goal. Other factors that should be considered in inventory valuation are:

- the condition of the goods;
- current market values; and
- replacement value.

The value placed on inventory is important because of its effect on gross margin and, in turn, on operating profit, as we learned in Chapter 3. For example, if the cost value of the closing inventory is *overstated,* the cost of merchandise sold for the period will be too small, and, in turn, gross margin and operating profit will be overstated. Overstated profits result in:

- payment of unnecessarily high income taxes and insurance premiums;
- unjustified capital expenditures;
- distribution as profits of the monies based on an overstatement of the value of stock on hand—in other words, "paper profit."

On the other hand, if the cost value of the closing inventory is *understated,* the cost of merchandise sold during the period will be overstated and gross margin and operating profit will be understated. Underevaluation of inventory value creates a type of hidden-profit reserve in case net sales and gross margin are less than anticipated. Understatement may, however, lead to an unnecessary curtailment of operating expenses because of understated gross margin.[1]

METHODS OF INVENTORY VALUATION

There are many different approaches to the problem of how an inventory should be valued. Those of most importance to retailers are:

1. The FIFO (first in, first out) method;
2. The LIFO (last in, first out) method;
3. The Cost-or-Market (whichever is lower) method;
4. The Original-Cost method;
5. The Retail method.[2]

[1] John W. Wingate, Elmer O. Schaller, and F. Leonard Miller, *Retail Merchandise Management* (Englewood Cliffs, N.J.: Prentice-Hall, Inc., 1972) pp. 185-86.
[2] Ibid., p. 187.

FIFO.   In evaluating inventory when the cost price is not recorded on price tickets and different portions of the stock have been purchased at different prices, the assumption is made that:

- the goods bought first are sold first,
- the most recent purchases are still in stock;
- their costs represent the cost of *all* items in the closing inventory.

LIFO.   In evaluating inventory by the LIFO method, the assumption is made that the customer who purchases an article from stock is buying an article the cost of which may not necessarily be the original cost of the item but what its current replacement would cost. Therefore, under this method the closing inventory is based on replacement cost.

Cost-or-Market.   Under the Cost-or-Market method, each unit of merchandise in the closing inventory is valued at either its original cost or its current market value, whichever is *lower.*

Original-Cost.   Under this method, each unit of merchandise in the closing inventory is valued at its original cost.

Retail Method.   Under this method, each unit of merchandise in the closing inventory is valued at its marked retail price.

Of these five inventory valuation methods, only the Original-Cost and Retail methods are described herein. The first three methods are chiefly the concern of professional accountants and outside the scope of this text.

The Retail Method

The Retail method of inventory valuation, usually referred to simply as the *Retail method,* is a method of merchandising accounting that makes it possible to approximate:

(1)   the total retail value of the inventory that should be on hand at any given time; and

(2)   the total cost value of that inventory without having to determine the cost of each individual item making up the inventory.

The Retail method is essentially a system for departmental rather than storewide inventory control because it is based on the assumption that the items making up the inventory are homogeneous in type and markup. As such, it is accepted today as standard accounting procedure in most departmentized retail organizations, because it provides merchants with the immediate information they need to:

- maintain satisfactory and on-going control of their merchandise inventories;
- be able to appraise and evaluate their merchandising operations on a continuing basis;
- identify problem areas so that appropriate remedial action can be taken before it is too late to rectify the situation.

More importantly, they are able to accomplish all this without having to resort to the taking of frequent, time-consuming, and costly physical inventory to provide the information.

Procedures.   Under the Retail method, each selling department is considered a separate accounting unit for which separate records are kept of the cost and retail values of the department's merchandise inventory, as well as data relating to departmental operating expenses and profit.

The Retail method involves:

(1) determining the total retail value of a department's inventory at the beginning of each accounting by either:
   (a) taking a physical inventory of merchandise on hand at retail value by listing each item at its marked retail price, and then totaling the listings, or
   (b) the Book Inventory method (obtained from various accounting records such as sales, purchases, and so on).
(2) keeping a perpetual (continuous) record of both the cost and retail values of the beginning inventory as well as additions to that inventory as these occur throughout a given period (total merchandise handled);
(3) determining the cumulative markup percentage on the total merchandise handled during the period (total retail minus total cost divided by total retail);
(4) deriving an estimated cost value of the ending inventory by means of the cumulative markup percentage (multiplying the total retail value of the inventory by the cost complement of the cumulative markup percentage).

Advantages. The major advantage of the Retail method is that it provides the means for calculating cost of merchandise sold without having to determine what was actually paid for each item in stock or its current market value. Since a determination of cost of merchandise sold must be made before gross margin and net operating profit or loss can be calculated (see Chapter 3), it becomes obvious that under the Retail method, departmental gross margin and net operating profit or loss may be estimated *at any time,* without having to actually count and list the stock on hand—that is, take physical inventory.

Other advantages of the Retail method are that it:

- simplifies and makes more accurate the taking of physical inventory and the preparation of budgets;
- provides for maintaining a perpetual Book Inventory system which is useful in planning purchases and obtaining a desired rate of stock turnover;
- facilitates the determination of stock shortages (see Chapter 9);
- makes possible a quick determination of inventory value for insurance purposes in case of fire or other type of loss.

The Original-Cost Method

Under the *Original-Cost* method of accounting, each item of merchandise received into stock is recorded at its billed cost, plus transportation cost, if known. And when price tickets are made up, the cost price of each item is usually indicated on the ticket in coded form or by a serial or reference number that refers to a separate cost record, such as an invoice, a purchase order, a cost journal entry, or a unit control record.

In order to determine the total cost of merchandise sold and ultimately gross margin and operating profit under the Cost method, the cost value of each item in the stock on hand as of a given date must first be determined and the individual costs totaled in order to arrive at the total cost value of the closing inventory. This figure is then subtracted from the cost value of the total merchandise handled during the preceding period in order to obtain the cost of merchandise sold during the period.

While the Retail method is the most widely used inventory valuation method today, it should be recognized that in some types of retail organizations, the older Cost method has been found to be more satisfactory than the Retail method, primarily because of significant differences in types of merchandise and the merchandising operations in various types of stores. For example, small stores or shops are usually not broken down into departments. Their buyers and/or store managers spend a good deal of time on the selling floor and in record keeping, and are in a position to judge the adequacy of the inventory on a day-by-day basis. Moreover, since the size of the inventory and the number of daily sales transactions are usually limited in such stores, so are their inventory control problems.

Furniture and appliance stores may be other exceptions to users of the Retail method. The type of merchandise handled in such stores is rarely subject to rapid or abrupt style change. Furthermore, the unit price of each item offered for sale is usually large, and the number of sales transactions per day is usually small in comparison to many other types of stores. Relatively little merchandise is sold "off the floor" because most of the items found there are usually considered samples. Generally, the bulk of the inventory is either stored in a warehouse or ordered directly from the factory after sales from the sample have been made. Inasmuch as the inventory control problem in such stores is limited, they usually find the Cost method a more satisfactory accounting system.

Other firms engaged in retailing such perishable products as fruit, vegetables, and flowers also find the Cost method more suitable because of the limited assortments and the extremely short "shelf life" of these types of products.

BASIC CONTROL DEVICES

As indicated earlier, retail merchandising includes the functions of both planning and control. The seasonal merchandise plan, as discussed in Chapter 4, is the retailer's major *planning* tool. The open-to-buy, also discussed in Chapter 4, is the retailer's major *control* tool once the preplanned season gets under way.

The two methods in general use today for helping retailers maintain stocks in a desired ratio to sales are known as (1) dollar control and (2) unit control. *Dollar control* refers to any type of system for recording stock and sales information in terms of dollar value and from which a variety of merchandising reports can be drawn. *Unit control* refers to any system for recording stock and sales information in terms of individual units of merchandise from which a variety of reports can be drawn.

Dollar Control

The seasonal merchandise plan is the basis of dollar inventory control throughout the season with the major elements being planned in dollars, while the supplemental elements are planned in relation to the net sales projection for the period.

Purpose. The major purpose of dollar control is to make certain that the dollar investment in the E.O.M. inventory does not exceed the planned figures as indicated in the seasonal plan. Once a season begins, the dollar plan for each of the various elements becomes their goal—the figure objective to be achieved and against which actual results are measured.

Control Devices. In order to maintain an effective and continuing control over inventory values, it is essential that frequent periodic reports on the results of current operations, as compared to planned projections, be prepared, analyzed, and evaluated with corrective action instituted as may be required. The chief and most frequently prepared dollar inventory control device is *open-to-buy* as discussed in Chapters 4 and 10. Other important dollar inventory control devices are:

1. buying plans (this chapter);
2. physical inventory reports (this chapter);

3. vendor analyses (Chapter 10);
4. markdown analyses (Chapter 10);
5. on-order reports (Chapter 4);
6. open-to-buy reports (Chapters 4 and 10);
7. slow-selling stock analyses (Chapters 8 and 10);
8. departmental operating statements (Chapter 10);
9. periodic sales and stock summaries (Chapter 10).

Since profit is universally expressed in terms of dollars, dollar control is the method preferred by most merchandise managers and controllers for regulating the activities of their buyers. Management executives want to make sure that the dollar value of sales achieved, markdowns taken, purchases committed for, inventories carried, average markup realized, direct expenses incurred, and other objectives are in line with each seasonal plan so that an operating profit will result. The success of department managers and buyers is largely measured in terms of how well they have achieved the dollar objectives indicated on each season's merchandise plan.

Unit Control

The term *unit control* refers to any system established by store management for recording the number of units of merchandise, each with certain specific characteristics, that are on order, have been received, sold, and are on hand, and from which system a variety of merchandising reports can be drawn. It is important to remember that unit control is a *merchandising tool,* not an accounting procedure.

Unit control is concerned with the unit items comprising an inventory assortment—the specifics of what and how much to buy within the limits imposed by dollar control. Accounting is concerned with the dollar cost and retail values of the total inventory investment.

Actually, the term "unit control" is somewhat of a misnomer, since any unit control system is not intended to exert "control" in and of itself. Perhaps a better term would be "unit records." Reports drawn from such records provide merchants with a variety of valuable, current, detailed information on sales, stock on hand, and on order in terms of units of merchandise, each with certain characteristics. This is information that dollar control cannot provide. With the availability of the type of information a unit control system can provide, retailers are better able to:

- see how closely their assortments are meeting customer demand;
- see how closely actual results are following planned projections;
- identify problem areas in the inventory assortment requiring prompt remedial action.

Purpose. The purpose of unit control is to so control buying that individual units of merchandise comprising the inventory assortment will be stocked in proportion to their individual rate of sale. For example, suppose that a China and Glassware Department had an inventory valued at $50,000. Although this inventory value may be well within the dollar limits of the department's seasonal merchandise plan, it does not indicate what the assortment consists of or how well it is balanced to the rate of sale of each of its various components. An effective unit control system for recording and reporting sales and stock information at regular intervals is the only means by which inventory content can be analyzed and evaluated. Dollar figures alone do not supply the needed information.

Unit control systems are used to assist buyers and department managers in isolating and identifying centers of demand around which properly balanced inventory assortments can be built or reshaped. Systems vary in format from store to store and from one type of merchandise to another. They also vary in the methods used for collecting and reporting data, as well as the amount of detail collected.

Some merchandise requires more detailed control than do others. For example, basic or staple goods (merchandise that is relatively slow to show style change or that which has a relatively steady rate of sale over a fairly long period of time) require a less detailed system of control than does ready-to-wear. High-unit-price merchandise, such as Furs or Furniture or Fine Jewelry, usually requires a system that includes much more detailed information than does low unit price merchandise, such as Notions or Greeting Cards.

Regardless of the system used or the type of merchandise involved, any unit control system is set up to show the following:

- net sales in number of units;
- stock on hand and on order in number of units;
- further dissection of stock and sales information in whatever detail is considered necessary to provide the essential facts needed to maintain an inventory assortment well balanced to rate of sale. Examples of further dissection are cost and retail price, vendor, classification, style number, size, and color.

Classifications. The first step in setting up a unit control system is to subdivide the department's or store's inventory into classifications based on the intended end use of each type of merchandise that is usually carried in each department's stock. A *classification* is defined by the National Retail Merchants Association as "an assortment of units or items of merchandise which are all reasonably substitutable for each other."[3]

The inventories of most selling departments are composed of a variety of types of merchandise, each of which, though generally related in nature, is intended for a somewhat different end-use purpose. For example, the various types of merchandise usually carried in a Women's Sportswear Department are slacks, shorts, shirts, sweaters, swim and beachwear, and so on. Each of these are distinctive types of merchandise that are regarded by customers as "Sportswear" yet they are nonsubstitutable as far as end-use purpose is concerned. For this reason, each type of merchandise is designated as a separate classification for purposes of unit as well as dollar sales and stock planning and control purposes. Similarly, a Men's Furnishings Department usually carries such nonsubstitutable types of merchandise as dress shirts, sportshirts, underwear, hosiery, sleepwear, jewelry, and cosmetics. In this case, too, each type of "Furnishings" is considered a separate, distinctive classification for which separate unit control records are kept and reports based on those records are drawn up. Generally broad classifications are subdivided into subclassifications, indicating more specific demand centers. For example, men's sportshirts might be subclassified as to short or long sleeves, sleepwear as to pajamas or nightshirts, jewelry as to tie tacs, stick pins, collar pins, bracelets, and so on.

Types of Systems. There are two basic types of unit control systems in use today for the recording of sales and stock data. These are known as:

(1) *perpetual control* (running or continuous entries made) and
(2) *periodic stock count control* (counts made at regular intervals).

The types of merchandise for which each is best suited and the procedures involved in maintaining each are described below.

Perpetual control. In this type of unit control system, separate records are kept by manual or machine means for each style by number, vendor, classification, cost price, retail

---

[3] *NRMA Standard Classification of Merchandise,* 2nd ed. (New York: Merchandising Division, National Retail Merchants Association, 1969), p. 15.

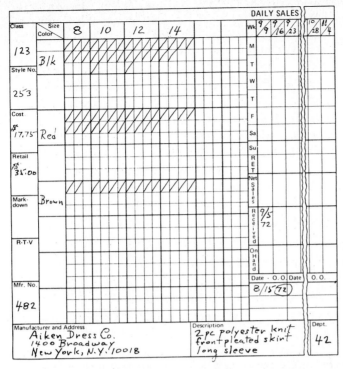

FORM 8-1A PERPETUAL UNIT CONTROL CARD:
STOCK RECEIVED (Manual System)

Mary D. Troxell, *Fashion Merchandising*, 2nd ed. (New York: Gregg
Division, McGraw-Hill, 1976), p. 257.

price, and brief description. Purchase orders, receipts of merchandise, customer returns, and sales, are recorded in terms of units as these transactions occur and stock on hand is computed.

In manual systems the number of units on order for each style are indicated by hand on a specially prepared record card or sheet by size and color, if these distinctions are important (see Form 8-1A). Merchandise on order entries are made from each purchase order at the time the order is written. Form 8-1B is an E.D.P. unit control purchase report after identical information from purchase orders is fed into a computer.

In a manual unit control system, the number of units on order in each color and size may be indicated on the style sheet or card by a single dot for each unit ordered. When merchandise is received against a P.O., each dot representing a unit on order is elongated into a slanting line to indicate that the merchandise formerly on order is now in stock. Dots that have not been changed into lines indicate merchandise that is still on order.

Sales of each style are recorded daily as these occur in a perpetual unit control system. Data on each sale may be obtained from a stub of the price ticket that is removed at the time of purchase, or from information recorded on duplicates of saleschecks, or from cash register tapes. Each sale is indicated by X-ing out an appropriate line on the item's style card or sheet. Customer returns are reentered in stock by making new slanting lines on the proper style card by size and color, if applicable. Units on order for each style are easily determined by counting the number of dots on each style card. Stock on hand in units can be quickly determined at any time by subtracting net unit sales from total units received to date.

Thus on Form 8-2 all purchase orders placed, receipts of merchandise, and sales are recorded as these occurred from August 5 through September 24, and stock on hand computed as follows:

Gross sales in units 9/11 thru 9/24	46
− Customer returns in units	− 0
= Net sales in units	46

Beginning stock on hand in units	0
+ Merchandise received during period	+72
= Total merchandise handled in units	72
− Net sales in units	−46
= Stock on hand in units	26
= Stock remaining on order in units	3

This system eliminates the need for taking actual stock counts other than annual or semiannual physical inventory. At that time, records of the actual number of units of merchandise on hand by classification, vendor, and style number (as indicated in the unit control records) are corrected to agree with the physical inventory count at the beginning of each new accounting period.

The merchandise for which perpetual unit control systems are best suited include:

- goods that are subject to frequent style change;
- good that are high or relatively high in unit price;
- goods in which acceptance of specific design features and color must be carefully watched;
- goods that have an irregular rate of sale.

Periodic stock count control. Under this system stock on hand is counted at regular weekly intervals and sales for the intervening period are computed. This is in direct contrast to the perpetual system, in which sales are recorded as they occur and stock on hand can be computed as required (see Forms 8-3A and 8-3B).

In this type of unit control system, departmental stock is first divided up into smaller areas and stock counts in each of these areas scheduled to be taken at certain regular weekly intervals.

In periodic stock count control, a count of the number of units on hand, by style or group of similarly priced merchandise, is made at specified weekly intervals and the results usually recorded on specially prepared style sheets kept in a loose leaf binder.

The department buyer or manager determines for each style or group of styles the maximum and minimum quantities that should be on hand at any time if there is to be enough stock to satisfy the anticipated rate of sale of each item. Additional units are ordered after counts have been made to bring the total stock on hand and on order up to the maximum desired.

The procedures for keeping periodic stock count unit control records are as follows:

- Stock on hand is counted at the end of each specified time period and the count recorded in the appropriate On Hand (O.H.) column on the record sheet.
- The number of units of merchandise needed to bring the stock up to the maximum amount desired is ordered and recorded in the O.O. column.
- Merchandise that has been received since the previous count was made is recorded as quantity received and the merchandise on order figure adjusted accordingly.
- Stock on hand is counted and recorded at the end of the next stock-taking period.
- Sales for the interval between counts are determined by adding the units of merchandise on hand at the previous count to the units received into stock

SELLING PRICE	CLASS	HOUSE	STYLE	STORE	NET STORE TOTALS	CODE	06	08	10	12	14	16	18
48.00	40	011	3003	A	18	02	2	3	4	4	3	2	
					25	04	3	3	8	6	3	2	
					16	22	1	4	5	5	1		
				B	24	35	3	4	5	5	4	3	
					10	02	1	2	2	2	2		
					6	04			3	3			
					5	35	1	1	1	1	1		
				C	10	02	1	2	2	2	2	1	
					8	04	1	2	2	2	1		
					8	22	1	1	2	2	1		1
			135		5	35	1	1	1	1	1		
38.00	82	041	0437	B	6	47		1	1	2	1	1	
28.00	53	042	2124	A	8	01			2	2	2	1	1
					13	02		1	3	3	3	2	1
				D	8	01		1	2	2	2	1	
				B	7	01		1	2	2	1	1	
					7	02		1	1	2	2	1	
				C	8	01		1	1	2	2	1	
			55		4	02		1	1		1	1	
38.00	53	042	2130	A	10	01		1	3	3	2		1
			22		12	02	2	1	3	3	2		1
32.00	82	042	2137	A	22	04		2	4	6	5	4	1
					16	26		2	3	4	4	3	
				D	8	04		1	1	2	2	2	
				B	8	04		1	2	2	2	1	
					6	26			1	2	2	1	
				C	1	00							
					4	04					2	1	
			71		6	26		1	2	2	1		
38.00	40	042	2138	A	16	04		2	3	4	4	3	
					12	26		2	3	4		3	
				D	8	26		1	2	2	2	1	
				B	8	04		1	2	2	2	1	
					8	26		1	2	2	2	1	
				C	8	04		1	2	2	2	1	
			67		7	26			2	2	2	1	
50.00	40	054	0305	A	14	02			3	4	4	3	
58.00	40	054	0311	A	1	00							
			8		7	02		1	2	2	2		
58.00	73	054	4124	A	15	40	2	2	3	3	3	2	

FORM 8-1B UNIT CONTROL PURCHASE REPORT (E.D.P. System)

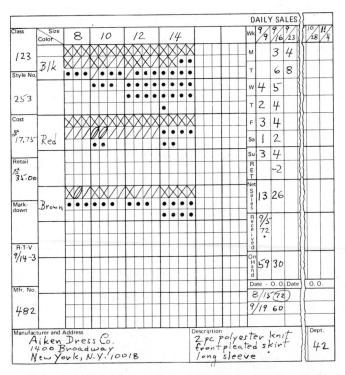

FORM 8-2 PERPETUAL UNIT CONTROL CARD: SALES,
STOCK ON HAND, AND STOCK ON ORDER
(Manual System)

Mary D. Troxell, *Fashion Merchandising,* 2nd ed. (New York: Gregg Division, McGraw-Hill, 1976). p. 257.

Department No.	15									

Vendor Ricci Glove Company
Gloversville, New York

Ship via Lee Transport

Manufacturer No. 102

Terms 6/10/E.O.M.

Class	Style	Cost	Unit Retail	Description	Color	Min. Pack	Coverage	
							Weeks	Units
268	140	17.50 dz.	$3.00	Stretch glove	White	1 dz.	6	36
268	140	17.50 dz.	$3.00	Stretch glove	Black	1 dz.	6	24
268	140	17.50 dz.	$3.00	Stretch glove	Beige	1 dz.	6	24

FORM 8-3A PERIODIC STOCK COUNT CONTROL

Mary D. Troxell, *Fashion Merchandising*, 2nd ed. (New York: Gregg Division, McGraw-Hill, 1976), p. 260.

since that count, and subtracting from this total the number of units on hand at the current count. The difference is recorded as the number of units sold during the period between counts.

Expressed as a formula:

$$
\begin{array}{lr}
\text{Stock as of previous count in units} & 36 \\
\text{+ Merchandise receipts since previous count} & +24 \\
\hline
\text{= Total merchandise handled in units} & 60 \\
\text{− Stock on hand at present count in units} & -30 \\
\hline
\text{= Sales for period in units} & 30 \\
\end{array}
$$

This system eliminates the need for actual stock counts to be taken more frequently than for the annual or semiannual physical inventory. After the latter are made, however, each on-hand "book" stock count is corrected to agree with the physical inventory count.

The merchandise for which periodic stock count control is best suited include goods that:

- have a relatively constant weekly rate of sale over an extended period of time;
- are moderate to moderately low in price, such as men's, women's, and children's hosiery or notions;
- are subject to a degree of fashion change (but not as readily as ready-to-wear), such as bed, bath, and table linens;
- are readily reorderable with short delivery periods;
- do not lend themselves to easy tagging by print-punch or multipart tickets, such as China and Glassware, Cosmetics, and grocery items.

There are two other unit control systems less frequently used, both based on the periodic stock count system. One is known as reserve requisition control, the other as visual (sometimes referred to as "eyeball") control.

Reserve requisition control. In a *reserve requisition system* only the back (reserve)

Department	15
Manufacturer No.	102

		Date 5/3				Date 5/17				Date 5/31			
Class	Style	O.H.	O.O. 5/6	Rec. 5/14	Sold	O.H.	O.O. 5/20	Rec. 5/28	Sold	O.H.	O.O. 6/2	Rec. 6/10	Sold
268	140 White	20	(12)	12	10	22	(12)	12	12	22	(12)	12	
268	140 Black	20			8	12	(12)	12	4	20			
268	140 Beige	30			10	20			8	12	(12)	12	

FORM 8-3B PERIODIC STOCK COUNT CONTROL

Mary D. Troxell, *Fashion Merchandising*, 2nd ed. (New York: Gregg Division, McGraw-Hill, 1976), p. 261.

stock—that held in the stockroom or warehouse—is counted. All merchandise on the selling floor (known as "forward stock") is considered sold. Reserve merchandise is counted at regular intervals, merchandise on order and received is recorded on appropriate style cards or sheets, and sales are computed either from the difference between the last and the current counts or by totalling up the stock requisitions for merchandise that has been delivered to the selling floor from the stockroom during the period between counts.

This method is best suited for boxed, prepackaged, or bulky merchandise, such as ladies' conventional hosiery and pantyhose, diapers, toys, sheets and pillowcases, furniture, and bedding.

Visual control. In the *visual system* no records are kept. Stock is checked by visual verification or occasional stock counts to see if the amount on hand is enough, too much, or needs replenishing. Visual or eyeball control is best suited for small, specialized stocks where variety is paramount and few of a kind of each item is ever kept in stock.

Unit Plans and O.T.B.

Dollar and unit control are interacting control measures. Unit control provides the means for making dollar control more effective. Plans made in dollars can be readily checked against actual operations in units.

Retailers are finding that the most meaningful dollar merchandise plans are those that have been "built up" from unit plans, that is, by first planning sales, B.O.M. stocks, and purchases in units by classification and price line, and then converting those unit figures into dollars. This is particularly true in the case of fashion departments, where close control of stocks in relation to rate of sale is of primary importance because of the fluctuating nature of demand for such goods.

Units can be readily translated into dollar amounts by multiplying the number of units at each price point by the applicable dollar figure. For example, assume that there is on hand in Classification 12 the following number of units at the indicated price points:

> 60 units at $ 5.00 each
> 90 units at $ 8.00 each
> 40 units at $10.00 each

By multiplying the number of units at each price point by the appropriate dollar figure, the dollar value of stock on hand in Classification 12 is found to be $1,420.00, as follows:

$$
\begin{array}{rcl}
60 \times \$5.00 &=& \$ 300.00 \\
90 \times \$8.00 &=& \$ 720.00 \\
40 \times \$10.00 &=& \underline{\$ 400.00} \\
\text{Total} & & \$1,420.00
\end{array}
$$

With dollar limitations on inventories, buyers and department managers find it easier to maintain a proper dollar balance among their many purchases throughout each accounting period if dollar plans are based on unit plans by classification and price line. Furthermore, unit-based plans represent a more realistic control device, since customers make their purchases in units of merchandise and buyers select and order merchandise for resale in terms of units with varying characteristics, to retail at various predetermined price lines.

Once a seasonal merchandise plan has been developed in terms of units by classification and price line, unit O.T.B. for the department as a whole or by classification can be readily calculated. The same formula as that used for calculating dollar O.T.B. is used for calculating unit O.T.B. Units are merely substituted for dollars. For example:

Planned net sales in units	= 1,000
+ Planned markdowns in units	+ 100
+ Planned closing inventory in units	+ 1,500
= Total stock requirements in units	= 2,600
− Inventory on hand in units	− 1,300
= Planned purchases in units	= 1,300
− Commitments this month in units	− 900
= Open-To-Buy current month in units	= 400

Dollar control is the method preferred by most merchandise managers and other management executives for regulating the activities of buyers and department managers. The latter, on the other hand, are guided in their day-to-day operations chiefly by unit plans and records, even though their buying and selling activities are evaluated on the basis of how well they have met departmental dollar objectives.

Automated and Electronic Procedures

The oldest, and still the most widely used, method for the recording of and reporting on unit control figures is the manual system. It still answers the needs of smaller retailers whose inventories and sales transactions are small to relatively small in number.

Automated Systems. The retail industry has been one of the last to adopt mechanized systems for record-keeping purposes. But as firms started to expand in terms of sales volume, as well as geographical location, several years ago some of the larger independent stores and chains began adopting some form of automatic punch card data processing (A.D.P.) as a means of obtaining faster merchandising information, particularly sales data.

Under this system, a standard tabulating card is punched from the information on the stub or other portion of the price ticket which is removed from goods at the point of sale. For greater speed and accuracy in the transfer of data from price tickets to punch cards, marking machines have been devised that in one single operation print the desired control data on each price ticket and also punch tiny holes in the ticket that represent the printed information in code (see Form 8-4A). Stubs or print-punch tickets are fed into a machine that prepares a standard punch card for each stub so processed.

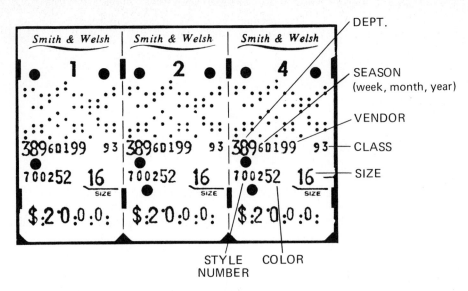

EXHIBIT 8-4A A.D.P. PRINT-PUNCH READY-TO-WEAR PRICE TICKET

The punch cards are sorted in any way desired for analysis, usually by merchandise classification, price line, vendor, season, and style number. Other data, such as size and color may also be included. After sorting the cards are fed into a tabulator that totals the number of each stockkeeping unit (S.K.U.) sold and prints out a report.[4]

Sensitized magnetic register tapes or codes on price tickets can also be used to produce punched tabulating cards.

Punch cards can also be prepared for customer returns from multiple-part print-punch tickets, thereby making it possible to prepare both gross and net sales reports.

A.D.P. can also be used to maintain a perpetual book inventory for each item by preparing punch cards for merchandise receipts from the records used in the preparation of the print-punch price tickets. Necessary additions to and subtractions from inventory may be made automatically to obtain the book inventory (see Chapter 9).

Despite the fact that most large department stores and chains have gone over to E.D.P., A.D.P. is still used for furniture and other types of hard goods where the goods on the selling floor are merely samples, with the stock subject to control being kept in a warehouse.

Electronic Systems. The newest and by far the most innovative development for recording unit control information and fast retrieval of that information for purposes of prompt evaluation is known as electronic data processing (E.D.P.). Electronically controlled registers, referred to as point-of-sale (P.O.S.) equipment, make it possible to collect an enormous amount of merchandise information at the point of sale in a number of ways.

1. One method is to use stubs or duplicate portions of price tickets that have been punched with the desired control information. These are removed and inserted into a P.O.S. recorder which automatically transcribes the data in code to tapes which are removed daily and sent to the computer center for processing.
2. A slower method is to punch keys on the sales register to record such inventory control data as style number, size, color, and so on. Such recording occurs after the usual sales data (department, classification, price, salesperson's number) has been rung up.

[4] John W. Wingate, Elmer O. Schaller, and F. Leonard Miller, *Retail Business Management* (Englewood Cliffs, New Jersey: Prentice-Hall, Inc., 1972), pp. 329-30.

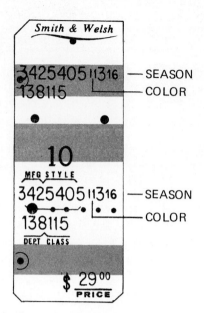

EXHIBIT 8-4B E.D.P. READY-TO-WEAR PRICE TICKET

3. An optic light "wand" that is attached to the register by a cord and held by hand "reads" specially prepared price tickets and automatically activates the electronic P.O.S. register to receive this information and transfer it to a magnetic tape recorder. The tape is then taken after business hours to a central computer for processing and the preparation of reports. The "wand" can also handle and even authorize charge sales, since it can scan and interpret color-coded bars on customers' credit cards. (See Form 8-4B.)

4. Another E.D.P. method is gaining acceptance in the grocery field. It involves an optical scanning device attached to a register which, when it is passed over the numbered vertical line or bar coding now being imprinted on most grocery item packages or boxes, feeds the coded information directly into a computer or onto tape for later processing.

Manual versus Mechanized Systems. Regardless of whether the method used for capturing, storing, and releasing merchandise information in report form is manual or mechanized, identical sources of unit control information, such as purchase orders, sales records, receiving records, and price changes, are used in each. The only difference is that in the manual method records are kept and reports made out by hand. In the case of data-processing systems, unit control information is fed into, the results tabulated by, and reports issued automatically by machines.

Major Advantages and Disadvantages of Mechanized Systems. The major advantages that machine data processing has over manual processing of unit control information are:

1. the speed with which the stock-sales information can be made available for study and remedial action, if necessary, and
2. the greater accuracy of the figures.

The major disadvantages of machine processing over manual processing are:

1. the greater cost of sophisticated machines, as compared with the relatively low cost of having clerical workers do the work;
2. if any wrong information is fed into the machine, the reports emanating from it will also be wrong;

3. the cost of installing and maintaining the necessary equipment (now being partially overcome by computer centers that permit the buying or sharing of computer use time, plus the increasing availability of minicomputers at correspondingly lower prices);

4. rapidly developing computer technology, plus the lead time required to build and install computerized units, often means that some models are already out-of-date by the time they are ready to be installed.

THE BUYING PLAN

The interacting aspects of dollar and unit control are best illustrated by the buying plan since the best ones utilize both methods of control. A *buying plan* is a general description of the types, price lines, and quantities of merchandise (in units as well as in dollars) a buyer expects to purchase for delivery within a specified period of time. The purpose of a buying plan is to keep buyers from overspending or buying merchandise they may find new and exciting but which would not fit into the department's carefully planned merchandise assortments.

Developing a buying plan is a tedious but very important responsibility but is made much easier if a seasonal merchandise plan has been made up in units as well as in dollars. Having the necessary unit information as to unit planned sales by classification and price line during the period for which buying is to be done, as well as planned closing stock for the period similarly broken down, the buyer needs only to have a count of stock currently on hand and on order to determine both unit and dollar O.T.B. for each of these categories.

There are no standardized forms for use in developing buying plans. Those used by small stores may be quite brief and informal. They may be drawn up completely in dollars, and at either retail or cost values. Others may be quite detailed and formalized. Form 8-5 is an example of a buying plan used by one medium-volume store for a brief pre-Easter market trip. Note that total planned purchases and O.T.B. are indicated on the buying plan in both units and dollars, as well as by classification and price lines within each classification. As we learned earlier in this text, the essential figures used in calculating O.T.B. are:

- the quantity of stock currently on hand and on order in terms of dollars and/ or units;
- a projection in number and retail value of those units that can reasonably be expected to be sold within a specified period of time for which buying is being done;
- the number and/or value of the units that should be on hand at the close of the period for which deliveries of purchases are to be made according to the buying plan.

THE PHYSICAL INVENTORY

In retailing, all merchandise planning and control calculations are based on a prior determination of the actual or estimated value of the stock on hand as of a given date. The actual counting and recording of each item, at either its cost or retail value, is referred to as the *physical inventory*. Calculation of the value of the stock that *should* be on hand as of any given date, according to the firm's accounting records, is referred to as the *book inventory*. Physical inventory will be discussed next. Book inventory is the subject of Chapter 9.

Taking physical inventory is an essential feature of retail merchandising and a key factor in the dollar control of retail inventories. All stores take a formal physical inventory

BUYING PLAN

Page 1

Dept. 42, Misses Dresses Date Feb. 20, 197-

Planned MU% 48.5

Buying trip to: New York

From: Feb. 24 To: Feb. 27

Reason for trip: Additional Easter Mdse; Review Mar. - Apr. O.O.; New Mdse for early Apr. delivery

Mo. of Delivery	O.T.B. 2/20/7- Planned Purchases	O.T.B. Balance	Actual Purchases Cost	Retail
March	$9,300	$7,900	$1,400	
April	13,600	6,700	6,900	

APPROVED: GMM ABD Date 2/22/7- DMM TJE Date 2/21/7-

(1) Class	(2) Unit Retail	(3) Description	(4) Actual Sales L.Y.	(5) Planned Sales T.Y.	(6) Planned Stock 4/15/7-	(7) Total (5+6)	(8) O.H. 2/20/7-	(9) O.O. 2/20/7-	(10) Total (8+9)	(11) O.T.B. (7-10)	(12) Plan to buy	(13) Purchases No.	Cost	Retail
123	22		141	150	250	400	176	90	266	134	Mar 60/Apr 60			
	26	Street, business and general occasion wear dresses	163	175	300	475	202	100	302	173	Mar 90/Apr 80			
	30		155	160	225	385	162	80	242	143	Mar 80/Apr 60			
	35		94	100	180	280	112	60	172	108	Mar 60/Apr 42			
140	30		42	45	80	125	94	36	130	—				
	35	Dressy and after-5 dresses	30	35	65	100	80	18	98	—				
	40		19	25	50	75	60	18	78	—				

FORM 8-5 BUYING PLAN

Mary D. Troxell, *Fashion Merchandising*, 2nd ed. (New York: Gregg Division, McGraw-Hill, 1976), p. 292.

once a year for tax purposes as well as for preparation of a Balance Sheet and Profit and Loss statements. In some cases more frequent inventories are taken, particularly if large stock shortages have been experienced in prior counts.

In departmentized stores inventory is taken and calculated separately by departments inasmuch as each selling department is regarded as an individual accounting unit. In non-departmentized stores, storewide counts are made and total dollar value calculated for the inventory of the store as a whole.

Physical inventory taken for dollar inventory control purposes is not to be confused with frequent and less formal stock counts that may be taken for unit control and reorder purposes.

Reasons for Taking Inventory

The basic reason for taking physical inventory, as stated above, is to determine the actual dollar value of stock on hand at the close of a fiscal or calendar year so that annual tax returns and such other financial statements as the Balance Sheet and Profit and Loss statements may be prepared. Other reasons for taking inventory are:

- to establish the dollar value of the inventory in connection with filing an insurance claim;
- as an aid in correcting errors that inevitably creep into the store's accounting records over a period of time; and
- to establish the value of the stock on hand for insurance purposes.

Since physical inventories are taken in units, as well as in dollars, they may also serve as a unit inventory control device, particularly when taken by classification, price line, and age or *season letter,* which is the term for the code appearing on each price ticket indicating the date the merchandise was received into stock (see Forms 8-4A and 8-4B). Form 8-6 illustrates the information generally recorded during a physical inventory count. Form 8-7 is an example of one large store's report to a department manager on the inventory results in her department. Physical inventory is taken every six months in this department and the results compared with the results of the two previous inventories.

The benefits to be obtained from taking physical inventory in units of merchandise are:

- to familiarize department personnel with exactly what is in stock;
- to aid merchants in analyzing the inventory assortment so that it may be brought into better balance with sales;

FORM 8-6 INVENTORY COUNT SHEET

Smith & Welsh

CONSOLIDATED INVENTORY REPORT

DEPT. 189 ACCESSORIES

DEPT. MGR. JANE DOE

MDSE. MGR. JOHN MANN

DATE OF INVENTORY	8/12/79		8/13/78		8/14/77	
	AMOUNT	%	AMOUNT	%	AMOUNT	%
BOOK INVENTORY	735,331		734,220		695,331	
PHYSICAL INVENTORY	723,090		721,090		693,090	
TOTAL SHORTAGE	12,241	1.07	13,130	1.15	2,241	0.26

MISSING MERCHANDISE REPORTED DURING FISCAL 19 79

PREVIOUS YEARS'

TOTAL NET SALES	1,142,128		1,139,209		870,128	
TOTAL MARKDOWNS	19,897	1.74	19,033	1.67	8,033	0.92

CLASSIFICATION ANALYSIS

LETTER	THIS YEAR	LAST YEAR
0		
1	211,089	214,656
2	160,210	158,210
3	182,079	187,612
4	169,712	160,612
5		
6		
7		
8		
9		
	723,090	721,090

730-7

STOCK BY LOCATION	1979	1978	1977
Store #1	195,397	213,394	235,915
Store #2	63,508	69,358	69,926
Store #3	66,296	72,402	68,188
Store #4	64,729	70,692	58,802
Store #5	73,965	80,778	65,016
Store #6	70,483	76,975	65,121
Store #7	63,690	69,556	65,062
Store #8	62,033	67,935	65,060
Store #9	62,989	—	—
Warehouses			

AGE ANALYSIS

SEASON			THIS YEAR	SEASON			LAST YEAR
SPRING 74 & OLDER				SPRING 73 & OLDER			
FALL	74	L	129	73	J		
SPR.	75	M	483	74	K		2,185
FALL	75	S	2,189	74	L		654
SPR.	76	A	655	75	M		4,267
FALL	76	B	4,275	75	S		10,219
SPR.	77	C	10,239	76	A		141,520
FALL	77	E	141,793	76	B		562,245
SPR.	78	H	563,327	77	C		
FALL	78	J		77	E		
SPR.	79	K		78	H		

FORM 8-7 CONSOLIDATED INVENTORY REPORT

- to aid in locating any odd lots of slow-selling merchandise and preventing any accumulation of old stock;
- to determine sales in terms of units of certain groups of merchandise handled for which no other type of unit control records have been kept (e.g., candy, greeting cards, sewing notions, certain hardware items, groceries, etc.)

Cost versus Retail Values

Although stores that utilize the Retail Method take their inventories at retail value, taking inventory at cost is not uncommon. Under the Cost Method, as previously stated, the cost price of each item of merchandise is usually listed on price tickets in one of two ways:

1. in coded form, or
2. with an identification figure that refers to an invoice, purchase order, or unit control record where the cost price is stated.

The most frequently used cost code is a letter code in which each separate letter indicates a specific number between 1 and 0. The letter code "MONEY TALKS," for example, indicates 10 separate numbers as follows:

$$\begin{array}{ccccccc} M & O & N & E & Y & & T & A & L & K & S \\ 1 & 2 & 3 & 4 & 5 & & 6 & 7 & 8 & 9 & 0 \end{array}$$

If these two words were used to represent the cost in code, and the cost price of an article was $10.75, the cost code would appear on the article's price tag as MSAY.

In stores operating under the Cost Method of inventory valuation, the total cost value of the inventory on hand at the end of a given period is calculated and that sum subtracted from the cost of merchandise handled throughout the entire period. The difference represents the cost of merchandise sold during that period.

In stores operating under the Retail Method, unit prices of merchandise on hand are listed at retail. Next, the total retail value is calculated. Then the approximate cost of the ending inventory is *calculated* by multiplying its total retail value by the complement of the cumulative markup percentage on total merchandise handled. Stated as a formula:

Formula:

$ Cost of stock on hand = $ Retail × (100% − Cumulative markup %)

Problem:

From the following figures, calculate the cost of a department's closing inventory:

Beginning inventory at cost	$ 6,000
Beginning inventory at retail	$11,000
Net purchases at cost	$ 3,000
Net purchases at retail	$ 5,600
Closing inventory at retail	$10,000

Solution:

	Retail	Cost
Beginning inventory	$11,000	$6,000
Net purchases	+ 5,600	+ 3,000
Total merchandise handled	$16,600	$9,000

$$\text{Cumulative markup \%} = \frac{\$ \text{Retail} - \$ \text{cost}}{\$ \text{Retail}}$$

$$= \frac{\$16,600 - \$9,000}{\$16,600}$$

$$= \frac{\$7,600}{\$16,600}$$

$$= 45.78\%$$

$ Cost of closing inventory = $ Retail × (100% − Cum M %)
. = $10,000 × .5422
= $5,422

209

Finally, the calculated cost value of the ending inventory is subtracted from the cost of total merchandise handled to determine the cost of merchandise sold (as in the Cost Method).

Procedures in Taking Inventory

For most accurate counts, inventories should be taken when no customers are in the store, and they should be completed in a single, continuous session—not one stock section of the selling floor one day and another section the next day.

Most stores establish a "cut-off date" several days before the actual physical count is to take place in order that the Accounting Department may have time to complete all in-transit "paperwork," such an invoices, price changes, and so on. After this cut-off date, no additional records relating to changes in the value of inventory should be processed or merchandise received into stock unless proper arrangements are made and inventory adjusted accordingly.

All participants should be well informed in advance of their duties and responsibilities with respect to taking inventory. Extreme accuracy is the essential element in having a "good" inventory.

Before the cut-off date, the buyer or department manager should see to it that all necessary markdowns are taken, as well as returns made to vendors. All merchandise should be checked to see that each item is correctly marked. Every drawer, shelf, cupboard, box, bag, nook, and cranny should be checked for departmental merchandise that may have been misplaced or overlooked. Every piece of merchandise on loan to other departments, such as the Display Department, the Advertising Office, or the Fashion Office should be accounted for on the proper inventory tags or sheets. Also to be accounted for is any of the department's merchandise being held in Will Call or in the Adjustment Department.

Consecutively numbered inventory sheets and/or tags are assigned to each selling department usually the day before the inventory is to be taken. Having drawn up a floor plan or chart of the department's selling floor and stockrooms, the buyer or department manager "lays" the numbered sheets and/or tags on every shelf, counter, rack, drawer, or other area where the department's merchandise is located and indicates on the floor plan the numbers of the sheets or tags assigned to each location. This is most important because at the conclusion of the inventory taking, the buyer or department manager is personally responsible for seeing to it that *every* numbered inventory sheet or tag issued to the department is returned to the Inventory Control office in numerical order with no numbered sheets or tags missing.

Inventory sheets, cards, and tags provide spaces for recording any and all information needed for purposes of analysis and evaluation. Such information usually includes classification, season letter, number of pieces at each marked price, and so on, as indicated on Form 8-6. Usually, participants work in teams—one person counts and calls while the other records the information. Both initial each sheet on which they have worked. Time permitting, the same or another team may spot check sheets on which information has already been recorded.

After all merchandise has been counted and listed, the inventory sheets are picked up in numerical order and the entire batch turned over to the Inventory Control office for extension and totaling of figures.

Some of the larger department stores and chains with computer facilities are employing E.D.P. in taking their annual or semiannual physical inventories. Here, as at point-of-sale, optical font readers are employed to read the coded price tickets, thus greatly reducing the time spent in inventory taking. Furthermore, the count is apt to be much more accurate than one taken manually.

Evaluating the Physical Inventory

When the total retail value of a department's merchandise inventory has been determined from a physical count, it is then compared with that of the book inventory as of the same date. When the physical inventory exceeds the book inventory, a stock overage is said to exist. When the physical inventory is less than the book inventory a stock shortage is said to exist.

Buyers and department managers are held personally responsible for the control of their inventories. Although the value of an inventory, as determined by a physical count, rarely agrees exactly with that of the book inventory (see Chapter 9), the extent of difference between the two is considered by store management as an important means of measuring the efficiency of a merchandising operation.

SUMMARY OF KEY TERMS

Book Inventory. The value of the stock that should be on hand as of any given date, according to the firm's accounting records.

Buying Plan. A general description of the types, price lines, and quantities of merchandise a buyer expects to purchase for delivery within a specified time period.

Classification. An assortment of units or items of merchandise which are all reasonably substitutable for each other.

Dollar Control. Any type of system (manual or mechanized) for recording sales and stock information in terms of dollar value and from which a variety of merchandising reports can be drawn.

Periodic Stock Count Control. Any unit control system in which stock on hand is counted and recorded at regular intervals, merchandise on order and received is recorded as these occur, and sales between counts are computed.

Perpetual Control. Any unit control system in which merchandise on order, receipts of goods, and sales are recorded as they occur and stock on hand is computed.

Physical Inventory. The actual counting and recording of each item in stock at either its cost or retail value.

Reserve Requisition Control. A form of periodic stock count control in which only merchandise in the stockroom or warehouse is counted at regular intervals and the stock on the selling floor is considered sold.

Retail Method of Inventory Valuation. A method of merchandise accounting that makes it possible to calculate the retail value of inventory on hand without having to take a physical count, and to determine the cost value of that inventory without having to determine the cost of each individual item of which the inventory is comprised.

Season Letter. A code appearing on each price ticket that indicates the month and year (and sometimes week) in which an item was received into the retailer's stock.

Unit Control. Any system (manual or mechanized) for recording the number of units of merchandise purchased, sold, on hand, and on order and from which a variety of merchandising reports can be drawn.

Visual System. A form of periodic stock count control in which no records are kept but stock is periodically checked by visual verification or occasional stock counts.

REVIEW QUESTIONS—Inventory Control and Devices

1. What are the four major objectives of retail inventory control?

   (1)

   (2)

   (3)

   (4)

2. What are the five major types of activities involved in inventory control?

   (1)

   (2)

   (3)

   (4)

   (5)

3. Set up two skeleton Profit and Loss statements showing how two firms (A and B), each having $100,000 in net sales, can have different operating profits—A with $10,000 and B with only $8,000.

4. The method of merchandise accounting that makes it possible to calculate the approximate retail value of inventory on hand without having to take a physical count is called the _____ _____.

5. The two basic methods for helping retailers maintain stocks in a desired ratio to sales are _____ _____ and _____ _____.

6. What is the major purpose of dollar control?

7. What is the major purpose of unit control?

8. Indicate the types of information that any form of unit control system is set up to show.

9. An assortment of units or items of merchandise which are all reasonably substitutable for each other is known as a _____.

10. Name and briefly describe the major difference between the two basic types of unit control systems.

    (1)

    (2)

11. Name at least two types of goods that are best suited for:

(1) perpetual control systems

(2) periodic control systems

(3) reserve requisition systems

(4) visual systems

12. (1) What is meant by the term "buying plan"?

(2) What is its major purpose?

13. (1) Why is it necessary to take periodic physical inventory?

(2) How often is it usually taken on a formal basis?

14. (1) What is meant by the term "season letter"?

(2) Describe its use as an inventory control device.

15. If a store used a cost code of MAKE PROFIT, what would be the cost of an item of merchandise on whose price ticket the cost was coded as MROP?

CHAPTER 9

INVENTORY CONTROL:
the book inventory

Many stores, particularly the larger ones, find it necessary to compute the value of their stock on hand more frequently than once or twice a year when storewide physical inventories are taken, for the following reasons:

- as an aid in maintaining predetermined relationships between actual sales and stock;
- for more frequent estimates of profit;
- to maximize collections from insurance companies in the case of insured losses.

During the time interval between physical counts, many transactions that affect the value of the inventory on hand occur. Sales are made to customers; some merchandise is marked down; additional stock is received; goods may be transferred to or received from other departments or other stores; occasionally some merchandise is returned by customers; and it may be necessary to return some merchandise to vendors. The details of every transaction involving the movement of merchandise into or out of stock, or changes in the price of that merchandise, must be recorded on documents specifically designed for reporting such transactions to the store's Accounting office. In the trade these documents having to do with the price and movement of merchandise are referred to as "paperwork." This "paperwork" is the life blood of the merchandising activity.

THE BOOK INVENTORY

The term Book Inventory (as defined in Chapter 8) refers to the value of stock that should be on hand at any time, according to the store's accounting records. If additions to and reductions in the value of the stock on hand are made as these changes occur and are reported to the store's Accounting office, and the book inventory is computed at regular intervals (daily, weekly, or monthly), this system is usually referred to as a *perpetual book inventory*. This is in contrast to book inventories that are prepared only periodically—usually only when a physical inventory is taken.

Book inventories may be kept manually or mechanically. The same information, obtained from the same documents, may be entered into a store's record-keeping system no matter whether the input is done by hand, machine, or electronic device. Whatever the method used, however, inaccuracy in recording, or failure to record, pertinent information will result in inaccurate book inventories.

Responsibility for the initiation and accuracy of most records used by a store's Accounting office in maintaining departmental book inventory is vested primarily in each departmental buyer, and represents a major part of each buyer's job. It is especially important that merchandising students acquire a thorough understanding of this particular area of a buyer's responsibility, since buyers frequently delegate responsibility for much of the record keeping to their assistants—an entry-level job for many Merchandising or Marketing students.

Retailers may take physical inventory as many times a year as they wish to verify the accuracy of their book inventories. But since the taking of meaningful physical inventory is costly and time consuming, it should be held to a minimum. When one has been taken, should there be a discrepancy between the total value of the physical inventory as of a given date and that of the book inventory as of the same date, the physical inventory figure is accepted as the correct one and the book inventory figure is adjusted to agree with it.

Following are examples of the principal documents in use by retail firms today for the purpose of maintaining book inventories for each of their merchandising departments. While each document is designed to serve a specific purpose, no standard format exists for any of them. Each store develops forms it finds suited to its own needs, which, although not exactly like those used in other stores, are fairly similar as to overall type and nature of information required.

Essential Records

Each of the following forms or documents in general use today by retail stores is designed to perform a specific function with respect to the merchandising activity in general and calculation of the book inventory in particular.

Receiving Documents. Although the merchandising process begins with the writing of a Purchase Order (see Chapter 5), a purchase is not considered finalized until the goods are actually received at the store or other designated receiving station, such as a warehouse, service building, or branch. In the trade the term "Purchases" designates merchandise received, while the term "Orders" designates merchandise for which P.O.s have been placed but the goods have not as yet been received. Merchandising paperwork, then, begins with the receipt of merchandise by the store.

While buyers and their assistants are not directly responsible for initiating the paperwork involved in the receipt of merchandise, getting it processed, or in payment of vendors' invoices, they are responsible for checking the accuracy of that paperwork.

Receiving Apron. A Receiving Apron, as indicated in Chapter 5, is prepared for each shipment of merchandise delivered to the store's Receiving platform. This document, of which Form 9-1 is a sample, consisting of multiple copies for distribution to various store areas, is consecutively numbered for control purposes, and generally requires all or most of the following data with respect to each shipment and its contents.

- name of vendor;
- name of carrier (trucking company, airline, parcel delivery service, etc.);
- date received;

RECEIVING RECORD

№ 16181 S

Received From _Aiken Dress Company_

Address _1400 Broadway_ City _New York, N.Y. 10018_

Date Received
9/5/7-

Department	Order No.	Transportation Charges		Buyers Approval or Remarks	Received Via
		Total Paid	Charge Shipper		
42	M184925	36.00		Jone Dean 9/16	I O U Service

Due Date	Terms	Invoice Passed	Discount		Amt. of Invoice	Retail Value	Pkg's. Pieces Cartons
			Date	Amount			
9/5/7-	8/10 EOM	9/12/7-	10/10	102.24	1,278.00	2,520.00	72 (hangers)

ATTACH INVOICE HERE

№ 16181 S

Received From _____

Vendor No.	Unit Cost	Color	Description			Size					Quantity		Class	Unit Price
						8	10	12	14		Amt.	Unit		
482	17.75	Blk	Style 253, 2 pc.			6	9	9	6		30	ea.	123	35.00
482	17.75	Red	Style 253, 2 pc.			6	10	8	4		28	ea.	123	35.00
482	17.75	Brown	Style 253, 2 pc.			2	4	4	4		14	ea.	123	35.00

Order Checked	Date	Mdse. Checked	Date	Price Tickets	Date	Mdse. Marked	Date	Cost Extension	Retail Extension	Merchandise Received/Date	
										Stock Room	Department
HLC	9/6	FBJ	9/6	NPR	9/6	mng	9/9	1,278.00	2,520.00	a JL 9/10	

FORM 9-1 RECEIVING APRON

Mary D. Troxell, *Fashion Merchandising,* 2nd ed. (New York: Gregg Division, McGraw-Hill, 1976), p. 263.

- number of pieces, cartons, packages comprising shipment;
- weight of shipment (if applicable);
- transportation charges;
- store order number;
- department to which consigned.

The Receiving clerk enters pertinent receiving information, attaches all copies of the Receiving Apron to the shipment, and routes the latter to the proper location for checking and marking. Each selling department is usually assigned a certain area for the receipt and checking of its purchases.

Merchandise Checking. At the checking location to which a shipment is assigned, merchandise checkers:

(1) account for the number of pieces or packages comprising each shipment, as indicated on the Apron;

(2) next open the shipment and check its contents against the packing slip or invoice (Form 9-2) if the latter is enclosed, and

(3) list the items and quantities received in the appropriate spaces provided on the Apron.

Once checking and listing is completed, the merchandise checker forwards the Apron, together with the invoice and/or packing slip enclosed with the merchandise, to the Order Checking Department for further processing. The merchandise is routed to a special marking area, where it is held until the marking clerk receives from the Order Checking Department information that is to go on each price ticket.

Order Checking. As indicated in Chapter 5, the Order Checking Department maintains files of all purchase orders and order cancellations by department name and number. Invoices that are received by first class mail (rather than being enclosed with the merchandise) are forwarded here and held in the appropriate departmental file until they can be matched with Apron copies sent to Order Checking by the merchandise checkers.

If a purchase order is not on file when the Apron copies arrive in the Order Checking department, "Hold for Order" is stamped on the Apron, which is then placed in the department's problem file, to wait for a purchase order.

From information obtained from the appropriate purchase order on file in the Order Checking Department, the following data are indicated by that department in appropriate spaces provided on each Receiving Apron:

- the retail price assigned to each item in the shipment;
- transportation costs of the shipment and who is responsible for paying same;
- verification of the department to be charged with the merchandise and who is to pay transportation costs;

```
                          DONNY BROOK
                         121 W. 34th St.
                        New York, New York
     New York, N.Y. 8/4/79                    DUNS # 698-9321

       SOLD TO   Smith & Welsh
                 8th & Market Sts.
                 Chicago, Ill. 60005
```

Term: 8/10 E.O.M.	F.O.B. Chicago	ORDER NO. 199971	DEPT. 189	SALESMAN James	VIA PACO

Style	Quantity	Description	Price	Extension Total
2390	144	S M L	9.00 ea.	
		Brown 16 16 16		
		Green 16 16 16		
		Black 16 16 16		

$1,296.00

INVOICE NO.
2561

THIS IS YOUR INVOICE

FORM 9-2 VENDOR'S INVOICE

- verification that proper carrier was used;
- terms of sale and due date of invoice.

If the merchandise received and the invoice are in agreement with the P.O. the Order Clerk attaches the Receiving Apron to the top of the vendor's invoice and forwards the combined documents to the Accounts Payable Department for further processing and payment of the invoice.

Most stores require that their buyers indicate on all copies of a purchase order (except the original copy which goes to the vendor) the retail price at which each item should be marked. This is known as "preretailing." If an invoice arrives and the buyer has not preretailed the order, the Order Check clerk stamps both the invoice and Apron "Hold for Retail" and places these documents in the department's problem file. It is the responsibility of the buyer or the assistant to provide the Order Checking Department with retail prices before incoming merchandise can be processed for delivery to the selling department.

Final processing of all invoices by the Accounts Payable department includes:

- verifying the extensions of total cost and total retail as indicated on the Apron;
- issuing any necessary claims to pick up transportation allowances or adjustments;
- calculating discounts and anticipation;
- assigning the date for payment of each invoice.

Therefore, in stores with an automated or electronic accounting system, all information on the Receiving Apron is transcribed onto a data-processing card or tape or fed into the memory bank of a computer, which, in turn, becomes the basic media for preparation of checks to vendors (Form 9-3), for the Purchase Journal (Form 9-6), and all other documents the store may employ in analyzing purchases.

Returns To and Claims Against Vendors. Buyers are responsible for initiating both of these documents (also referred to as "Chargebacks"), which usually also serve as the store's invoices to vendors.

Form 9-4 is the Return-to-Vendor form used by one large retail organization for merchandise being returned to vendor for cause. Reasons generally accepted for returning merchandise to a vendor are that it:

- is not as ordered;
- is not as sampled;
- was shipped after cancellation date;
- was not ordered.

It is necessary for buyers to obtain permission from vendors to return merchandise, however. Permission is usually signified by the vendor providing the buyer with an authorization sticker that must be attached to the outside of the package containing the return. Packages without such stickers are usually refused by the vendor.

Although there is no standard format for Return-to-Vendor forms, Form 9-4 is typical of those in general use today. Most are multicopy and are usually consecutively numbered for inventory control purposes.

Many stores use the same form for processing a Claim-Against-Vendor as that used for making a return by simply indicating on the face of the form the nature of the transaction. Some of the larger stores have a special Claim form, of which Form 9-5 is an example.

9/10/79   0786543

SMITH & WELSH

CHICAGO, ILLINOIS

P AY TO THE
ORDER OF

0698-9321

DONNY BROOK
121 W. 34TH ST.
NEW YORK, N.Y. 10019

SMITH & WELSH

Ralph Brown

Treasurer

⑆0310⑈0001⑆   000⑈0406⑈

F70-4 (150M 10-63) DESCRIPTION	DEPT. NO.	INVOICE NO. OR DATE	AMT. OF INVOICE	DISCOUNT— ANTICIPATION	TRANSPORTATION	BALANCE (NET AMOUNT)
	189	2561	1,296.00	103.68		1,192.32s

DETACH BEFORE DEPOSITING

FORM 9-3 STORE CHECK WITH ATTACHED VOUCHER

This distinction between a Claim and a Return is that a Claim does not involve the return of merchandise to a vendor. Important reasons for writing claims include:

- short shipment of merchandise;
- error in cost price of merchandise;
- error in charging transportation costs (amount, who pays, etc.);
- receipt of damaged merchandise;
- rebate granted by vendor not appearing on the invoice.

The Purchase Journal. The departmental Purchase Journal (sometimes referred to as a "Merchandise Journal" or "Bill Sheet") is a record of each merchandise department's purchases, claims against and return to vendors during a specified period. This report may be prepared with the aid of standard accounting office machines or data-processing equipment and is controlled and distributed usually on a weekly or semimonthly basis by a store's Accounts Payable department.

Buyers and department managers are responsible for examining each Purchase Journal promptly and carefully, since net purchases are a major factor in calculating a department's book inventory. Neglecting to accurately check the Purchase Journal could result in inventory shortages due to errors or omissions such as:

- one department being charged with another department's merchandise;
- failure to receive credit for merchandise returned to the vendor;

FORM 9-4 RETURN TO VENDOR

VENDOR

REFER ALL CORRESPONDENCE
TO: Accounts Payable Department
PHONE:

Smith & Welsh

8th & Market Sts.
Chicago, Ill. 60005

TODAY'S DATE 7/9/79

For Mdse. Dept. Use

CODES		CODE
CHARGE VENDOR		2 2 0
RETURN	220	VENDOR DUNS NUMBER
SHORTAGE	221	6 1 9 6 1 7 4
DAMAGE	222	251672
ALLOWANCE	*223	
REBATE	*227	MDSE. DEPT.
CREDIT VENDOR		6 7 7
CANCEL of CL 211		
HOLD FROM CHECK		S DIV. DEPT.
ALLOWANCE	*224	
REBATE	*228	EXPENSE CODE
OVERAGE	*210	
*DISCOUNT MUST BE ZERO		

CHARGE OR CREDIT TO (IF OTHER THAN SHIP TO)
(NAME AND ADDRESS MUST BE PRINTED)

NAME *NATIONAL PRESTO INDUSTRIES*

ADDRESS *617- WHITLOCK ST.*

CITY *EAU CLAIRE, WISCONSIN 54702* STATE ZIP CODE

SHIP TO: (NAME AND ADDRESS MUST BE PRINTED)

SHIP TO *SAME*

STREET

CITY DEPT. NO.

STATE Mr.
Attention of Ms. ZIP CODE

☑ RETURN
☐ SHORT
☐ DAMAGED
☐ OTHER (Explain)

RETURN APPROVED

DMM *Campbell* ACCTS. PAY. *D. W. Cunningham* CONTROLLER
AMT. OVER $200. AMT. OVER $1,000.

STYLE NO.	ITEMS	QUANTITY	UNIT COST	COST EXTENSION	UNIT RETAIL	RETAIL EXTENSION		
140	Pots	50	2 40	1 20 00	4 00	2 00 00		

IF NOT CORRECT USE THIS REFERENCE NO.

251672

INBOUND FREIGHT		
TOTAL	1 20 00	
OUTBOUND FREIGHT		

	RETAIL EXTENSION		
TOTAL RETAIL @	2 00 00	
TOTAL COST @	1 20 00	
DISC. RATE %	8 00 00 0	
DISC. AMT. $	1	
VENDOR TRANS.	2 80 0	
DEPT. TRANS.	1	

DEPT.	RECEIVING NO.	RECEIVING DATE	VENDOR'S INVOICE NO.	INVOICE DATED
677	946-63	5/12/79	29369	5/4/79

YOUR ACCOUNT IS BEING: **Charged*** X _____ **Credited** _____

* If charged please remit. Any replacement goods must be accompanied by an invoice.

IF A RETURN: BUYER MUST FILL IN REASON

☒ IMPERFECT ☐ NOT AS ORDERED ☐ ON CONSIGNMENT
☐ OTHER (SPECIFY)

Arrangements made with *M. Sopolski*

Buyer *G. E. Wilde*

See our letter of *7-2-79*

CARRIER *REA*	PICK-UP DATE 7/9/79
# CARTONS 5	WEIGHT 35#
FRT. CHG. 2.80	BY *F. Wiggins*
PICKED UP BY:	
MUST SIGN ALL COPIES	

WHO PAYS FRT. CHG. ☑ VENDOR DEPT.

HASH TOTAL

TAX CODE

USE FOR EXPENSE CLAIMS ONLY

Note: Enter discount rate or discount amount. Do not enter both. Indicate by numbers only. Do not use Alpha Characters.

- over- or undercharges due to incorrect extension of cost and/or retail figures on an apron or invoice.

Although there is no standard format for the preparation of purchase journals, Form 9-6 is a typical example of this type of discount, which usually includes the following information with respect to purchases:

1. vendor's Duns number;
2. vendor's name;
3. document reference number (Apron, Return-to-Vendor, or Claim number);

4. markup percentage on each purchase;

5. retail of each and total purchases;

6. cost of each and total purchases;

7. cash discounts earned;

8. anticipation discount earned;

9. transportation charges paid by department.

Following is a brief description of each of the above entries:

Vendor's Duns number. Every business firm has an assigned and universally accepted identification number. This number, known as the firm's *Duns number,* provides an efficient means for coding, processing, filing, tracing, and controlling financial documents via data processing systems. The most important factor to be observed with respect to a Duns number is accuracy. The use of an incorrect number will result in the appearance of the wrong vendor on the Purchase Journal and sometimes payments to an incorrect vendor. Invoices are usually filed in a store's Accounts Payable Department under the vendor's Duns number.

Vendor's name. By examining the vendor's name or Duns number on the department Purchase Journal, the buyer or department manager can determine whether the resource indicated is the one from which the purchase was actually made. As indicated above, the

FORM 9-5 CLAIM AGAINST VENDOR

Smith & Welsh

DIV. 21	MDSE. MGR. GROUP ACCESSORIES		WEEK 4	PER. 07 19 79	W/E DATE 8/28/79		PAGE 006	DEPT. 189

RESOURCE NO	NAME	REF. NO.	M.U. %	$ RETAIL	$ COST	$ DISCOUNT	$ ANTICIPATION	DEPT. TRANSP.	ADV. HELD
	PTD. FORWARDED		43.9	75,377.57	42,248.96	3,379.92		12.00	
0812959	JET SET (PR. CHG.)	155046	-	27.27	-	-	-	-	
0812959	JET SET (PR. CHG.)	155047	-	4.04 CR.	-	-	-	-	
1920545	ALMCEE	9197321	44.1	2,249.49	1,258.63	100.69	-	-	
2236952	TOP FORM	8578-50	40.4	600.00 CR.	357.50 CR.	-	-	-	
2599370	ROSENFELD	125678	43.9	2,398.35	1,346.65	107.73	-	-	
5173915	MINI	876243	44.8	4,229.25	2,333.78	186.70	-	-	
6989321	DONNY BROOK	947231	43.8	2,304.00	1,296.00	103.68	-	-	
7914948	S & C TRANSFER	0160955	40.1	599.00	359.00	-	-	-	
8123648	SCANNON	124785	44.0	424.11	237.50	19.00	-	-	
	POSTED TOTAL THIS WK.		44.3	11,627.43	6,474.06	517.80	-	-	
	PERIOD TO DATE		44.0	87,005.00	48,723.02	3,897.72	-	12.00	

Dun's No.	Vendor	Apron or Claim Number	Markup Percent	Retail Value	Cost Value	Cash Discount Earned	Anticipation Earned	Transportation Charges Paid by Store

FORM 9-6 PURCHASE JOURNAL

Duns number used indicates the specific vendor from which merchandise has been purchased.

Reference number.　The number appearing in this column is that of each transaction document, whether it be a Receiving Apron, Return-to-Vendor, or Claim number.

Markup percent.　This refers to the markup percentage on each transaction. If the markup, as indicated on the Purchase Journal, is considerably higher or lower than the departmental markup as indicated on the Operating Statement, this suggests possible errors resulting from incorrect extension of cost and/or retail dollars copied from aprons and/or invoices.

Retail dollars.　Receiving Aprons, Returns-to-Vendors, and Claims are recorded at retail value and appear as debits or credits in the retail column of the Purchase Journal.

Cost dollars.　The cost value of purchases, returns-to-vendors, and sometimes claims are listed in the "Cost" column of the Purchase Journal. Credits that appear with a minus sign preceding the amount indicate a reduction in the cost value of purchases.

Cash discount.　The "Discount" column on the Purchase Journal shows the dollar amount of discount earned on each purchase.

Anticipation discount.　The amount appearing in this column of the Purchase Journal indicates additional discount allowed and taken by the Accounts Payable Department for prepayment of invoices.

Transportation charges.　If an amount appears under "Department Transportation" on the Purchase Journal, this indicates the amount the store has paid as an incoming freight charge for each shipment. The department manager or buyer should verify the transportation terms stated on the Purchase Order, and if such terms are F.O.B. destination, issue a Claim against the vendor for any such freight charges paid in error by the store.

The buyer or department manager should promptly report to the Accounts Payable Department any errors found in the Purchase Journal so that resulting errors in the Book Inventory can be corrected. Special forms are used by some retail firms for reporting Purchase Journal errors to the store's Accounts Payable Department.

Transfers of merchandise.　Buyers or department managers are responsible for initiating and/or approving documents having to do with the transfer of merchandise from one location to another or from one selling department to another selling department.

Transferring merchandise from one selling department to another.　The buyer or department manager originating the transfer prepares a multicopy, serially numbered transfer document, of which Form 9-7A is a typical example, indicating the following:

- department to be charged with the merchandise;
- department receiving credit for the merchandise;
- quantity and description of merchandise being transferred;
- unit cost, total cost, unit retail, and total retail;
- buyer's or department manager's signature of issuing department as well as receiving department.

The buyer or department manager receiving merchandise from another department should verify that the items, quantities, and extensions are correct, then affix his/her signature in the proper space on the Transfer form, and forward it to the Statistical Department of the Accounting office for posting as a credit to the book inventory of the issuing department and as a charge to the book inventory of the receiving department.

Transferring merchandise between various locations of the same department.　This refers to merchandise transferred between the parent store and branch locations of the same department or between the same department in two branches. Form 9-7B is a typical example of the form in general use of this type of transaction, particularly among the larger,

FORM 9-7A TRANSFER FROM ONE DEPARTMENT TO ANOTHER

FORM 9-7A TRANSFER FROM ONE DEPARTMENT TO ANOTHER

branch-operating stores. Usually on an intra-store transfer, unit and total cost entries are omitted, with the merchandise being transferred at retail prices only. The reason for this is that the merchandise has already been charged at cost and retail to the department's book inventory; it is not being transferred out of the department but rather to a different selling location of the same department. In effect, this type of transfer is mainly a memorandum, indicating a shift in location of certain goods and is useful mainly for unit control purposes.

Price Changes.   The dynamic nature of retailing makes the repricing of merchandise, subsequent to its original pricing, a frequent requirement. As indicated in Chapter 7, price adjustments are constantly being made to either increase or decrease the original retail price placed on merchandise. Price changes must be accurately recorded and promptly reported to the store's Statistical Department if an accurate perpetual Book Inventory is to be maintained. For example, if a badly soiled garment were reduced $10 from the marked retail price because of its condition and sold at the reduced price, but the markdown was not recorded on a Price Change form, the result would be $10 stock shortage in the department's book inventory.

FORM 9-7B TRANSFER OF GOODS FROM ONE LOCATION TO ANOTHER

Price changes must also be carefully considered and anticipated in planning initial (or purchase) markup on the seasonal merchandise plan (see Chapter 4) and must be carefully controlled in line with planned figures if the desired operating profit is to be attained.

Sales Records. Every sale must be recorded on a store's salescheck form, the cash register, or in some cases both. Buyers or department managers or their assistants are responsible for forwarding a sales tally envelope (Form 9-8A) for each salesperson in their department to the Sales Audit Department at the close of each business day.

DEPARTMENT MANAGER'S DAILY SALES REPORT

Ring off total of the Department Sales Key of every Register including out-posts, deduct voids if any, and list below. List by register the Transactions and $ Sales in the columns provided. Turn in each evening for Daily Flash Reports. (Turn in two copies if you have out-posts.) Fill in all information required.

DATE _____ DEPT. _____

| DEPT. MANAGER | | | | FOR SALES AUDIT |
REG.	TRANS.	SALES		USE ONLY
ADJUSTED GROSS SALES				

DEPARTMENT MANAGER'S SIGNATURE   PHONE EXT.

FORM 9-8A DEPARTMENT DAILY SALES REPORT

Saleschecks are not standardized, either as to format or extent of information required. Form 9-8B is typical of saleschecks in general use today by medium- and large-volume stores. Saleschecks used in smaller stores may require considerably less detailed information, while those in very large stores, particularly those using "on-line" electronic registers (registers connected directly to a computer) or other types of data processing systems, may be even more detailed.

FORM 9-8B SALESCHECK

Each selling department's sales and sales credit adjustments are audited (Form 9-8C) daily by the Sales Audit Department which, in turn, reports each day's net sales by departments to the store's Statistical Department for processing as a reduction in the retail value of the appropriate department's Book Inventory.

Forms 9-8D and 9-8E are examples of sales credit forms in general today.

Form 9-9 is an example of a monthly report by the Sales Audit Department of the dollar value of merchandise returns by customers to two departments in the parent store and the same departments in the branch stores.

Calculating Book Inventory at Retail

Calculating book inventories at retail is an integral part of the Retail Method of inventory valuation as previously described. And the term book inventory, you will recall, refers to the dollar value of the stock that is supposed to be on hand, according to the accounting records kept of all inventory-related transactions that have occurred during any given period (see Form 9-10).

The simplest way to calculate the retail value of book inventory is to

(1) determine total merchandise handled during the period; and

(2) subtract from this figure the sum of *all* transactions which decreased (reduced) the retail value of the stock available for sale during the period.

Transactions that Increase Retail Inventory Value. The following transactions *increase* the retail value of the book inventory:

- *Purchases* increase the value of the stock on hand because they represent the value of additional merchandise that has been received into stock since the beginning of the period.

- *Transfers In,* like Purchases, increase the value of the stock on hand because they represent merchandise that has been brought into a department's stock during the period from other selling departments of the home store or from other stores or branches.

- *Additional Markup* also increases the retail value of stock on hand, because it represents an increase in the retail price of goods over the price at which those goods were marked when they were originally brought in to stock.

- *Customer Returns* increase the value of the stock on hand because merchandise previously considered sold was subsequently returned for credit, thereby reducing gross sales and increasing stock on hand by an identical amount of the return.

- *Transportation Costs* increase only the *cost* value of the inventory, *not* the retail value.

Transactions that Decrease Retail Inventory Value. The following transactions *decrease* (reduce) the retail value of a department's book inventory:

- *Net Sales.* As previously stated, all sales of merchandise are reported daily to a store's Sales Audit Department on saleschecks or register tapes. The total of all sales made is referred to as gross sales. Returns from and allowances to customers (credits) are also reported to and recorded in the Sales Audit Depart-

SALES REGISTER ERROR REPORT

DEPT. #_____ DATE _____

REGISTER #_____DRAWER LETTER_____

CLERK #_____

SALESCHECK

☐ 1. FAILURE TO MARK SALESCHECK
       CHG.   PD.   COD

☐ 2. UNDER RING _____

☐ 3. OVER RING _____

☐ 4. INFORMATION IN "HOW SOLD" BOX

    ☐ (A) PAID CHECK MARKED "CHARGE"

    ☐ (B) CHARGE CHECK MARKED "PAID"

☐ 5. ILLEGIBLE PRINTING AND NUMBERS

☐ 6. C.O.D. ERRORS

    ☐ (A) XXX USED IN DRIVER COLLECT
               BOX ON A C.O.D. EXCHANGE

    ☐ (B) C.O.D. NOT FRANKED FOR FULL
               AMOUNT

    ☐ (C) DRIVER COLLECT AMOUNT
               INCORRECT

☐ 7. HANDLING CHARGE OR DEPOSIT MISSING

SALES AUDIT CHECK-OFF

☐ RE-ADDED

    ☐ CASH

    ☐ CHARGES

    ☐ C.O.D.'S

☐ COMPARED FRANKING WITH WRITTEN AMOUNT

☐ LOOKED FOR UNFRANKED CHECKS

☐ CHECKED FOR MISSING CHECKS

☐ CHECKED DATES FOR LATE CHECKS

....

NET OVERAGE $_____ NET SHORTAGE $_____

REASON FOR OVERAGE OR SHORTAGE

☐ MISSING SALESCHECKS

☐ LATE SALESCHECKS

$_____ #_____

$_____ #_____

$_____ #_____

☐ CASH
    PAID TAKES
      PLUS
    PAID SENDS
      PLUS
    DEPOSITS VS.
    CASH REPORTED

OVER $_____

SHORT $_____

OTHER COMMENTS:

BALANCED BY_____ CHECKED BY _____

INTERVIEWED BY_____ DATE _____

F 2122A

FORM 9-8C DEPARTMENT DAILY SALES ERROR REPORT

FORM 9-8D CREDIT FORM (CASH REFUND)

ment. Returns and Allowances are deducted from gross sales to obtain Net Sales, as indicated by the following formula:

Net sales = Gross sales − Returns from and allowances to customers

The retail value of the book inventory is reduced by the amount of net sales made during each accounting period.

- *Returns-to-Vendors* decrease both the cost and retail value of the book inventory because they represent merchandise that is no longer in stock because it has been returned to its vendors.
- *Transfers Out* decrease the retail value of the stock available for sale because they represent merchandise that is no longer in a department's stock because it has been sent to other departments of the home store or to other stores or branches.
- *Merchandise Markdowns* decrease the retail value of the stock on hand because they represent downward revision in the retail prices (value) of goods currently

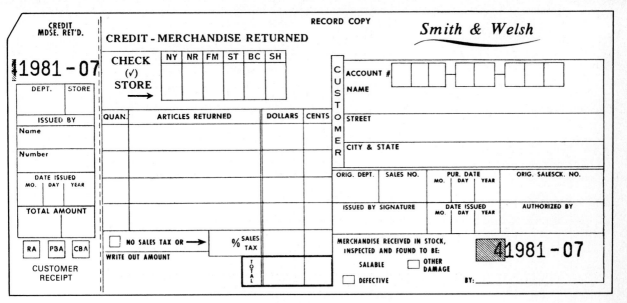

FORM 9-8E CHARGE CREDIT FORM

Return Sales Report　　　Period 02 1977 PG 46

ST	OV	DEP	Gross Sales	Returns ($)	PCT
P	23	172	6,358	419	6.6
A	23	172	1,715	133	7.8
J	23	172	1,990	112	5.6
W	23	172	1,785	99	5.5
C	23	172	4,474	234	5.2
S	23	172	4,100	135	3.3
P	23	172	2,875	194	6.7
N	23	172	4,137	246	5.9
E	23	172	2,358	29	1.2
TOTAL		172	29,792	1,601	5.4
P	23	189	40,267	3,050	7.6
A	23	189	13,214	499	3.8
J	23	189	15,037	1,663	11.1
W	23	189	11,278	582	5.2
C	23	189	23,100	762	3.3
S	23	189	22,227	1,413	6.4
P	23	189	13,473	388	2.9
N	23	189	15,558	679	4.4
E	23	189	13,221	339	2.6
TOTAL		189	167,375	9,375	5.6

(1) Store identification
(2) Merchandise Division Number
(3) Department Number

FORM 9-9 DEPARTMENTAL MONTHLY RETURN SALES REPORT:
DOLLARS AND PERCENT OF GROSS SALES

in stock. As explained in Chapter 7, net markdowns equal gross markdowns minus markdown cancellations, or as a formula:

Net markdowns = Gross markdowns − markdown cancellations

- *Employee and Special Discounts* also decrease the retail value of a department's book inventory by the amount of the discount allowed. As stated in Chapter 7,

Dept. _159_   DEPARTMENTAL INVENTORY LEDGER   Year Ending _Jan. 31, 197-_

Period Ending	Purchases and Transfers			$ Freight Costs	$ Add'l. Markup	Accumulated			$ Net Sales	Deductions at Retail				EOM Inventory		
										Markdowns		Shortage Reserve				
	$ Cost	$ Retail	% Markup			$ Cost	$ Retail	% Cum. Markup	Net Sales	$	% Sales	$ Shortage Reserve	$ Total	$ Cost	$ Retail	% Maint. Markup
	(1)	(2)	(3)	(4)	(5)	(6)	(7)	(8)	(9)	(10)	(11)	(12)	(13)	(14)	(15)	(16)
Beg. Inv.	32,276	52,227	38.2	—	—	—	—	—	—	—	—	—	—	—	—	—
Feb.	6,000	10,000	40.0	37	120	—	—	—	11,500	590	5.1	173	12,263	—	—	—
YTD	38,276	62,227	38.5	37	120	38,313	62,347	38.5	11,500	590	5.1	173	12,263	30,802	50,084	38.5
Mar.	7,200	12,000	40.0	45	—	7,245	12,000	39.6	13,000	650	5.0	195	13,845	—	—	—
YTD	45,476	74,227	38.7	82	120	45,558	74,347	38.7	24,500	1,240	5.1	368	26,108	29,571	48,239	38.7
Apr.																
YTD																
Oct.																
YTD																
Nov.																
YTD																
Dec.																
YTD																
Jan.																
Year																

KEY:

YTD = Year to Date
Column 1 = Billed Cost of Purchases
Column 2 = Retail Value of Purchases
Column 3 = $\dfrac{\text{Col. 2} - \text{Col. 1}}{\text{Col. 2}}$
Column 6 = Col. 1 + Col. 4

Column 7 = Col. 2 + Col. 5
Column 8 = $\dfrac{\text{Col. 7} - \text{Col. 6}}{\text{Col. 7}}$
Column 9 = Net Audited Sales
Column 10 = From Markdown Book
Column 11 = $\dfrac{\text{Col. 10}}{\text{Col. 9}}$

Column 12 = as % of Col. 9
Column 13 = Col. 9 + Col. 10 + Col. 12
Column 14 = Col. 15 x complement of Col. 8
Column 15 = Col. 7 − Col. 13
Column 16 = $\dfrac{\text{Col. 15} - \text{Col. 14}}{\text{Col. 15}}$

FORM 9-10 BOOK INVENTORY

Mary D. Troxell, *Fashion Merchandising*, 2nd ed. (New York: Gregg Division, McGraw-Hill, 1976), p. 273.

Employee Discount is the trade term for the reduction in the marked retail price of merchandise that most retailers grant their employees and dependents of those employees. Many stores also grant discounts to other favored customer groups, such as the clergy and certain charitable organizations.

- *Stock Shortage Reserve.* A recurring but very undesirable reduction in inventory value is known as stock shortage. *Stock shortage* is the trade term for the condition that exists when the value of the Book Inventory exceeds (is greater than) that of the Physical Inventory.

Most stores set up a reserve fund for anticipated stock shortage when drawing up seasonal merchandise plans (see Chapter 4). The anticipated shortage is based primarily on each department's previous experience, industry averages, and current business trends. The stock shortage provision is expressed as a percent of net sales. At the end of each accounting period, net sales for the period are multiplied by the shortage reserve percentage, and the retail value of the book inventory is reduced by an equivalent dollar amount.

The purpose of establishing a stock shortage reserve is not to condone inventory shortage or to establish an acceptable limit, but rather to spread the anticipated loss over an entire 6- or 12-month period instead of having to make a single, usually large, adjustment in inventory value when physical inventory is taken and the book inventory figure is adjusted to agree with the results of the physical count.

Calculating Book Inventory at Retail

Formula:

$$\begin{aligned} \text{Book inventory} = \;&\text{(Beginning inventory + net purchases}\\ &\text{+ net transfers in + additional markup)}\\ &- \text{(net sales + net markdowns + employee}\\ &\text{discounts + stock shortage reserve)} \end{aligned}$$

Problem:

If a Drapery Department had the following retail figures for March, determine its Book Inventory as of March 31:

Inventory March 1	$137,000
Gross purchases, March	68,500
Transfers in	150
Transfers out	100
Returns-to-vendor	2,500
Additional markup	175
Gross sales	65,000
Customer returns and allowances	2,000
Gross markdowns	1,800
Markdown cancellations	450
Employee discounts	250
Stock shortage reserve, March	2%

Solution:

		Retail
Inventory March 1		$137,000
Gross purchases	$68,500	
Less R-T-V	2,500	
Net purchases		66,000
Transfers in	$ 150	
Less transfers out	100	
Net transfers in		50
Additional markup		175
Total merchandise handled, March		$203,225
Less total decreases, March		65,860
Book inventory March 31		$137,365

		Retail
Gross sales	$65,000	
Less customer returns and allowances	2,000	
Net sales, March		$63,000
Gross markdowns	$ 1,800	
Less cancellations	450	
Net markdowns		$ 1,350
Employee discounts		250
Stock shortage reserve		1,260
Total decreases in stock, March		$65,860

PRACTICE PROBLEMS—Book Inventory at Retail

1. Find the August 31 book inventory for a Floor Covering Department that had the following figures for the month of August:

Net sales	$ 90,000
August 1 inventory	120,000
August purchases at retail	100,000
Returns-to-vendor	9,000
Transfers out	1,000
Markdowns	2,000
Employed discounts	1,000

_____
(Answer)

2. Find the book inventory on November 30 of a Gift Department with the following figures for November:

Net sales	$163,000
Purchases at retail	99,600
Transfers out	1,400
Returns-to-vendor	2,600
November 1 inventory	124,000
Net markdowns	1,600
Employee discounts	400
Stock shortage reserve	2,500

_____
(Answer)

3. The inventory on February 1 of a Luggage Department was $25,000. For the 6-month period ending July 31, $40,000 worth of purchases at retail were received; net sales for the period were $35,500; markdowns taken amounted to $2,300; employee discounts were $200; returns-to-vendor were $350; and transfers out were $750. What was the book inventory at the end of the period?

_____
(Answer)

4. On August 1 the inventory in a Women's Coat Department was $175,000. Purchases for the 6-month period ending January 31 were $490,000; net sales $400,000; markdowns $30,000; returns-to-vendor $10,000; transfers to the store's Fantasia Boutique $15,000; and employee discounts $6,000. What was the book inventory on January 31?

_____
(Answer)

5. Find the book inventory from the following departmental "book figures":

Net sales	$45,000
Opening inventory	65,000
Retail purchases	55,000
Returns-to-vendor	4,300
Employee discounts	300
Markdowns	1,100
Transfers out	600

_____
(Answer)

Calculating Book Inventory at Cost

Up to this point we have been dealing only with retail figures. Sometimes, however, it is necessary to know the cost equivalents of retail figures. One of the advantages of the Retail Method is that it makes it possible to determine the cost equivalent of the retail value of a department's book inventory without having to determine the cost of each individual item in stock. This is accomplished by first finding the cumulative retail markup percent on total merchandise handled during the period and then multiplying the book inventory at retail by the cost complement of the cumulative retail markup percent, or

$$100\ \% - \text{cumulative markup percent}$$

Under the Retail Method the store's Accounting Office maintains a perpetual (running) record, at both cost and retail, of each department's purchases, returns-to-vendor, and transfers to and from other departments, stores, or branches. Inbound transportation costs are recorded at cost only—as an additional cost of purchases. Any additional markup taken on goods after they were first received into stock and all other inventory transactions are recorded at retail value only, such as net sales, net markdowns, and so forth.

Formula:

Book inventory at cost = Book inventory at retail
        × cost complement of the cumulative markup %

Problem:

What would be the cost value of the book inventory for a department with the following figures?

	Cost	Retail
Beginning inventory	$25,000	$ 48,000
Net purchases	50,000	100,000
Inbound transportation costs	450	
Additional markup		1,000
Net transfers in	550	1,000
Total deductions from stock		106,000

Solution:

	$ Cost	$ Retail	CM %
Beginning inventory	$25,000	$ 48,000	
Net purchases (receipts from vendors less returns to vendors)	$50,000	$100,000	
Inbound transportation	450		
Additional markup		1,000	
Net transfers in (transfers in less transfers out)	550	1,000	
Total additions to stock	51,000	102,000	
Total merchandise handled	$76,000	$150,000	49.3
Total deductions from stock		− 106,000	
Book inventory at retail		$ 44,000	

Book inventory at cost = $44,000 × (100% − 49.3%)
        = $44,000 × 50.7%
        = $44,000 × .507
        = $22,308

238

PRACTICE PROBLEMS—Calculating Book Inventory at Cost

1. If the book inventory in a Wig Department, at the close of a 6-month period, was $28,000 and the cumulative markup percentage was 51.0%, what was the cost value of the ending inventory?

_____
(Answer)

2. From the following figures, determine a department's closing book inventory at cost:

	Cost	Retail
Beginning inventory	$10,000	$17,000
Net purchases	20,000	40,000
Closing inventory		18,000

_____
(Answer)

3. From the following figures determine the:

(a) closing inventory at retail and

(b) closing inventory at cost

(a) _____
(Answer)

(b) _____
(Answer)

	Cost	Retail
Beginning inventory	$15,000	$28,000
Net purchases	$30,000	$59,000
Net sales		$42,000

4. At the start of a 6-month period a department had an inventory amounting to $29,600 at retail and $15,200 at cost. Purchases during the period amounted to $48,200 at retail and $25,000 at cost. Sales were $44,000 and markdowns $2,600.

(a) Find the book inventory at retail.

(a) _____
(Answer)

(b) Find the book inventory at cost.

(b) _____
(Answer)

5. Find the book inventory at cost for a department with the following retail figures:

Gross sales	$106,000
Purchases	93,000
Opening inventory	88,000
Customer returns	4,500
Cumulative markup %	45.0%

_____
(Answer)

STOCK SHORTAGES AND OVERAGES

As previously stated, a retailer operating under the Retail Method may take physical inventory as many times a year as he wishes to verify the accuracy of his "book" records and then adjust his book inventory figure to agree with the physical inventory figure. It should be noted that taking physical inventory is not the means of correcting inventory shortage nor practices which lead to shortage. It simply points out how much shortage exists.

In the normal course of business the results of a physical inventory rarely tally precisely with the book inventory figure. If the total physical inventory figure is *less* than the book inventory figure, the discrepancy is called *stock shortage*. If the total physical inventory is *more* than the book inventory, the discrepancy is called *stock overage*. Very simply stated, a stock shortage means that there is less inventory actually on hand than there is supposed to be, according to the accounting records that have been kept. Conversely, a stock overage means that there is more inventory actually on hand than there is supposed to be, according to the accounting records.

Overages are rare. They are most likely to occur in stores with several branches, where a stock overage might be created by transferring merchandise to one branch but charging it in error to a different branch. In such a case, the branch that actually received the merchandise would have an overage, while the branch to which the transfer was charged would have a shortage.

Shortages are common and increasing among stores of all types at an alarming rate. Shortages *decrease profit* because they increase the cost of merchandise sold without a corresponding increase in net sales, and thus, in turn, decrease gross margin. For this reason, stores strive to hold storage figures to a minimum by:

- stressing greater accuracy in counting and listing physical inventory;
- exercising more care in recording purchases, price changes, and sales data;
- taking greater precautions against theft, such as using sensitized price tags, increasing security staffs and measures, and so on.

While stock shortages may not be directly the fault of the buyer or department manager in whose department they occur, more buyers and department managers have been fired for excessive shortages than for any other reason—simply because shortages reduce profits, and profit is the buyer's or department manager's responsibility.

Major Causes of Shortages

The two major causes of stock shortage and stock overage are (1) clerical errors and (2) physical merchandise losses. Common clerical errors include:

- salescheck and credit errors;
- errors in calculating the retail value of invoices;
- errors in charging or crediting departments;
- errors in recording merchandise transfers;
- failure to take or properly record markdowns;
- errors in recording returns-to-vendor;
- errors in recording physical inventory.

Physical merchandise losses occur through:

- pilferage (internal theft);
- shoplifting (theft by ostensible customers);
- failure to obtain receipts for merchandise loaned;
- breakage and spoilage, principally in transit;
- providing samples of yard goods, perfume, and so on, from regular stock.

Calculating Stock Shortage

Formulas: (for calculating stock shortage in dollars and as a percentage of sales):

(a) $ Stock shortage = Book inventory at retail − physical inventory at retail

(b) Stock shortage % = $\dfrac{\text{\$ Stock shortage}}{\text{\$ Net sales}}$

Problem:

Find (1) the stock shortage in dollars, and (2) the stock shortage in percent for a department with the following retail figures:

Beginning inventory	$110,000
Net sales	100,000
Purchases	60,000
Physical inventory	69,000

241

Solution 1:

Beginning inventory		$110,000
Purchases	+	60,000
Total merchandise handled	=	$170,000
Net sales	−	100,000
Book inventory	=	$ 70,000
Physical inventory	−	69,000
Stock shortage	=	$ 1,000

Solution 2:

$$\text{Stock shortage \%} = \frac{\$ \text{ Stock shortage}}{\$ \text{ Net sales}}$$

$$= \frac{\$1,000}{\$100,000}$$

$$= 1.0\%$$

Stock Shortage Reserves

Since stock shortages can be determined only when a complete physical inventory is taken, which is usually only once or twice a year, most stores set up interim monthly bookkeeping reserves for anticipated shortages. This means that between physical counts a predetermined percentage of net sales is allocated to a stock shortage reserve fund on a monthly basis. The purpose of this reserve is to offset the actual difference between the book inventory and the actual physical inventory when the latter is taken.

SUMMARY OF KEY TERMS

Chargeback. A store's invoice to a vendor. Another term for return-to-vendor or claim-against-vendor.

Perpetual Book Inventory. The book inventory system in which additions to and deductions in the value of stock on hand are recorded as these changes occur, and the value of that stock is calculated at regular, short-term intervals, such as daily, weekly, or monthly.

Preretailing. Indicating on each purchase order the unit retail price at which each style being ordered should be marked when it is received at the store.

Purchase Journal. A record of all merchandise received into stock and charged to a department's book inventory during any given period. Returns-to-vendor and claims-against-vendor may also be included on this type of report.

Stock Overage. A condition that exists when the value of the physical inventory is greater than that of the book inventory.

Stock Shortage. A condition that exists when the value of the physical inventory is less than that of the book inventory.

Stock Shortage Reserve. A bookkeeping procedure in which a monthly percentage of net sales is placed in reserve to offset the anticipated stock shortage likely to be found when a physical inventory is taken and its value compared with that of the book inventory.

REVIEW QUESTIONS—Book Inventory; Stock Shortages
and Overages

1. The accounting system in which additions to and reductions in the value of the stock on hand are made as these changes occur and are reported to the Accounting Office is

   usually referred to as a _____ _____ _____ .

2. Responsibility for the initiation and accuracy of most of the figures used in compiling book inventories is vested mainly in the

   (a) store's accounting office
   (b) merchandise manager
   (c) buyer
   (d) none of the above

   _____
   (Answer)

3. The documents having to do with the price and movement of merchandise are referred

   to in the retail trade as _____ .

4. What is a Purchase Journal and why is it an important inventory control device?

5. Name and describe five types of documents used in calculating a department's Book Inventory.

   (1)

   (2)

   (3)

   (4)

   (5)

6. When the physical inventory figure is less than the book inventory figure, the discrepancy is called a _____ _____ .

7. When the physical inventory figure is more than the book inventory figure, the discrepancy is called a _____ _____ .

8. Indicate with an "X" in the proper column below the effect of each of the following on a department's Book Inventory:

	Increases	Decreases	No Effect
(1) Purchases			
(2) Transfers in			
(3) Returns-to-vendors			
(4) Employee discounts			
(5) Markdowns			
(6) Additional markups			
(7) Gross sales			
(8) Customer returns			
(9) Stock shortage reserves			
(10) Merchandise on order			

9. One of the major advantages of the Retail Method is that it makes it possible to determine the approximate cost of the inventory on hand without having to determine the cost of each item in stock. True _____; False _____

10. Stores never take physical inventory more than once a year. True _____; False _____

REVIEW PROBLEMS—Book Inventory;
Stock Shortages and Overages

1. If the closing book inventory is $36,000 and the physical inventory $31,500 (both retail), what is the shortage percentage if sales were $150,000?

_____
(Answer)

2. If a book inventory indicates an on-hand stock of $64,260 as of July 31, and a physical inventory on that date indicates an on-hand stock of $62,450, what is the opening inventory figure for the period beginning August 1?

_____
(Answer)

3. From the following figures, find both the dollar and percentage shortage or overage figure:

Opening inventory	$22,000	$ _____
Retail purchases	17,500	Shortage or Overage
Net sales	18,000	
Markdowns	300	% _____
Employee discounts	600	Shortage or Overage
Physical inventory end of period	19,200	

4. A Household Appliance Department had gross sales of $59,000 and customer returns and allowances of $2,500. If the buyer's B.O.M. inventory was $25,000 at retail with a markup of 40%, his net purchases cost $31,500 and were marked to retail at $58,000, what was his E.O.M. book inventory at both cost and retail?

Cost $_____

Retail $_____

5. From the following information determine a department's closing book inventory at:

(a) Retail

(a) _____
(Answer)

(b) Cost

(b) _____
(Answer)

	Cost	Retail
Opening inventory	$10,000	$19,000
Net purchases	20,000	37,000
Net sales		32,000
Net markdowns		2,000

6. A gift shop had gross sales of $68,000 and customer returns and markdowns of $3,000 each. The buyer's beginning inventory was $24,000 at retail which represented a 47.5% markup. Net purchases were retailed at $80,000 at 50% markup. What was the buyer's closing book inventory at (a) cost and (b) retail?

(a)   Cost _____

(b)   Retail _____

7. A Drapery Department had an inventory on February 1 of $185,000. Gross purchases for the following 6-month period amounted $500,000, gross sales were $387,000, returns from customers $12,000, markdowns $27,000, returns-to-vendors $11,000, transfers to the Furniture Department $14,000, and employee discounts $6,500. What was the closing book inventory at retail on July 31?

_____
(Answer)

8. From the following figures, determine the closing book inventory:

Markdowns	$ 12,000
Purchases	315,000
Returns-to-vendors	20,000
Employee discounts	2,000
Goods on loan	1,500
Returns from customers	25,000
Transfers in	8,000
Transfers out	4,000
Gross sales	290,000
Opening inventory	180,000
Stock shortage reserve	1.5%

_____
(Answer)

9. A small boutique shop had an opening inventory of $45,000 at cost and $70,000 at retail. Net purchases during the 6-month period August 1 to January 31 amounted to $53,000 at cost and $90,000 at retail. Transportation on purchases cost $2,000. Net sales during the period totaled $85,000. Net markdowns amounted to $5,000 and discounts to employees and favored customers totaled $1,000. The closing physical inventory on January 31 amounted to $67,200 at retail. What was the shop's:

(a) January 31 book inventory at retail?   (a) _____

(b) Stock shortage for the 6-month period?   (b) _____

(c) Closing physical inventory at cost?   (c) _____

(d) Cost of merchandise sold?   (d) _____

(e) Gross margin?   (e) _____

CHAPTER 10

PERIODIC REPORTS ON THE MERCHANDISING OPERATION

Retailing is a business operation. Merchandising is a primary retailing function. Therefore merchandising is a business function, and good business practice implies that management:

1. formulate policies to govern the firm's activities;
2. prepare carefully considered operating budgets;
3. develop systems for keeping essential business records;
4. prepare regular periodic reports based on those records in which actual result figures can be compared with budgeted figures; and
5. make decisions as to any remedial actions relating to the business operation in order to improve working conditions and profit.

Since buyers and department managers are responsible for operating at a profit, they regularly receive a number of periodic summary reports on the financial aspects of their merchandising operation. Copies of such reports also go to top management of the firm, as well as to the buyer's and department manager's boss—the merchandise manager.

For the buyer or deparment manager these reports serve as important guides in operating the department or store more profitably. And as far as store management is concerned, they provide the means for evaluating each individual merchandising operation.

In medium- and large-volume stores there are likely to be a variety of such reports. Also they are likely to be more formal and detailed than those developed for use in smaller stores. Regardless of how formal or detailed the reports may be, however, they should be immediately and carefully studied by buyers and managers as the means of identifying potential problems that may be forestalled by taking corrective action before a problem gets out of hand.

Reports on actual results from the current operation are made more meaningful when figures for the same period last year are included for comparative purposes.

The reports referred to here fall roughly into two categories: financial and managerial. The major financial reports to which we refer are:

- Departmental Operating Statements (actually monthly P.&L. Statements);
- Open-to-Buy Reports;
- On-Order Reports;
- Sales Reports;
- Stock and Sales Reports;
- Return Sales Reports.

The major managerial reports to which we refer are:

- Basic Stock Lists;
- Age-of-Stock Reports (also known as Prior Stock Lists);
- Vendor Analysis;
- Markdown Analysis.

FINANCIAL REPORTS

Financial reports deal directly with the financial aspects of a business operation: monthly Operating Statements; Open-to-Buy and On-Order reports; Sales reports by classification and price line (with additional breakdown as required); Stock and Sales reports by style, classification, and price line; and Customer Returns reports. Each of these reports is usually issued in terms of actual dollars or units or both, with last year's figures for the same period included for comparative purposes. It should always be remembered that the name of the retailing game is "Beat Last Year!"

Department Operating Statement

The Accounting Department of each store prepares from its records a monthly Department Operating Statement for each of its selling departments. Each is a summary of all the financial aspects of a department's total merchandising operation during a given calendar or "4-5-4-week" month. A copy of each statement goes to the department buyer or manager, the divisional and/or general merchandise manager, and the president or general manager of the store.

The format adopted for such summaries varies from store to store. In general, however, those of large-volume, branch-operating retail organizations tend to be more complex and detailed than those of smaller-volume stores with few, if any, branches. Exhibit 10-1 is an example of a Department Operating Statement that might be used in a medium-sized store.

Whether detailed or simple, the Department Operating Statement is by far the most important of all periodic merchandising reports the buyer receives. This is because it represents, in summary form, every financial aspect of the buyer's job performance, usually in comparison to the current seasonal merchandise plan and/or last year's figures for the same period. To the student of retail merchandising, the Operating Statement is the most important document with which he/she should become acquainted. With an understanding of the inter-relationships of the various components involved and their effect upon ultimate profit, he/she will be prepared to detect and evaluate weaknesses, strengths, and potential problems as far as operating profit or loss is concerned in any size or type of retail operation.

DEPARTMENTAL OPERATING STATEMENT

Department No. 20

Month *March* Year 197-

Line		This Month				Year to Date						Line
		Plan		Actual		Plan		Actual		Last Year		
		$	%	$	%	$	%	$	%	$	%	
1	Gross Sales	38,000	108.0	39,476	108.6	69,120	108.0	71,396	108.2	72,669	108.3	1
2	Customer Returns	3,000	8.0	3,142	8.6	5,120	8.0	5,411	8.2	5,569	8.3	2
3	NET SALES	35,000	-9.3	36,334	3.8	64,000	-4.6	65,985	3.1	67,100	2.1	3
4	Beg. Stock @ Retail	66,500	39.6	65,816	39.6	82,800	—	81,950	39.5	86,520	39.2	4
5	Net Retail Purchases	60,200	40.0	58,960	40.0	76,400	40.0	76,102	40.0	78,559	39.5	5
6	End. Stock @ Retail	86,900	39.9	83,541	39.8	86,900	—	83,541	39.7	89,720	39.3	6
7	Markdowns	4,450	12.7	4,565	12.6	7,660	12.0	7,868	11.9	7,590	11.3	7
8	Employee Discounts	350	1.0	336	.9	640	1.0	658	1.0	669	1.0	8
9	Shortage Reserve	525	1.5	545	1.5	960	1.5	990	1.5	1,141	1.7	9
10	Workroom Costs	350	1.0	340	.9	640	1.0	690	1.0	672	1.0	10
11	Cash Discounts	2,890	8.3	2,830	7.8	3,667	5.7	3,653	5.5	3,707	5.5	11
12	GROSS MARGIN	13,056	37.3	13,446	37.0	22,912	35.8	23,092	35.0	23,322	34.8	12
13	Advertising	1,120	3.2	1,417	3.9	2,048	3.2	2,111	3.2	2,416	3.6	13
14	Special Events	210	.6	291	.8	384	.6	396	.6	537	.8	14
15	Buying Salaries	1,155	3.3	1,200	3.3	2,112	3.3	2,178	3.3	2,214	3.3	15
16	Buyer's Travel	175	.5	218	.6	320	.5	397	.6	402	.6	16
17	Selling Salaries	2,660	7.6	2,834	7.8	4,864	7.6	5,015	7.6	5,299	7.9	17
18	Stk & Cler. Salaries	280	.8	284	.8	512	.8	530	.8	604	.9	18
19	Supplies	70	.2	75	.2	128	.2	135	.2	135	.2	19
20	Delivery	140	.4	185	.5	256	.4	270	.4	268	.4	20
21	Other Direct Expense	1,050	3.0	1,091	3.0	1,920	3.0	1,982	3.0	2,015	3.0	21
22	TOTAL DIRECT EXPENSE (13 thru 21)	6,860	19.6	7,595	20.9	12,544	19.6	13,014	19.7	13,890	20.7	22
23	DEPT. CONTRIBUTION (12 minus 22)	6,196	17.7	5,851	16.1	10,368	18.2	10,078	15.3	9,432	14.1	23
24	Indirect Expense	4,095	11.7	4,178	11.5	7,488	11.7	7,536	11.5	7,851	11.7	24
25	TOTAL EXPENSES (22 plus 24)	10,955	31.3	11,773	32.4	20,032	31.3	20,620	31.2	21,741	32.4	25
26	OPERATING PROFIT (12 minus 25)	2,107	6.0	1,673	4.6	2,880	4.5	2,492	3.8	1,581	2.4	26

EXHIBIT 10-1 DEPARTMENTAL OPERATING STATEMENT
Mary D. Troxell, *Fashion Merchandising,* 2nd ed. (New York: Gregg Division, McGraw-Hill, 1976), p. 283.

Although there is no standard format for the Operating Statement, most include planned and actual retail figures, in dollars and percentages, for the current month this year, last year, and year-to-date for all phases of the merchandising operation, such as:

- gross sales;
- customer returns and allowances;
- net sales;
- beginning and ending stocks;
- net purchases;
- net transfers (if any);
- net additional markup (if any);
- net markdowns;
- employee discounts;
- stock shortage reserve;
- workroom costs;
- cash discounts earned;
- gross margin;
- major direct expenses itemized, such as selling salaries, buying salaries, buyer's travel expense, stock and clerical salaries, advertising, supplies, and so on;
- other miscellaneous direct expenses—not itemized;
- total direct expenses;
- buyer's (department's) contribution to storewide expenses and profit;

- itemized or nonitemized indirect expenses, such as utilities, maintenance, management salaries, insurance, protection department, display department, and so on;
- total direct (controllable by buyer) and indirect (noncontrollable by buyer) expenses;
- net departmental operating profit before taxes.

One large, branch-operating West Coast department store attaches so much importance to the Department Operating Statement that they give each of their management trainees a copy of a guide on how to reduce cost of sales and expenses, and how to maximize operating profit (see Exhibit 10-2).

Open-To-Buy Reports

Open-to-buy is the retailer's primary inventory control tool, as discussed in Chapters 4 and 8. It is a "result" figure—the figure obtained when merchandise on-order for delivery during a specified period is subtracted from planned purchases for that same period.

As previously discussed, open-to-buy may be calculated in units as well as in dollars. Form 4-7, is an example of one large store's O.T.B. report in dollars as of the end of the second week of May 1977. Exhibit 10-3 is an example of a computerized departmental Unit open-to-buy Report as of Feb. 21, 1977, for the balance of that month plus the months of March through July. Exhibit 10-4 is an example of an O.T.B. report frequently used by small stores.

A selling department with O.T.B. can continually bring in new, fresh merchandise to "spruce up" the stock on hand, thereby stimulating interest and enthusiasm for the merchandise among salespeople and customers alike. Reorders of fast sellers can be made and sales, in general, improve.

An overbought condition, on the other hand, means that there is no money for reordering fast selling merchandise or to bring in new, fresh stock. The department's total allowance for purchases for that period is tied up in slow-moving stock that daily grows less appealing and is apt to become shopworn. Nor is there money to make opportune "buys" should these become available. This condition is usually self-perpetuating. Sales decline, markdowns increase, interest on the part of both customers and salespeople wanes, insurance and interest costs rise, and the overbought condition usually worsens.

Merchandise On-Order Report

Most stores require a weekly list of outstanding orders. In some stores the buyers or department managers are responsible for compiling such a list. In other stores the job is handled by the Order Checking Department or the Merchandise Manager's office. Orders scheduled for delivery in future months, as well as the current month, are listed separately by:

- vendor
- purchase order number
- total cost of each order
- total retail of each order
- scheduled month of delivery

Form 4-8 is an example of a weekly dollar On-Order report. A unit On-Order Report is incorporated in Exhibit 10-4.

OPERATING STATEMENT — Total All Stores Combined

Dept.		MONTH %	%		YEAR TO DATE %	%	
1. Net Sales and % Inc. or Dec.	Gross Sales less returns (line #2). The real volume done.						1
2. Mdse. Returns and % to Gross Sales	Purchases returned by Customers.						2
3. No. of Transactions & Average Sale	Total recorded by Salespeople. Average Sale equals Gross Sales divided by # of Transactions.						3
4. Markdown and Allowances	A necessary calculated risk – plan ahead; move non-selling or slow-selling merchandise.						4
5. Employee Discounts	Employees are Customers also.						5
6. Inventory Shortages	The difference between the physical inventory and the book inventory – be alert and prevent						6
7. Total Retail Deductions	Computed by the Statistical Department – taken from Stock Ledger.						7
8. Purchases and Markup	Total merchandise bought in time period – aim for high initial markup, watch transportation chg.						8
9. Stock – End of Month & Cum. Markup	Ending Book Inventory – keep in line with sales, watch for necessary adjustms. on Model Stock Plan?						9
10. Workroom Cost	If applicable, Alterations, Furniture repair, etc.						10
11. Other Cost of Sales	Costs incurred other than cost of merchandise or workroom costs, i.e., repair work outside store.						11
12. Gross Margin and % to Sales	Net Sales minus Net Cost of Goods Sold, before operating costs are deducted.						12
13. Discounts – % to Purchases	Work with Resources to increase cash discount – works directly to increase profit.						13
14. Telephone Charges	Based on actual long-distance charges – plan your calls, make use also of mail, telegram, etc.						14
15. Interest	Charged at rate of 2% (at cost) per month of Department's ending inventory – keep stock in line.						15
16. Taxes and Ins. on Mdse.	Pro-rated to the department on the basis of beginning inventory at cost – penalty if overbought.						16
17. Payroll Tax	Unemployment and F.I.C.A. (4.8%) based on monthly payroll.						17
18. Space Charge – Bldg.	Charge per square foot; suburban stores pro-rated on basis of month's sales – make use of space.						18
19. Space Charge – Ser. Bldg.	Charge per square foot – keeping stock in line will eliminate the need for extra space.						19
20. Maintenance Expense	Charge on a square foot basis – janitors, carpenters, etc.						20
21. Newspaper Advertising	Cost per column inch – make ads sell for you; work with resources for advertising allowances.						21
22. Advertising Preparation	Based on total number of column inches – save the time of both you and advertising.						22
23. Window Display	Actual usage charged – make best use of the space and inform your salespeople of displays.						23
24. Signs	Based on cost of 100 word sign units per department – keep signs brief, to the point, and clean.						24
25. All Other Direct Publicity	Charges for direct mail, radio, television, models, broadsides, etc.						25
26. Travel	Department's share of Divisionals and Buyers travel – plan trips carefully.						26
27. Receiving and Marking	Cost distributed on basis of actual number of pieces of merchandise marked – use pre-ticketing.						27
28. All Other Direct Buying	Salaries of Buyer and Asst. plus share of Div-sional's stock control, classification clerical.						28
29. Stock & Clerical Salaries	Charge for stock personnel who actually work for the department – check the necessity of such.						29
30. Salespeople's Salaries	Actual payroll expense and commission; largest expense – analyze schedules.						30
31. Wrapping and Packing	Includes courtesy gift wrap – encourage "takes" and "Clerk wraps".						31
32. Delivery	Chg'd on basis of current month's deliveries multiplied by a fixed package rate – sell "takes".						32
33. All Other Direct Selling	Charged as incurred, i.e., selling supplies, salaries of clerical instructor, inventory, etc.						33
34. Total Direct Expense	Total of Lines #14–#33.						34
35. Indirect Expense	Expenses not chargeable to specific departments; pro-rated on year-to-date sales.						35
36. Total Expense	Total of Lines #34 & #35; subtracted from Gross Margin to arrive at line #37, the most important.						36
37. Net Profit and % to Sales	The amount remaining after subtracting all cost of sales & expenses. % equals Net Profits divided by Net Sales.						37

EXHIBIT 10-2 BUYER'S GUIDE TO THE OPERATING STATEMENT

Dept. 42 Casual Dresses   WEEK ENDING FEB. 21, 197—

CODE	PRICE RANGE	E.O.M. INV. 1/31/7–	FEB. ON ORDER	AVAILABLE FOR SALE	PLANNED SALES	ANTICIPATED MARK DOWNS	PLANNED 2/28/7– INV.	OPEN TO RECEIVE FEB.	MAR.	APR.	MAY	JUNE-JULY	OPEN TO BUY MAR-JULY
700	14.00	771	100	871	500	40	750	419	300	800	1000	100	2885
702	18.00	621	85	706	425	30	900	649	500	1000	250	0	2625
704	22.00	1412	210	1622	800	70	1500	748	200	1400	1400	50	3410
706	26.00	3201	610	3811	1600	120	3000	909	800	800	0	0	4310
707	30.00	2120	350	2470	1000	80	2500	1110	1000	750	500	0	4820
708	35.00	1409	300	1709	600	50	1200	141	150	150	100	100	2530
TOTAL MISSY		9534	1655	11189	4925	390	8850	3976	2950	4900	3250	250	20580
710	14.00	494	500	994	700	50	1050	806	1000	1000	500	500	3405
712	18.00	1464	1000	2464	1000	80	1500	116	850	850	550	550	4460
714	22.00	2026	800	2826	1100	100	1700	74	1500	1200	700	0	4795
716	26.00	2251	100	2351	850	70	1500	69	1000	200	100	0	3620
TOTAL JUNIOR		6235	2400	8635	3650	300	5750	1065	4350	3250	1850	1050	17280
TOTAL CASUAL		15769	4055	19824	8575	690	15600	5041	7300	8150	5100	1300	37860

EXHIBIT 10-3 UNIT OPEN-TO-BUY REPORT

Mary D. Troxell, *Fashion Merchandising,* 2nd ed. (New York: Gregg Division, McGraw-Hill, 1976), p. 283.

Sales and Stock/Sales Reports

As previously discussed, open-to-buy may be calculated in units as well as in dollars. control. Therefore, actual sales in relation to planned sales are studied closely because of their effect on other elements of the merchandise budget and more particularly in relation to their effect on operating profit. Formats used for reporting sales and stock as well as sales vary widely, as do the periods covered and the amount of detail included. Basically,

The Boutique
Dollar Open-to-Buy

Department _____   Week Ending _____

1. Physical inventory on hand this Monday				
2. On order this Monday				
3. Total inventory and on order (lines 1 plus 2)				
4. Planned sales this week (Monday thru Saturday)				
5. Planned closing physical inventory at end of this week (Saturday)				
6. Planned on order at end of this week				
7. Planned total closing inventory and on order at end of this week (lines 5 plus 6)				
8. Planned total closing inventory and on order and planned sales for this week ending Saturday (lines 7 plus 4)				
9. Open to buy for this week (lines 8 minus 3)				

EXHIBIT 10-4 WEEKLY DOLLAR OPEN-TO-BUY CONTROL

however, sales reports fall into two categories: (1) "Flash" sales and (2) periodic audited sales reports.

Flash Sales. Daily reports of dollar sales (Exhibit 10-5) by departments are developed from the saleschecks and cash register tapes for the previous day and are circulated early the following business day to all merchandising executives. For comparison purposes, these reports may also include dollar sales for the corresponding selling day in the previous year and year-to-date sales figures. These reports are particularly useful in stores that employ the older, manual system of record-keeping. In stores that employ newer mechanized systems, it is possible to get more detailed and current sales information to buyers, department managers, and merchandise managers considerably faster than under the older manual system of record-keeping.

Smith & Welsh

STORE	DOWNTOWN FLASH NET SALES CURRENT PERIOD DOLLARS (00)	% CHANGE	Y-T-D NET SALES YR. THRU CURRENT PERIOD % CHANGE	TOTAL DOWNTOWN + BRANCHES FLASH NET SALES CURRENT PERIOD DOLLARS (00)	% CHANGE	Y-T-D NET SALES YEAR THRU CURRENT PERIOD DOLLARS (00)	% CHANGE	BEGINNING OF MONTH RETAIL STOCK DOLLARS (00)	B.O.M. STOCK TO SALES RATIO
Q				360.1	6.4	2713.6	10.1	756.1	2.1
Y	29.5	-65.4	42.2	122.4	-71.8	1294.8	-45.5	191.2	1.6
G									
O									
U	33.7	-33.7	22.3	251.6	-9.7	1166.1	-7.0	363.1	1.4
J	23.1	6.6	3.3	80.0	-10.0	671.2	12.0	153.5	1.9
W	24.0	15.9	20.6	344.8	11.9	2496.4	23.9	410.7	1.2
B	22.6	-28.0	3.2	81.0	-6.4	662.4	-4.1	152.3	1.9
P	43.4	3.8	-14.4	271.1	40.6	1676.9	15.2	557.7	2.1
V	49.0	16.9	3.2	490.4	3.8	3416.2	14.4	838.7	1.7
S	25.4	-1.9	6.3	209.3	20.4	1376.9	15.5	620.2	3.0
I	18.7	-33.1	-4.5	297.0	9.1	1744.1	-4.5	475.3	1.5
R	23.9	-36.1	-4.9	173.9	-36.8	1710.3	-1.0	475.6	2.7
C	31.5	8.3	-7.9	322.4	9.0	1744.1	-4.5	475.3	1.5
M	27.4	-16.6	33.2	190.7	10.6	930.0	-18.1	367.2	1.9
Z	25.0	86.6	-1.3	148.2	90.5	848.2	25.7	83.4	.6
CC				142.0	9.1	973.1	15.6	162.3	1.1
X	16.6	-19.5	-10.2	199.7	5.0	1086.6	9.6	274.1	1.4
L	15.3	4.8	2.2	66.4	4.1	387.9	-2.8	133.0	2.0
T	18.1	4.0	25.6	349.5		1136.8		482.3	1.4
K	30.2	39.2	17.9	136.7	61.4	897.4	11.1	352.2	2.6
F									
BB	16.3	20.5	7.1	99.1	15.2	589.4	24.5	140.1	1.4
E	17.7	21.7	40.6	105.7	27.1	865.0	21.6	234.4	2.2
AA	6.7	-19.5	-32.0	60.4	-17.2	426.8	-14.1	110.1	1.8
H	16.7	-2.3	-12.1	82.2	-8.9	601.8	1.8	74.8	.9
DD									
EE	13.9	11.2	-16.2	78.9	10.3	657.1	10.1	148.5	1.9
GG				57.7	46.1	412.7	112.1	90.7	1.6
FF									
D									

4-5-4 PERIOD 11/28/78 to 1/1/79 (December) 19 78 PAGE
DEPT. 364 Misses' Casuals & Knits-Moderate-Ready-to-Wear 32

EXHIBIT 10-5 FLASH SALES REPORT

Periodic Stock and Sales Reports.   More detailed sales reports, usually including some stock on hand information, may be issued daily, semiweekly, weekly, biweekly, or monthly. Under manual systems the reports are usually issued weekly, semimonthly, or monthly. Since A.D.P. and E.D.P. systems can produce reports so much faster, however, summary reports under either of these two systems are usually issued more frequently.

Exhibit 10-6A is an example of a computer-prepared 3-day stock and sales Style

01

Smith & Welsh

DEPT 349

3 DAYS ENDING 123177

SELLING PRICE	CLASS	HOUSE	STYLE	STORE	NET SALES LAST 3 DAYS	THIS WEEK	ONE WEEK AGO	2 WKS. AGO	TOTAL LAST 4 WEEKS	TOTAL TO DATE	ON HAND	INITIAL DATE OF RECEIPT	TOTAL	CUSTOMER RETURNS	ACTIVITY INDICATOR	COMMENTS
28.00	53	042	2103	1		1		2	3	50	16	081177				V9
				2						4		090877				T9
				3						7	4	090877				T9
				4						4		081177				T9
				5						11		081477				T9
				TOT		1		2	3	76	20			16	SLOW 1	
32.00	53	042	2104	3						6		081177				V9
				4						11		082877				T9
				5						3		082877				T9
				TOT						0	20			13	SLOW 2	
28.00	53	042	2124	1	3	6	4		10	10	11	120877				R4
				6			1		1	1	7	120877				R4
				2	1	1			1	1	5	121177				R3
				3	2	2	1		3	3	11	120877				R4
				4	2	3	1		4	4	8	120877				R4
				5	1		1		1	1	13	121177				R3
				TOT	9	12	8		20	20	55			2		
36.00	53	042	2126	1	3	7	3	13	33	33	5	112477				T3
				3				1	1	1		112777				T3
				4	4	5		3	9	9	6	112777				T3
				5		1	1	1	4	4	4	112077				R9
				TOT	7	13	4	18	47	47	15			4		
28.00	53	042	2128	1	4	7	-1	2	10	20	9	111377				T1
				6			1	1	4	12		111377				T2
				2	3	5		4	11	15	9	111377				T2
				3			2	3	7	13	9	111377				R9
				4			3 1	8	12	24	12	111377				T1
				5	1		4	3	13	19	10	111377				T6
				TOT	8	12	5	21	57	103	49			21		
38.00	53	042	2130	1	3	4	3		7	7	11	120877				T2
				3	1	1	1		2	2	6	112777				R7
				4			1	1	2	2	6	112777				R7
				5	1	1			1	1	3	121577				T2
				TOT	5	6	5	1	12	12	26			1		
48.00	53	082	0255	1						2	2	101377				T1
				3						2		101677				T9
				4						2	1	101377				T9
				TOT					0	4	3			4	SLOW 3	
48.00	53	085	0842	1	-1	-1		-1	-2	1	9	111377				T3
				2					1	1		111777				T3
				3			1		3	4	4	111377				T8

EXHIBIT 10-6A STYLE STATUS REPORT

Status Report from a large East Coast, branch-operating department store and developed through E.D.P. Information in terms of units includes:

- selling price of each unit;
- classification;
- vendor's "house number";
- vendor's style number;
- store identification number;
- unit sales last 3 days;
- unit sales this week;
- unit sales 1 week ago;
- unit sales 2 weeks ago;
- total unit sales last 4 weeks;
- total unit sales to date (since first in stock);
- units on hand as of reporting date;
- date of initial receipt of each style;
- total customer returns;
- activity indicator.

Exhibit 10-6B is quite similar to Exhibit 10-6A in type of information presented. It is also a summary report and is electronically processed. However, it differs in a few respects, such as affording:

- a brief description of each item;
- cost price per unit;
- number of units on order.

Return Sales Report

As explained in Chapters 3 and 4, customer returns and allowances decrease gross sales and therefore anticipated retail income. Since they reduce gross sales they exert a negative effect on potential operating profit. It is therefore imperative that customer returns and allowances be carefully watched by the department buyer or manager and everything possible be done to keep them at a minimum.

Major causes of customer returns and allowances are:

- faulty merchandise;
- poor selling techniques;
- not competitively priced;
- poorly kept stock (soiled, wrinkled, etc.).

Exhibit 10-7 is a sample of one store's return sales report. Note that it includes:

- store identification letter;
- merchandising division number;
- department number;
- $ gross sales;
- $ returns;
- % returns to gross sales.

```
Smith & Welsh

                    DEPARTMENT 494      07/10/77
VEND 324  - REGULAR                                      PAGE  8533

       WKS FRM                          ******SALES BY WEEK******
       RECEIPT   TOTAL    ON     ON    THIS   LAST    2 WK    3 WK   CURR
  STR  1ST LST   SALES  ORDER   HAND   WEEK   WEEK    AGO     AGO    STAT

  ...CLS 660   STY 02601   SS STRIPE          RET 36.00 CST 17.75......
  00    5   5      1       0      1      0      0       0       0
  01    5   5      2       0      2      1      0       0       0     F
  02    5   5      2       0      2      0      1       1       0     S
  03    5   5      1       0      3      1      0       0       0     F
  04    5   5      2       0      2      0      0       1       1     S
  05    5   5      1       0      3      0      0       0       0     S
  06    5   5      1       0      3      0      1       0       0     S
  07    5   5      1       0      3      0      0       0       0     S
  08    5   5      1       0      3      0      0       1       0     S
  09    5   5      1       0      3      0      0       0       0     S
  5-27  5-27     13 *     0 *    25 *   2 *    2 *     3 *     1 *SLOW
  RTM        2

  ...CLS 660   STY 02604   SS VERONA STRP    RET 36.00 CST 17.75......
  00    2   2      5       0      7      1      1       3       0
  01    2   2      0       0      4      0      0       0       0
  02    2   2      1       0      3      0      0       1       0
  03    2   2      0       0      4      0      0       0       0
  04    2   2      2       0     10      1      0       1       0
  05    2   2      3       0      1      2      1       0       0     F
  06    2   2      1       0     11      1      0       0       0
  07    2   2      2       0      2      1      1       0       0     F
  08    2   2      0       0      4      0      0       0       0
  09    2   2      0       0      4      0      0       0       0
  6-21  6-21     14 *     0 *    50 *   6 *    3 *     5 *     0 *

  ...CLS 660   STY 02605   SS BLOCK ARNEL    RET 36.00 CST 17.75......
  00    5   5      3       0      1      0      1       2       0
  04    5   5      3       0      1      1      0       0       2     F
  05    5   5      2       0      2      0,     0       1       0     S
  06    5   5      0       0      4      0      0       0       0     S
  07    5   5      1       0      3      1      0       0       0     F
  5-27  5-27      9 *     0 *    11 *   2 *    1 *     3 *     2 *

  ...CLS 660   STY 04439   SS SOLID RIBBED   RET 30.00 CST 14.75......
  00    9   9      6       0      0      0      0       0       0
  04    9   4      6       0      1      2      0       0       0     F
  05    9   9      6       0      0      0      0       0       0
  06    9   9      3       0      0      0      0       0       0
  07    9   9      2       0      1      0      0       1       0
  08    9   9      3       0      0      0      0       0       1
  09    9   9      3       0      0      0      0       0       0
  4-27  4-27     29 *     0 *     2 *   2 *    0 *     1 *     1 *FAST
```

EXHIBIT 10-6B STYLE SUMMARY REPORT

The student should recall that only in the case of Customer Returns is percentage calculated on gross sales. All other factors affecting operating profit are calculated as percentages of net sales.

MAJOR MANAGERIAL REPORTS

Store management and individual buyers use a number of reports other than the strictly financial ones described above in measuring the success of a department's merchandising operation and in guiding it toward even greater accuracy in meeting consumer demand and greater operating profit. Chief among this type of report are Basic Stock Lists, Slow-Selling Stock reports, Vendor Analyses, and Markdown Analyses.

Smith & Welsh

RETURN SALES

DEPT.: 446, 447   PERIOD: 01 1979

ST	DV	DEP	GROSS SALES	RETURNS	PCT
PH	10	446	37,668	2,056	5.5
A	10	446	10,646	926	8.7
J	10	446	9,134	906	9.9
W	10	446	9,485	637	6.7
C	10	446	12,708	906	7.1
S	10	446	12,373	928	7.5
P	10	446	7,261	459	6.3
N	10	446	8,449	471	5.6
E	10	446	5,548	324	5.8
TOTAL		446	113,272	7,613	6.7
PH	10	447	33,631	3,145	9.4
A	10	447	11,277	1,475	13.1
J	10	447	10,895	1,388	12.7
W	10	447	10,513	896	8.5
C	10	447	20,096	1,917	9.5
S	10	447	20,803	1,871	9.0
P	10	447	13,878	1,098	7.9
N	10	447	13,990	1,151	8.2
E	10	447	12,598	899	7.1
TOTAL		447	147,681	13,840	9.4

EXHIBIT 10-7 DEPARTMENT MONTHLY RETURN SALES REPORT (DOLLARS AND PERCENTAGES)

Basic Stock Lists

Basic stock is merchandise that enjoys such consistent demand that it should be kept in stock at all times throughout a year or special selling season. A basic may be a specific item or a group of substitutable items, such as men's white dress shirts or jeans for men, women, boys, and girls.

When a store is frequently out of an item that enjoys consistent demand, customer goodwill, as well as sales, is at stake. For this reason some stores require, and all stores encourage, their buyers and department managers to maintain a list of specific items in their departments that are considered basic each selling season of the year, and to set up dates for periodic stock counts or similar methods for making sure that there is always an adequate supply of such goods on hand.

There is no established system or format for basic stock reports. But whatever the format or system used, maintenance of adequate basic stock inventory should have priority on each department's open-to-buy.

Slow-Selling Stock Reports

Slow-selling merchandise is defined as merchandise that has been in stock so long as to endanger making a profit from its eventual sale. Slow-selling reports, of which Exhibit 10-8

			ANNUAL INVENTORY		MAY 15		JULY 15		SEPT. 15			

Smith & Welsh **SLOW MOVING STOCK**   SEASON LETTER _____ STORE NO. _____ DEPT. NO. _____

LOC. OF STOCK	CLASS	DESCRIPTION	Quan.	Unit Price	Quan.	Unit Price	Quan.	Unit Price	Quan.	Unit Price	Quan.	Unit Price
		TOTAL										
		RECORDED BY										

EXHIBIT 10-8 SLOW-SELLING STOCK

is an example, are those that provide the retailer with information in summary form of the amount of stock in units and in dollars in each of a number of seasons prior to the current one. Since each price ticket contains a season letter indicating when the item was received into stock, (see Forms 8-4A and 8-4B), this information is easily obtained either from periodic stock counts or from physical inventory records. Reports are created by listing the stock by age (season) groups, totaling each group, and then showing what percentage of the total inventory each age group constitutes. These reports are then spot-checked periodically, indicating what steps have been taken to dispose of the slow sellers.

In an effort to minimize slow sellers in fashion departments, some of the larger general merchandise chains require any merchandise remaining in a store's stock six weeks after its receipt from the Fashion Distribution Center is subject to an automatic markdown system until its final removal from stock.

Vendor Analysis

A retailer should rate vendors in terms of how accurately their merchandise meets the needs of the store's customers—*never* on the basis of personal relationships.

In an effort to evaluate the department's vendors, a buyer may, with the help of the store's Accounting office, maintain records of dealings with each vendor. While there are no standardized forms on which to record the essential information, most forms in use today for this purpose (Exhibit 10-9) indicate:

- vendor's name and address;
- vendor's house and/or Duns number;

VENDOR ANALYSIS

DEPT 189 — 2ND QUARTER ENDING 7/31/79 — YEAR TO DATE — DATE

RESOURCE NUMBER	NAME	2Q NET PURCHASES RETAIL	2Q COST	2Q TRANS $	2Q M.U. %	2Q DISC. % TO COST	2Q ANTL. $	2Q % RTNS. TO COST PURCH.	YTD NET PURCHASES RETAIL	YTD COST	YTD TRANS $	YTD M.U. %	YTD DISC. % TO COST	YTD ANTL. $	MARK DOWNS $	TO RET/PURCH.	VENDOR MARGIN %	REMARKS
215-3385	ALLIED FELT CORP	-	-	-	-	-		-	.1	.1		48.1	-		-	-	48.1	
226-4471	THE VILLAGER	4.5	2.1	-	52.3	-		-	4.5	2.1	-	52.3	-		242	5.4	46.9	
232-1818	MALAMUT & CHANEN	.3	.2	-	45.3	2.2		-	.6	.3	-	45.2	2.2		-	-	46.4	
238-7389	E I DUPONT				-	-		-					-		-	-		
290-0389	KLOPMAN MILLS INC	1.1	.6	-	41.4	3.0		-	1.1	.6		41.4	3.0		-	-	43.1	
290-0405	BURLINGTON INDUSTR	6.1	3.6	20	40.7	3.0		.8	14.9	9.0	51	39.6	2.7		-	-	41.3	
290-0611	J P STEVENS & CO INC				-	-		-	2.9	1.6	22	45.0	1.0		250	8.5	37.0	
312-4831	DAN RIVER MILLS				-	-		-	2.2	1.2	8	44.6	-		-	-	44.3	
335-9239	INDIAN HEAD MILLS	25.4	13.9	74	45.1	3.0		2.6	60.9	32.9	211	45.7	3.0		100	.2	47.3	
590-0204	LANDAU WOOLEN CO	.1			46.4	-		-	.2	.1	1	45.2	-		-	-	45.2	
590-1160	GOTTSCHALK & CO	.5	.3		43.4	2.8		-	5.4	3.1	16	42.8	3.0		-	-	44.5	
590-4065	LOOMBEST FABRICS	1.1	.6		45.8	2.9		-	2.6	1.4	4	45.6	2.9		-	-	47.2	
590-4883	DONNY BROOK FABRIC	4.8	2.7	11	44.4	-		1.1	12.4	6.7	29	46.0	-		-	-	46.0	
590-8504	MARRIELO FABRICS				-	-		-				-	-		-	-	-	
591-1250	VALTEX FABRICS INC	1.5	.8	7	45.9	3.1		-	1.5	.8	7	45.9	3.1		-	-	47.5	
591-2274	JANICE INTERNATIONA				-	-		*	-.3	-.2	5	-	-		-	-	-	
698-6186	ISIDOR KAPLAN	26.1	14.0	216	45.6	-		3.0	45.6	24.6	319	45.3	-		1667	3.7	41.7	
698-9396	RAILWAY EXPRESS			6	-	-		-			7	-	-		-	-	-	
698-9693	ROSEWOOD FABRICS	8.2	4.6	51	43.0	3.0		.4	23.0	12.9	142	43.4	3.0		-	-	45.2	
891-7460	BENROSE FABRIC CO				-	-		-	2.2	1.2	6	45.3	3.0		-	-	47.0	
999-9989	CUSTOMER ALLOWANC														167			
999-9997	DEPT RESPONSIBLE														9414			
	TOTAL DEPT SUMMARY	179.1	96.2	741	45.9	2.2		1.7	428.9	232.8	1739	45.3	2.3		13530	3.2	43.5	

EXHIBIT 10-9 VENDOR ANALYSIS

- year-to-date purchases at cost;
- year-to-date purchases at retail;
- year-to-date markup on retail;
- transportation arrangements and costs;
- cash discount and anticipation earned;
- year-to-date dollar markdowns;
- year-to-date markdown percentage to purchases;
- year-to-date returns and claims;
- year-to-date advertising allowance.

Since buyers do business with many vendors over the period of a season or year, this type of report is especially helpful in bringing into focus the overall value of each vendor with whom the store has done business, and focusing attention on the business aspect of the relationship rather than on purely personal ones.

Markdown Analysis

Markdown analyses and the reasons for taking them yield valuable clues as to a buyer's proficiency in gauging customer demand, the quality of departmental supervision, and the extent to which various vendors have contributed to the department's maintained markup and operating profit—to creating a problem or helping to solve one.

There is no standard form used for analyzing markdowns. However, the Vendor Analysis, as just described, provides for calculation of markdowns taken on purchases from each vendor. In addition, many price change forms (see Chapters 7 and 9) provide space for indicating the reason(s) for taking the markdowns entered on each form. Suggested reasons might be:

- remainders of promotional purchases;
- slow-moving or inactive stock;
- special sales from stock;
- competitive price adjustments;
- broken assortments and remnants;
- shopworn, soiled, or damaged;
- unpopular color, size, fabrication;
- allowance to customer;
- salvage.

Periodic review of markdowns taken and the reasons for same may indicate that the buyer or department manager should take corrective steps as to:

- stockkeeping procedures;
- vendors used;
- purchasing colors, fabrics, sizes more closely related to demand;
- buying too many units on initial order;
- shopping competition more carefully.

SUMMARY OF KEY TERMS

Average Gross Sale. Dollar sales divided by number of sales transactions.

Basic Stock. Merchandise that is in such consistent demand that it should be kept in stock at all times throughout a year or special selling season.

Buyer's Contribution (to Operating Profit). The difference between gross margin and total controllable expense.

Controllable Expense. Same as direct expense (see Chapter 3)—those expenses over which the buyer or department manager can exercise considerable control.

Department Operating Statement. The equivalent of a monthly departmental Profit and Loss Statement.

Flash Sales Report. A daily report showing unaudited departmental sales totals in dollars for the previous day.

Key Resource. A vendor with whom a store has done a substantial share of its business in recent years. Also referred to as a "preferred" resource.

Noncontrollable Expense. Same as indirect expense (see Chapter 3)—expenses that are storewide in nature and over which a buyer or department manager has no control.

Slow-Selling Merchandise. Merchandise that has been in stock so long as to endanger making a profit on it.

Name_____ Date_____

REVIEW QUESTIONS

COMPLETION—Write your answers on lines provided.

1. Merchandise which is in such consistent demand that it should be kept in stock at all times during a year or special selling season is referred to as _____ _____.

2. A buyer's contribution to operating profit represents the difference between _____ _____ and total controllable expense.

3. The equivalent of a monthly P & L Statement is known as an _____ _____.

4. A store's or department's _____ _____ represents the difference between gross margin and total expenses.

5. _____ _____ is another term for direct expense.

6. Daily reports showing unaudited sales totals for the previous day are referred to in the trade as _____ _____reports.

7. A vendor with whom a store has consistently done a substantial share of its business is referred to as a _____ _____.

8. _____ _____ merchandise can be described as goods that have been in stock so long as to endanger making a profit on it.

9. Expenses that are storewide in nature and over which a buyer has little or no control are known as _____ expenses.

10. In business the term "bottom line" refers to _____.

TRUE-FALSE—Circle your choice of answer.

T F 1. The Operating Statement is primarily a sales report.

T F 2. Open-to-buy is a retailer's primary inventory control tool.

T F 3. Flash Sales reports are developed from the previous day's unaudited sales-checks and cash register tapes.

T F 4. On-Order reports are developed primarily to see how much merchandise has been ordered from each vendor.

T F   5. Stores employing electronic data processing systems can get summary Stock-and-Sales reports out much quicker than can those using a manual system of record-keeping.

T F   6. Customer returns and allowances are calculated as a percentage of net sales.

T F   7. Adequate basic stock inventory should have priority on a department's or store's open-to-buy.

T F   8. Promptness of delivery of orders is an important consideration when rating vendors.

T F   9. Periodic markdown analyses reveal the percentage of each vendor's merchandise that had to be marked down.

T F   10. Last year's summary results are of little value when evaluating this year's periodic reports on the merchandising operation.

MULTIPLE CHOICE—Circle your choice of answer.

1. Periodic reports on the results of a merchandising operation
   a. are standardized throughout the industry.
   b. are issued monthly.
   c. vary from store to store in format and detail.
   d. are prepared by the buyers.

2. Open-to-buy for a specified period can be calculated
   a. only at the beginning of that period.
   b. at any time during that period.
   c. only in dollars.
   d. only in units of merchandise.

3. Most stores require an On-Order report to be made up
   a. weekly.
   b. semi-monthly.
   c. monthly.
   d. seasonally.

4. Flash Sales reports are usually issued
   a. weekly.
   b. semi-monthly.
   c. monthly.
   d. daily.

5. A major cause of customer returns and allowances is
   a. faulty merchandise.
   b. poor selling techniques.
   c. merchandise not being competitively priced.
   d. all of the above.

6. Basic Stock refers to merchandise that
   a. has a high rate of stock turnover.
   b. has a low rate of stock turnover.
   c. is in consistent demand throughout the year or other specified selling season.
   d. is low in price.

7. Slow-selling merchandise adversely affects a department's or store's
   a. rate of stock turnover.
   b. open-to-buy.
   c. assortment planning.
   d. all of the above.

8. The basis for rating vendors should be
   a. how accurately their merchandise meets customer needs.
   b. personal relationship with the buyer.
   c. geographical location.
   d. their terms of sale.

9. Periodic review of markdowns taken afford valuable clues as to
   a. final profit.
   b. the rate of stock turnover.
   c. why they were taken.
   d. monthly markdown percentages.

10. Most financial summary reports on the merchandising operation
    a. are limited to this year's actual results in dollars or units or both.
    b. include last year's figures for the same period for comparative purposes.
    c. are issued monthly.
    d. are unavailable to buyers.

INDEX

269

M

Maintained markup, 140
Managerial reports, 258-61
Markdown analysis, 262
Markdown cancellations, 167, 174-76
Markdowns, 167-74
    amount to be taken, 174
    calculations, 167, 169-71
    causes of, 171-72
    defined, 168
    percentage, 170-71, 174
    planning, 75-76
    purposes of, 168-69
    retail inventory value and, 232-33
    timing of, 173-74
Markup cancellations, 167, 178-79
Markups:
    additional, 167, 177-78, 230
    average, 138-40, 146-49, 151-52
    cumulative, 139
    initial, 83, 138-39
    interrelationship with cost and retail price, 134-35
    maintained, 140
    percentage, 135-36, 139-41, 226
M.D. (*See* Markdowns)
Medium volume stores, 17, 18-19
Memorandum, 121
Men's and Boys' Wear Departments, 19
Merchandise Budgets, 21
Merchandise checking, 219-20
Merchandise Control Clerk, 24-25
Merchandise features, analysis of, 22
Merchandise managers, 32
Merchandise plan (*See* Seasonal merchandise plan)
Merchandise pricing (*See* Pricing)
Merchandise ordered, 99, 101
Merchandise quality, pricing and, 133
Merchandising (*See* Retail merchandising)
Merchandising and Operating Reports, 69, 75
Merchandising Division, 17
    organizational chart of, 20, 21
    staff aides to, 25-27
Merchandising profit (*See* Profit)
Mom-and-Pop store, 17
M.U. (*See* Markups)

N

National chains, 19
National Retail Dry Goods Association, 97
National Retail Merchants Association, 69, 70, 196
Net operating loss, 45

Net operating profit, 45
Net payment date, 113, 114-15, 118
Net purchases, 38-39
Net sales, 35, 44, 46-48
Net terms, 104, 108

O

Objectives, merchandising, 15-16
On-Order Report, 86, 252, 254
On percentage method, 105-6
Opening inventory, 39
Open-to-buy (O.T.B.), 84-90, 194
    calculating, 84, 88
    converting at retail to cost, 89-90
    unit plans and, 201-2
Open-To-Buy Report, 85, 252, 254
Operating expenses, 32, 43-48
Operating income, 32-35, 44, 46-48
Operating profit (*See* Profit)
Operations Division, 25
Order checking, 220-21
Order Checking Department, 101-3, 220, 252
Organization for merchandising, 17-25
    branch systems, 20
    chain store systems, 18-20
    executives, responsibilities of, 20-25
    medium- to large-volume stores, 17, 18-19
    organization chart of merchandising division, 20, 21
    small stores, 17
    store divisions, interdependence of, 25
Original-cost method, 192, 193-94, 208-9
O.T.B. (*See* Open-to-buy)
Outstanding checks, 88-89
Overage, stock, 240
Overbuying, 87, 172
Overstated profits, 191

P

Paper profit, 191
Paperwork, 217, 218
Percentages, 6-8
Periodic Profit and Loss Statement, 45
Periodic reports, 249-67
    basic stock lists, 259
    Department Operating Statement, 250-53
    financial, 250-58
    key terms, summary of, 263
    managerial, 258-61
    markdown analyses, 261
    On-Order, 86, 252, 254
    Open-To-Buy, 85, 252, 254